To [...]

with the compliments
of the author

March 1955

# TOWARD A DEMOCRATIC WORK PROCESS

# TOWARD
# A DEMOCRATIC
# WORK PROCESS

## THE HORMEL - PACKINGHOUSE
## WORKERS' EXPERIMENT

HD
6515
:F68
B65

## By Fred H. Blum

*Lecturer, Pendle Hill; Consultant, Research Center
for Group Dynamics, University of Michigan*

198566

HARPER & BROTHERS PUBLISHERS NEW YORK

*Library of Congress catalog card number: 53-8534*

*To*
*Frances G. Wickes*
*and to*
*The People of Austin, Minnesota*

# Contents

Preface                                                                 xi

Introduction                                                           xvii

1. The Rise of a Company and of a Union                                  1

Austin and the Hormel company
The rise of the union
The strike of 1933 and the recognition of the union
Transition and consolidation

2. A New Era of Industrial Organization                                 14

First changes in the traditional organization of work
The Working Agreement
Two interlocking systems of control
Modifications in workers' relatedness to the work process
The Master Plan
Joint Earnings and Profit-Sharing Trust
Hormel Business Improvement Project and Committee
Business Improvement Committee and grievance machinery
The emerging pattern of labor-management relations

3. "You Can't Run a Place Like That Without a Union"                    36

The union's objectives
Workers' feelings about the union
The union's role in the work process: rights and security
Group belongingness, and the world of labor
Participation in union affairs
The meaning of the union
Cultural forces and the role of the union

4. *"A Company Hard to Beat"*                                    56
   The policy of a fair deal
   Workers' feelings about the company
   Management and "the company"
   Involvement and feelings of partnership
   Profit-sharing and guaranteed wages
   Workers' desire for a "know-how" and "say-so"
   Participation in the company
   Cultural factors: conclusions

5. *The Game of Work*                                            74
   The work environment
   Likeness and differences of workdays
   The desire for "a break"
   Fatigue
   Boredom and the passing of time
   Factors giving meaning to work
   The experience of the game of work

6. *The Flight from and to Work*                                 94
   Work and off-work activities
   "Separation" of work and life
   First tendency: The desire to "get away from it all"
   Second tendency: Carry-over of work attitudes into leisure
        time
   Third tendency: The desire for creative activities
   The need to be occupied

7. *Alienation from Work*                                        112
   Technical and social division of labor
   Productiveness
   Money-service orientation
   Work—a "general good"
   Mechanical experience of work
   Production for what?

8. *"A Christian Gentleman"*                                     123
   The game of work
   The company and the desire for independence

The union and the need to be free
Satisfactions derived from work
Meaningless work—and a creative life
For a more democratic organization of work

9. *Victim of a Foe Unseen*                                  136
The experience of work
The meaning of the union and the company
Work interfering with life

10. *A Would-be Salesman*                                     146
A good job—or "the same old rut"?
The company: good earning opportunities
The union and the labor movement
What way out?

11. *The Meaning of the Austin Experience*                    157
Austin's achievements
The underlying causes
Democratization of the work process
The Austin experiment and the traditional organization of
    industry
The general significance of the Austin experiment
Unsolved problems
Management's and the union's role in solving these problems

12. *Creative Self-Expression in a Democratic Work Process*  172
Democratic values—objectivity and neutrality
Reverence for life—in the industrial scene
Group discussions and democratic consciousness
Human values in the concrete-technical work process
Democratization of the organized work process
A community of people and ideas

*Epilogue: Toward a Democratic Work Process*                 192
The scarcity and eternity of time
Work in an industrial culture
A meaningful life
Humanization of work

Problems to be met
Ways of solving these problems
Blueprint or experimentation?
A cooperative commonwealth of people

*Appendix I: Earning Opportunities and other Benefits of    208
the Hormel Workers*

*Appendix II: Research Methods*                              214

*Notes*                                                      219

*Index*                                                      225

# *Preface*

This study owes its origin to my association with the Guaranteed Wage Study undertaken by the Office of War Mobilization and Reconversion. While investigating the economic aspects of guaranteed wages, the question often arose as to the impact of the kind of security given by wage guarantees on workers' attitudes. Such vital questions as the effect of guaranteed wages on productivity, wage policy, and labor-management relations could not be answered in the absence of a knowledge of the impact of wage security on workers' attitudes toward management, the union, and toward their work.

After the completion of the Guaranteed Wage Study, an opportunity for an independent attitude study was given. The Geo. A. Hormel & Co. in Austin, Minnesota, was chosen for this study because it has the most developed guaranteed wage plan, is generally most advanced in labor-management relations, and because the Hormel workers are organized in a strong union affiliated with a national labor organization.

In order to be in the best position to understand workers' attitudes, I decided to work in the plant, to share the life of the workers as much as possible, and thus to create a human basis for a scientific inquiry. This experience of factory life has fundamentally influenced the research and changed its general orientation. Whereas at the beginning the main question was to throw light on the solution of certain economic problems arising out of the business cycle, the emphasis now shifted toward the much broader problems of a democratic organization of the work process. The *experience* of the degree to which human values are absent from the industrial scene and the recognition that the present organization of industry—even at its best—allows little creative self-expression convinced me of the necessity to examine industrial relations from the point of view of their compatibility with democratic values. The study which was begun with guaranteed wages as its main theme became, therefore, more and more focused on democracy in industry, and only incidentally on the contribution which guaranteed wages could make to its achievement.

My greatest indebtedness for making this project possible goes to Frances G. Wickes, whose interest in my work, profound psychological insight and help, even financial assistance have been with me from its beginning. In her interpretation of C. G. Jung she has assimilated the best he has to offer and related it to her deep experience of life. My basic orientation is Wickesian because no interpretation of the unconscious has reached into equal depth of personal and collective *human* experience. As far as an understanding of the *social* collective is concerned, I have freely drawn on the most significant recent contributions: Erich Fromm and Harry Stack Sullivan. The Washington School of Psychiatry, where I became acquainted with their work, has greatly contributed to the formulation of the general theoretical framework underlying this study.

During the first two years—in 1948 and 1949—the Eastman Foundation provided sufficient funds to allow me to devote a considerable part of my time to this study and to carry through the field work in Austin. I should like to mention in particular the late Carrol Dunham, Mrs. Eastman, and Mr. Brownlee from the Board of Home Missions of the Congregational and Christian Churches. Their interest and that of the other members of the Board of Directors of the Eastman Foundation, Mr. R. P. Windisch and Mrs. French, have seen this research through its most difficult initial years.

During 1950 a joint union-management grant made it possible to spend the whole year in Austin. My special thanks for this grant go to Mr. Jay C. Hormel, Chairman of the Board of Directors of the Geo. A. Hormel & Co., and to Mr. Ralph Helstein, President of the United Packinghouse Workers of America, C.I.O. (from now on referred to as U.P.W.A.). During 1951 and 1952

Lois and George Hogle, of New York, gave generously as special expenses had to be covered, and the seemingly unavoidable delay in the completion of the manuscript occurred.

The joint union-management grant was given in full knowledge of the objectives of the study. It gave me complete freedom in the conduct of my research and in the manner in which I would choose to present the results. The right of the company and of the union to object to specific findings was explicitly recognized but, unless convincing evidence could be presented, I was merely obliged to mention their objection. As it turned out, there were only a few instances in which the company and the union raised objections which led to modifications in my presentation. Ultimately, I was "only responsible to my own conscience." It is hoped that this precedent will encourage social research made under similar sponsorship.

This study has been carried through independently, yet it would not have been possible without the cooperation of the Geo. A. Hormel & Co. and of Local 9, U.P.W.A. I had complete freedom to enter the plant whenever I wanted, to work there, to talk to people, or just to observe factory life. I am particularly indebted to Mr. Fayette Sherman, the Personnel Director of the Hormel company, and to Mr. Frank W. Schultz, the President of Local 9, for their most generous cooperation. Their understanding was of invaluable help in the general conduct of the research and in gaining the confidence of the workers, as well as of the supervisory staff. The workers who have liberally given of their time to tell me about their life—particularly those who came to the weekly group sessions for about a year—are entitled to my special gratitude. During these meetings they discussed my findings and offered many suggestions for making the work process more democratic.

The values underlying the group work and this project in general may be simply expressed by what Albert Schweitzer calls "Reverence for Life," a reverence whose human-religious foundation gives to democratic values their genuine character and deepest meaning. I have freely criticized both the company and the union whenever the scientific evidence has shown that they do not live up to these values. I have tried, however, to take always an attitude of complete human understanding without letting my criticism of ideas and actions degenerate into a criticism of the people themselves. I have, furthermore, striven to be constructive in terms of the values underlying this study.

The responsibility for what I am saying is my own though I have benefited by the advice and help of many people. Professor Clark Kerr, then Director of the Institute of Industrial Relations, now Chancellor at the University of California, in Berkeley, introduced me originally to Mr. Jay C. Hormel and Mr. Frank W. Schultz. He has followed my work with sympathetic criticism. Professor E. Wight Bakke, from the Labor and Management Center at Yale University, has generously put at my disposal the services of the Labor and Management Center and has assisted in research design and the development of research methods. I have been inspired by his new approach to labor-management relations and he has given me freely from his wide experience in social research. The same is true of Professor C. Wright Mills from Columbia University, whose experience in intensive interviewing was particularly helpful. Of great value for the conduct of the field work have been various people associated with the Research Center for Group Dynamics at the University of Michigan in Ann Arbor, particularly Drs. Ronald Lippitt, Alvin Zander, and E. R. P. French. Their action-research approach with which I became familiar at the Second National Training Laboratory for Group Development, and the ideas of the late Kurt Lewin, the founder of the Research Center, have greatly influenced my own thought. Margaret Mead, a storehouse of ideas, should also be mentioned. Professors Paul Taylor, Carl Landauer, VanDusen Kennedy, and Robert Nisbet from the University of California in Berkeley deserve special thanks for working their way through the manuscript when it had reached its greatest bulk.

The actual write-up of the data began at the island summer residence of C. Wright Mills on Lake Temagami, Canada, where he helped with the structuring and editing of the manuscript. During the final preparation of the manuscript, Mrs. Gretl Heinz gave unstintingly of her time to criticize sympathetically but relentlessly its form and content. Her insight and understanding have contributed greatly.

Anybody familiar with the problems of field research will understand the contribution made by those who took shorthand and transcribed thousands of pages of more or less illegible notes. During the first period of field work Mrs. Ruth Ball, of Austin, gave more than her due to this study. After her family obligations had to take first place, Mrs. Miriam Phifer carried on the work with the greatest diligence.

All quotations in this book that are not specifically marked as being taken from published material are statements made by the workers. In Chapter XII, which deals with the group work, first names have been used. These names are fictitious except for my own first name, which I left unchanged, since I believe that the reader is entitled to glimpse the role I played during the group sessions. In Chapters VIII to X minor changes have been made to assure anonymity of the workers.

F.H.B.

# Introduction

Work is an activity which absorbs about half of our waking life and considerably more of our energy. It creates, moreover, basic attitudes by channeling our energy towards certain objectives and drawing it away from alternative goals and values. We characterize people by their profession, thus taking their work as a symbolic expression of their being. The values which give meaning to our life cannot, indeed, be separated from those which give meaning to our work.

Modern industrialism has given a peculiar significance to work by giving it a central place in the life of people. "There is no other period in the history in which free men have given their energy as completely for the one purpose: work. The drive for relentless work was one of the fundamental productive forces, no less important for the development of our industrial system than steam and electricity."[1]

Yet while our libraries abound in investigations of technology and technical efficiency, only a few books deal with the human aspects of industrial organization and even less deal with the role of work in the life of the people. This is not accidental: when the industrial revolution triumphed, "a new species of creature arose. Formerly the laborer was the central figure, he worked according to the laws of his being and his tools worked as he required their services. Now the machine is the central figure, and labor follows the laws of the machine's being and works as it requires his services."[2]

The machine took the place of man because the *organization* of industry made it the central figure. Steam, electricity, and machines are, after all, mere instrumentalities. Their ethical coloration depends upon the purpose which they serve: they may be used to alleviate the burden of daily work and thus create the basis for creative self-expression, or they may be allowed to set the pace of life and submerge it in the meaninglessness of their own movement. In this sense the ethical-spiritual orientation of industry touches deeper roots and is more decisive for the role of work in our life than is its material basis.

This book is mainly concerned with the impact of the *organized* work process on the life of the workers, the attitudes it evokes in them, and the values which it fosters and which it gives the greatest chance to develop. "Ultimately," Max Weber said, "every form of social organization . . . must be examined in terms of the type of man to whom it gives . . . the greatest chances to survive."[3] We are, therefore, interested in exploring to what extent the present organization of industry develops democratic values by fostering a creative self-expression of the workers.

In a democratic society the difficult task of giving meaning to life by choosing between ultimate values is up to the individual. Such a society must, therefore, respect an area within which the individual conscience is supreme. And the deepest self-expression will always be outside the realm of social relatedness. But for most people self-expression is contingent upon a certain type of relatedness to the social process. This is certainly true of work: Our role in the work process, our opportunity to express ourselves and to be meaningfully related and positively identified with a community of work, is essentially a problem of social-industrial organization.

The following statement shows the intimate connection between the social organization and the values which we can realize in our life. "A democratic situation activates in man certain psychic forces and potentialities which also exist in an authoritarian situation—because they exist in all men. But an authoritarian society does not use these forces to build up the social structure, they unfold their social effects only in a democratic situation. . . . Every social organization appeals to certain psychic forces and binds them to its peculiar social structure. . . ."[4] To enable people to feel, think, and act democratically, the organization of industry must, therefore, be based on democratic values.

When we speak about democratic values, we do not refer primarily to what is sometimes considered the core of democracy: a parliamentary machinery. The essence of democracy is an ethical-religious conception of the dignity of the individual and of his creative self-expression and self-realization. To be creative does not mean to produce great works in the field of the arts, the sciences, or other endeavors; it means to develop freely what is peculiarly one's own in a give-and-take with one's fellow man. The cook in the Joseph Mankiewicz film "No Way Out" is creative because she has developed her potential and makes her contribution to her community with a radiant joy. The antithesis of such a creativity is the compulsive performance of a task which has no meaning.

Genuine creativity is only possible in a democratic society which is organized in such a way as to allow man to be an "end" in his own right rather than a mere means for the demands of a state or of an organization of industry which subordinates him to machines. Democracy and creativity are, therefore, synonymous terms for the purposes of this study. They both denote a peculiar kind of relatedness of the individual to himself, to his fellow man, to the group in which he belongs, and the society in which he lives—a relatedness which allows him to develop his emotional, intellectual, and aesthetic potentialities to the fullest.

To indicate concretely what such a conception of democracy-creativity means in the industrial field is the purpose of this study. Its scope, however, is limited; it deals with the organized work process and not with the problems of the over-all organization of industry. Though fully realizing the contingency of the organization of the factory upon the over-all market organization, our central focus is on the factory—the basic unit of the organized work process. No matter what changes in the over-all organization of industry may be necessary to make the work process more democratic, the factory remains the pulse which indicates the degree to which democracy in all actuality prevails in industry.

This study diagnoses the conditions prevailing in one factory. Yet the methods of diagnosis used throw light on the general problems which arise as an attempt is made to realize more fully democratic values in the organized work process. Problems of actual change are only dealt with incidentally though the whole research project on which this study is based has been designed as an action-research project whose aim is therapy rather than diagnosis only.

Since this study arose out of my interest in guaranteed wages, their place in this inquiry should be indicated briefly. Wage guarantees may be considered as a technical device to increase workers' security. But they have more far-reaching implications. In an economy which subordinates man to capital values by treating human beings as variable costs and machines as overhead costs, guaranteed wages try to bring a human element into an industrial system traditionally insensitive to such concerns. The demand for wage guarantees is, therefore, a demand to make man the master and center of the socio-economic organization rather than the weakest link in an uncontrollable chain of events. Guaranteed wages thus conceived lead naturally to the central problem raised by a democratization of the work process: How must industry be reorganized in order to allow workers a creative self-expression in their work and in their life?

In asking this question, we must look to the future. It is true that in the era preceding the industrial revolution the worker was the central figure in the sense that the technique was subordinated to his craftsmanship. And the pre-industrial revolution worker derived a great deal of satisfaction from the concrete expression of his craft. But for the majority of the people, work without modern machinery meant drudgery and low standards of living. And even the craftsman was not a free man. His consciousness "lay dreaming or half awake beneath a common veil . . . Man was conscious of himself only as a member of a race, party, family or corporation, only through some general category."[5]

To conceive of a return to the pre-machine age constitutes, therefore, an undesirable step backward. Both materially and spiritually it would lead us away from a democratic society. Instead of trying to escape the arduous problems of today by looking back to a glorified past we must harness all our ingenuity and energy to explore how industry has to be reorganized in order to assure its contribution to the development of a democratic consciousness. And we must act accordingly. Eventually we must replace the "new species of creature" which arose from the industrial revolution by a new democratic species of man who is conscious of himself as an individual, yet integrated in a group and involved in his society according to the laws of his own being.

# TOWARD A DEMOCRATIC WORK PROCESS

# CHAPTER 1

# The Rise of a Company
# and of a Union

## AUSTIN AND THE HORMEL COMPANY

Austin, Minnesota, is located on the banks of the Cedar River in the central plains of the United States. The first records go back to 1853 when Austin Nichols settled in this area. The town is surrounded by the rich south Minnesota and north Iowa farm land. Corn, grain, soy beans, and livestock are typical products of its neighborhood.

As the county seat of Mower County, Austin was a small administrative and trading center of about 4000 people when, in the fall of 1891, two men started to hammer and saw among the scrub oaks of the northeastern part of town. The two men—George A. Hormel and George Peterson, his right-hand helper—converted a small creamery building into a "packing house." Six men started to work there late in 1891—after most of the equipment was obtained from a defunct packing house in a nearby town.

Two years after the business had begun to operate, the country was struck by the panic of 1893. In addition to the general decline in business activity the competition within the industry became particularly keen, since the improved refrigeration car enabled the big packers to sell directly to many smaller communities. "Hundreds of developing packing plants west of the Mississippi went down before the twin scythes of hard times and modern efficient competition. Four west-of-the-Mississippi packing plants survived. The Hormel company was one of them."[1] The new business not only survived these stormy days; it even expanded. The first brick building was started in 1892 and from then on the expansion never came to an end, in spite of temporary setbacks and hard times. A news item of 1896 illustrates the development of the early days.

> Geo. A. Hormel & Co. conduct one of the principal industrial establishments of the city. Its growth has been phenomenal. The success has been due entirely to the well-directed efforts of Mr. Hormel, whose energy, enterprise and ability as a thoroughgoing businessman is well known.[2]

The growth of the packing house and the development of Austin went hand in hand. In 1893 the company slaughtered and dressed 3000 hogs; at the turn of the century somewhat over 30,000. After World War I it reached the half-million mark, during the depression of the thirties it packed more than a million hogs a year, and when the country emerged from World War II, slaughtering of hogs neared the two million mark. The community grew correspondingly: at the turn of the century it had over 5000 inhabitants; it reached 10,000 in 1920 and during the thirties "Austin enjoyed a percentage increase in population of 49.1 per cent, almost twice that of the Minnesota city showing the next highest increase."[3] In 1940, about 18,000 people lived in Austin and the preliminary census figures for 1950 show a population of 23,000.[4]

As of 1950, Austin has twenty-seven manufacturing establishments. They include stone, clay, lumber and similar products, printing and publishing, as well as a railroad repair shop. But the only really important firm is the Hormel company which is packing and, since 1928, canning meat. Over 4000 workers earn their livelihood there. Most of the people who are gainfully employed in nonmanufacturing establishments service those who work at the Hormel company.

The community consists of a well-amalgamated mixture of English, German, Scandinavian, and Irish origin. About 60 per cent belong to various Protestant denominations and the rest are

Catholic. According to the Chamber of Commerce, Austin is "a typical American city, with no section or area classified as being predominantly one nationality."[5] At first glance it does not, indeed, seem much different from other midwestern communities. But a more systematic trip through the town reveals more new houses—and more one-family houses—than similar cities have. The city records verify this impression: about 75 per cent of the Austinites live in their own homes.[6] This is a higher percentage of home-ownership than that of any comparable city in the United States.[7]

There are no slum areas or neglected houses in town. A visitor coming to the city during the early thirties would have seen some people living in shacks and tents on the fair-grounds at the outskirts of town. But even at that time, Austin was better off than comparable cities in the State of Minnesota. In 1937, for example, it had "a smaller absolute number of unemployed than any other city in the state with a population of 10,000 and over. Its proportion of unemployed ranged between one and two percent, which was considerably lower than the proportion in any other city in Minnesota."[8] And today it belongs to one of the most prosperous communities in the United States.[9]

Anyone walking nowadays along Main Street watching the well-dressed and seemingly well-contented people who mill around the stores, banks, and offices can hardly visualize the inner tensions and the open strife and conflicts which marked the history of Austin. The headquarters of the union are inconspicuously located on one of the side streets leading to the plant. The factory itself—up to eight stories high and stretching over forty acres—is impressively situated along the Cedar River. The view from the bridge is peaceful, undisturbed by the squealing of the hogs which farmers deliver at the other end of the packing house, and unaffected by the human drama which has been—and still is being—played in these neat looking buildings.

Yet this drama makes Austin a "typical American city" since it reflects the material achievement, the economic power, as well as the socio-economic, psychological, and ultimately spiritual problems with which this country is faced.

Free enterprise is an epithet which has been applied most consistently to our socio-economic organization. The Hormel company has been from its beginning in the spotlight of the competitive struggle; within the short span of two generations it has been built up literally from scratch to a 300 million dollar-a-year operation.[10] This "phenomenal" expansion was due to the best free enterprise has to offer: thrift, hard work, and the unusual business ingenuity of its founder, George A. Hormel, and his son, Jay C. Hormel.

The memory of George A. Hormel lives on among those workers who have been with the company for many years. They remember particularly his frugality, his insistence on savings—and his startling ways of demonstrating these attitudes. A typical story which workers told me goes as follows: "One day, while walking through one of the departments, he saw meat on the floor. He took the facsimile of a dollar bill out of his billfold and tore it up in front of the workers. When they looked at him astonished, he said: 'You think I am crazy because I tear up a dollar bill. But this symbolizes what you do when you throw meat on the floor.'"

The company operated for ten years as an individually owned firm, was incorporated in 1901, and reincorporated under a Delaware charter in 1929.[11] Its recent growth and development is inextricably related to the personality of Mr. Jay C. Hormel, who became its President in 1929. In 1946, at the death of his father, he became Chairman of the Board of Directors. The Hormel family owns the majority of the stock, and Mr. Hormel takes such an active part in the conduct of the business that he has the last word in all significant policy decisions. The company preserved, therefore, to a large degree the characteristics of a firm owned and operated by an entrepreneur: the business genius of one man is in command of the organization. Jay C. Hormel has, moreover, taken a keen, active interest in the workers, in labor-management relations, and in the socio-economic problems posed by the rise of unionism.

## THE RISE OF THE UNION

The conditions prevailing in the factory before unionization were characterized by Mr. Jay C. Hormel as a "benevolent dictatorship." The workers who were closer to the scene were less conscious of their benevolent character. The most sensitive among them and those who were strongly imbued with the ideal of a free, self-reliant individual, called the factory system "sheer tyranny." The managerial authority exercised in the factory was, indeed, complete and all-embracing. Foremen had the right to hire and fire workers and to determine the conditions of work. Their unbridled authority ranged from personal family problems —such as occasional denials to go to a funeral of a family member—to attempts to influence workers' political ideas. This is a typical story of that period: "The last time the company tried to influence our votes was before Roosevelt was elected. The work was stopped for 10 minutes; we were assembled in small groups; foreman and supervisors gave speeches telling us to vote Republican. We voted for Roosevelt anyhow, only the bosses voted Republican and it cost the company a hell of a lot of money."

The strength of workers' feelings about the conditions prevailing before the formation of the union in 1933 can be gauged from the vivacity and emotional involvement with which some of the workers talked to me about those times—more than fifteen years afterwards. "Supervisors and foremen bossed you around. One day it was very hot. The foreman said, pointing at people: 'You have a new cap tomorrow and you . . . and you have your mustache cut off.' The foreman pointed his finger at an old fellow who had a torch in his hand and who was sweating all over. Next day he had his mustache cut off, you bet. You were a dime a dozen. There were hundreds of people outside the plant waiting for work. When you didn't like something, you were told, 'Get out of here.'" Another worker said: "One day the company collected for the community chest for the poor people and they set up an insurance plan. A fellow could not live on what he got, and they wanted to take money out of our paycheck. *We* were the poor people. My gosh, that is human nature, if a fellow can take so much and no more. My gosh, there comes a time when something snaps in him. When we got the union, I felt a man alone cannot do it. . . ."

This quotation refers to the specific incident which led to the formation of the union: the insurance plan. But long before this event, workers formed "informal groups" to protect themselves as much as possible against the arbitrary authority of the foreman. The transformation of these informal groups into a formal organization of workers, a union, is well described in the official union record. To quote:

The talk about a union kept stewing until Thursday, July 13, 1933, when three men on the Hog Kill were "told" by a supervisor to sign up for a $1.20 weekly deduction for Hormel's newly innovated Old Age Retirement Plan. . . . One of the fellows did sign, but the others stood their ground and refused to sign. A large group of protesting, aroused and indignant workers gathered around the supervisor and the killing floor was shut down. They told the supervisor to give the fellow back his card and let him tear it up and to stop trying to make people sign the cards, or they would not work.[12] This demonstration was planned in advance, and a large share of these fellows had pledged to stick together even though they did not have a union. The supervisor was thunderstruck by this display of unity and gave the fellow his card back. The killing floor, which was shut down for about 10 minutes, started again.[13]

The exact course of events is controversial but there is no doubt that the instructions given by the company to the foreman, namely to "sell" the plan, were not carried through within the usual limitations of a sales talk. There is also no doubt that the intentions of the company were good and that the insurance plan was advantageous for the workers.[14] It is, indeed, not without a certain irony that the company's attempt to introduce an insurance plan which would have cost the workers only 20 cents a week* became the stumbling block for the formation of the union. Yet workers were upset about the reduction in their take-home pay and irked because they were again told to do something. "Company tried to spend the money for us instead of you doing it yourself." According to management, these feelings were influenced by misunderstandings about the nature of the plan and intensified by some commercial insurance companies who saw in a company-sponsored plan a dangerous competitive precedent.

* The insurance cost amounted to $1.20, but $1.00 was added to the workers' pay.

However, the insurance plan could not have led to the formation of the union if there had not been an explosive situation due to deeper lying causes: low wages and resentment of the authoritarian boss system. One practice prevailing at that time illustrates procedures resented by the workers: foreman would "trade" workers, one laying them off, the other hiring them—at a lower wage rate.

A systematic analysis of the answers to the question, "Why did you join the union?" bears out this interpretation. Two arguments go like a continuous thread through the manifold answers to this question: wages were low and we were pushed around. Many times this thread comes to the surface; sometimes it is hidden. But it never seems to be lost: "I thought it was a damned good idea for protection, did not want to be laid off, tired of buying alcohol for the boss—every third week—to hold my job." Another worker said: "Well, for one thing I got transferred out from the . . . into the . . . department. My wages were 45 cents an hour. They cut my wages down to 32½ cents an hour with the promise it would be up in a short time. Things got worse, hours less, no guarantee. I made nine dollars a week or less.[15] You didn't dare to kick, or boss told you: 'If you don't like it, you get the hell out of here. We find all kinds of guys a dime a carload.' That's what they *did* tell us, and the wages did not go up." A final quotation: "I joined the union because we had hard times in the plant, wasn't making any money, hard to do anything with the boss, better have a union."

It is, therefore, not astonishing that hundreds of workers went on the evening of the Hog Kill incident—in 1933—to a meeting in the Sutton Park at the southeastern part of town. This meeting was followed by other meetings in the park, and on the court-house lawn in the center of town. Within a few days a Charter was prepared and the union was formed. It was an industrial union, organized along the lines of the I.W.W. (Industrial Workers of the World). Its name was The Independent Union of All Workers (I.U.A.W.). Its object, "to enlist all workers and farmers into one great union."[16]

The mood of the workers who took an active part in the formation of the union is well expressed in the following story:

"When the union was organized, there was a meeting in the park. I saw a man walking his way toward the park; his back was bent from the toil of pulling trucks, but he walked with a purpose toward this meeting. I don't know what his thoughts were, possibly better days to come . . . the speaker spoke about the benefits of organization. You could see the purpose in the eyes of these fellows. I looked at their eyes. New hope was shining in them. They crowded in to pay their dues and the organization was born."

Needless to emphasize that not all workers were so strongly motivated as this worker was. Some coasted along from the beginning—and they still do so: "I was pretty young; everybody else joined. I joined with them." There is even one worker who did not dare to go against his fellow workers and who up to this day projects on the union his resentment of his own lack of courage. Others did not join because they did not care or did not dare or could not see any advantages in unionization.

The company was caught napping by the unionization. It was hard to take because Mr. Jay C. Hormel felt that he had done a great deal to help workers during the difficult times of the depression. Indeed, the company had started to experiment with wage guarantees before unionization and the insurance plan was, as already pointed out, advantageous for the workers. The wages paid by the company were, as we will see shortly, the highest in the industry and Mr. Hormel was working out a plan to increase the purchasing power of the farmers in order eventually to be able to raise the wages of the workers. It should also be noted that the Hormel company was the last firm in the industry to cut wages, when in 1931 it was forced to do so because it lost over half a million dollars.

But the cards were stacked against the company. The New Deal was at its height. The atmosphere created by Washington was favorable to unionization and the government protected workers who wanted to join unions. The local scene helped to aggravate the smoldering conflicts. In near-by Minneapolis the Dunn brothers organized unions imbued by a militant ideology and the Farmer-Labor Party was active all through the state. The Minnesota farmers were restless and eager to resort to strike action. When the union was formed the agricultural neigh-borhood of Austin was swept by farmers' open resistance to low prices and foreclosures. The newspaper headlines announced "Farmer Holiday" again and again.

## THE STRIKE OF 1933 AND THE RECOGNITION OF THE UNION

A period of feverish activity followed the chartering of the union. Membership meetings took place every week. A strike vote taken in September to gain recognition for the union and for seniority rights led to an immediate agreement with the com-pany (September 23, 1933), in which it recognized the

Independent Union of All Workers No. 1, of Austin, Minnesota, and recognizes its right to organize as such to bargain collectively with said company through representatives of its own choosing in connec-tion with all matters pertaining to the interests and welfare of the members of said Union, employed by the Geo. A. Hormel & Co., and it does recognize and adhere to the provisions of law regarding the right of labor to organize and the provisions of the N.R.A. Code and subscribed by it.

Said Geo. A. Hormel & Co. further agrees to and subscribes to the principle of seniority. . . .

It is further agreed that no matters shall be permitted to lead to a strike . . . without first being submitted to arbitration.[17]

The agreement was made during an all-night meeting to which Mr. Jay C. Hormel called fifty prominent businessmen of the town. In the course of an address, he said in regard to the union:

There has been a number of things corrected which I was par-ticularly happy to find out about and things which I would not have found out about if there had been no union. When the union was organized I was fearful of its use. My first impulse was to draw away from it because I have known of unnecessary trouble resulting from unions, but I like the idea now even though the organization set up in this city is not included in the regular labor federation. I like the idea of having this local union here in Austin where the town is de-pendent on the plant and the plant dependent on the town and where the union is dominated and conducted by local people rather than by paid organizers from the outside. . . .

I will not be guilty of having anyone come here to take the place of these Austin people, to throw brick bats at other Austin people and cause friction and trouble. I am not going to get mixed up in a fight in my home town.[18]

The Austin daily newspaper lauded the agreement for taking Austin "out of the 'strike city' class and placing it in the column of those where all labor troubles and disputes will be settled by arbitration. . . ."[19]

However, this was not to happen immediately. A strike vote taken in November, 1933, to enforce the implementation of the September agreement led to a strike which was not authorized by the Executive Board of the Union.[20] The strike was short but violent. The pickets "cleaned out the foremen and also escorted Mr. Hormel . . . and other company executives out of the plant."[21] The events are controversial, particularly the circumstances under which Mr. Hormel left the plant. But there is no doubt that the strikers were in complete control of the plant. "At midnight a table was carried to the gate and was used as an improvised platform by Jay Hormel and Frank Ellis, business organizer of the Independent Union of All Workers, who talked to the men, each stating their attitude on the strike."[22] Mr. Hormel assured the workers that no unannounced attempt would be made to break the strike. He said, "There will be no work in the plant until I give you twenty-four hours' notice." He also pointed out that "some work would have to be done in the plant 'to clean up things' and that the office force must be permitted to enter the plant."[23]

This nightly meeting at the factory gates did not improve the tense situation. While the pickets walked around the bonfires to protect themselves against a bitter cold, the Sheriff sent the following message to the State Governor:

Situation here so unruly that deputizing of un-uniformed and poorly armed citizens would precipitate guerrilla warfare with pitiful casualties on both sides, especially because men have been told that law-enforcement agencies would not interfere with them. Therefore, in order to avoid needless bloodshed, I appeal to you to dispatch militia to take situation in hand before nightfall at latest.[24]

Since the Governor did not respond, "frantic calls" were being broadcast over the radio station. " 'Governor Olson, call Austin 2334,' the radio announcer said."[25] The Governor sent a representative to Austin who told Mr. Hormel that "while he could not speak for the Governor, he was satisfied the Governor would not call out the militia unless Mr. Hormel would arbitrate . . . the demands of the union."[26]

The uncertainty and restlessness reached its height when "more than 300 National Guardsmen were mobilized . . . in readiness to move by truck to Austin. . . ."[27] Before the troops went into action, the Governor of Minnesota, Floyd B. Olson, came to Austin personally and brought about an agreement between the company and the union. All questions in dispute were to be submitted to an Arbitration Board. This agreement was submitted to a rank and file meeting at which Governor Olson addressed the workers. In the course of his speech he said:

To be frank you were in illegal possession of the plant; you had taken over someone's property. . . .

I am a friend of labor. If you sign this agreement, I assure you that you will use arbitration. . . .

You can't strike against the findings of the board of arbitration, but if the code is put into operation, and you can prove that the company violated the code, you can, of course, strike. . . .

I don't want to be put on the spot because if I have to choose between my duty and sympathy, I will be obliged to choose duty.[28]

After Governor Olson had finished his talk, the workers voted overwhelmingly to accept his proposal for arbitration. The company agreed to re-employ all strikers without discrimination after the workers had given the company full possession of the plant. The episode ended with a statement by Mr. Hormel to the press: "I am glad the controversy is settled without bloodshed"[29] and a remark by the business manager of the union: "The solidarity of the organization has taught the scabs a lesson. Do not be antagonistic toward them, treat them kindly and educate them."[30] Last but not least, it ended with an arbitration award of a 2- to 4-cent wage increase. This award was relatively small because wages at the Hormel company were found to be higher than at other companies.[31]

TRANSITION AND CONSOLIDATION

The atmosphere in the city at the time of the strike has been summarized in these words: "With the Hormel Plant in control of the strikers, the refrigeration system turned off, endangering meat valued at $3,600,000 and a call being made for National Guard and Federal troops, the anxiety of Austin people reached a pitch that was probably never equaled in the history of the city."[32] Indeed, there has never been a similar upheaval and there is unlikely ever to be one again—unless strange things happen in the city of Austin.

However, the years following the strike were still unruly. The drives to organize the uptown workers were supported by mass meetings (1936), accompanied by rioting and by the burning in effigy of the judge in front of the Court house (1935). Injunctions and the formation of anti-union organizations such as the "Secret 500" and the "Citizens' Alliance" (1938) created new tension. There were, furthermore, a series of sit-down strikes in the plant. The outstanding sit-down strike was one which occurred in the sausage department in January, 1936, and led to a union shop agreement between the company and the union.[33] Company officials emphasized that the union shop was granted without any concessions from the union. The plant was now 100 per cent organized and the union had the security to enter a period of more constructive labor-management relations.

Shortly afterwards, in May, 1937, when John L. Lewis had declared the C.I.O.'s intention to organize the packing industry, the Independent Union of All Workers affiliated in a rather close vote with the C.I.O. It became Local 183 and, later on (1939), Local 9 of the United Packinghouse Workers of America (U.P.W.A.). This affiliation was in agreement with the company's desire to have competitive wage rates. In fact, Mr. Jay C. Hormel urged the union to join with other existing unions in order to make it possible for him to pay higher wages and still compete effectively.

While strengthening the position in regard to the company, the union penetrated more deeply into the life of the community, the state, and the nation. Already, in 1934, it had decided to go into political action and to run a candidate in the city election. The *Austin Daily Herald,* the only paper in town, did not take a friendly attitude toward the union and its attempts to play a role in the community. To counteract this "one-sided" influence the union started its own weekly, *The Unionist,* in 1936. Weekly radio broadcasts by the president of the Local starting in 1947 strengthened the union's influence on public opinion. The Local endorsed Franklin Delano Roosevelt for a second and third term. The first of these endorsements was made in defiance of the then President of the C.I.O., John L. Lewis.

During the war, Local 9 did all it could to support the war effort. It endorsed a "United for Victory," rally and bought a considerable amount of war bonds. Not less important were its constant efforts to speed up production. The Executive Board issued a "strong resolution stating it will not support slacker elements."[34] By that time the union had become an accepted part of the community which boasts to be one of the strongest union towns in the country. Already, by 1943, only four local firms remained on the "unfair list" of non-unionized firms.

Yet these events followed basic changes in the relationships between the workers, the company, and the union. Before peace came to the city of Austin, the conflicts of the thirties had to find a constructive solution in a new organization of the work process. As efforts were made in that direction, the nature of the conflicts changed imperceptibly: whereas the strike of 1933 brought long-suppressed tensions into the open, the strife which persisted at the end of the thirties marked the birthpangs of efforts to create a new form of industrial organization. The Working Agreement between the company and the union and the master plan of Mr. Jay C. Hormel are the tangible results of these efforts.

# CHAPTER 2

# A New Era of Industrial Organization

## FIRST CHANGES IN THE TRADITIONAL ORGANIZATION OF WORK

No less dramatic than the outward happenings in Austin were the changes in the invisible organizational web relating workers to the work process, to management, and now to a union "of their own choosing." Traditionally, workers were loosely related to the enterprise "on an hourly basis." They were merely means without any authority, without any control over the work process, and hence without any ability to express their own needs and aspirations in their working life.

The first significant modification of this traditional organization was the introduction of guaranteed annual wages. The company's attempts to overcome the worst excesses of the traditional organization came as a direct repudiation of the recommendations of an efficiency expert:

The idea of the Hormel Annual Wage Plan was born in an episode which occurred in the early 1920's.

Geo. A. Hormel & Company, grown since its start in 1891, had employed an efficiency expert. This man has pointed out the savings which would come by measuring the workman's time by the *tenth* of the hour instead of by the half hour. This was a shock to Mr. Hormel when he recalled that his grandfather had started work by the year, his father by the month. Then came per hour, now per tenth.

14

Of course, the efficiency expert pointed out, office help should still be employed by the week or month or year, because they are "company people"! Mr. Hormel wondered. The true cause and effect *might* be the other way around.

The unfairness of asking workmen to take the hazards of uncertain employment was brought out in an episode which occurred in 1929.

The Hormel company had hit upon a brand-new product—a boom product—canned chicken. Wholesalers bought, retailers bought, housewives bought. The company doubled and quadrupled its production line; then went to three shifts. Then the boom busted. The housewife, having the security of a chicken on her pantry shelf, kept it there.

The retailer and the wholesaler stopped buying, and Hormel laid off its extra help. Many went quietly on their way—all but one man. That man headed straight for the front office and said: "You can't do this to me."

"Can't do what to you?" asked Mr. Hormel.

"You can't turn me out in the street. You wouldn't turn a horse out in the street. You can't do it to me."

"You can go back where you came from, can't you?" queried Mr. Hormel.

"No!" said the man. "My town has 1200 people. Before I got out of school, I was selling home-popped popcorn out of a basket. I finally got a little stand, selling peanuts, popcorn, chewing gum, and pop. I just got to where I could count on $9.00 or $10.00 a week when you sent a man along who said you would pay me $20.00 a week to help you can your chicken. He didn't tell me you would only keep me a couple of months—just long enough to ruin my business—then turn me out in the street!"[1]

Whether truth or fiction, this story illustrates management's ideas in instituting a wage guarantee in 1931. In doing so, management gave up "the right to revalue each worker and lay him off if currently the company is not profiting from his employment."[2]

Under the original plan which was put into effect in the smokehouse and the fresh sausage department, workers were guaranteed a straight weekly wage. The number of hours to be worked was left open, only the *annual* workload was stipulated. Workers, furthermore, could be transferred freely from one department to another. By the end of 1933, almost all departments worked under such a guaranteed wage system.[3] In the folklore of the factory, this system has ever since been called "straight time" because workers' pay was "straight"—not varying according to the number of hours worked.

One of the first demands of the newly organized union was "to abolish straight time." This request was in agreement with the feelings of most workers. "We were skeptical, at first, afraid that there was a catch to it." One worker even mentioned his "skepticism of straight time" as a reason for joining the union. Workers' distrust and their negative feelings were partly a result of their general attitude towards management— an attitude engendered by the authoritarian factory organization—and partly dissatisfaction with the arbitrariness of the transfer regulations and the indefiniteness in regard to the number of hours to be worked.[4] Fear of a speed-up also played a role. The opposition to losing overtime, however, did not exist since the guaranteed wage came into operation before the wage-hour law made the payment of overtime mandatory.

However, as seasonal layoffs recurred, some workers asked, "Would we be laid off if we still were on 'straight time'?" The answer was: "Of course not." They pondered this reply and thought about the recurrent periods of idleness. It was a painful feeling that their jobs were uncertain, and that the times when they brought home a decent income were rare and far between. These ideas prompted them to take up the problem in the meetings of the newly organized union and to work out a scheme which preserved the advantages of the company's initial proposal without having its major disadvantages. First reinstated in the hog kill, the new guarantee system spread slowly but steadily over the whole plant.

At the same time the so-called "sunshine bonus" was transformed into a group-incentive system. When guaranteed wages were first introduced, the workload was stipulated for each gang. When workers had completed their task, they could go home—no matter how many hours it took them to complete it. They were compensated for their extra effort in terms of free time. They went home earlier than they were used to for a while and then asked, "Could we continue to work and be paid for the additional output rather than enjoying the sunshine?" Management's answer was: yes, of course. As a result, a group-incentive system remunerating workers with additional income was worked out.

The emerging guaranteed-wage–group-incentive system functions as follows: Workers have a guarantee of a minimum weekly income from their regular scheduled work hours, no matter how many hours they are actually working. They are paid, in addition, for whatever the work-group produces above the hourly work requirement, stipulated in a union-company contract. How much workers produce above the minimum is a matter of group decision. The company has no direct influence on this decision as long as the minimum work standards are maintained. Since, as we will see later on, production above minimum standard is considerable, the speed of work is, for practical purposes, self-determined. Necessary transfers are regulated by the seniority principle. The details of this system are explained in Appendix I.

The Working Agreement

Though initiated by management, the guaranteed wage became part of the Working Agreement between the United Packinghouse Workers of America, Local 9, C.I.O. and the Geo. A. Hormel & Co., Austin, Minnesota—an agreement which radically modified the organization of the work process.

From the beginning to their successful conclusion in 1940, the negotiations leading to this agreement took place in a spirit of mutual understanding. "We have a common problem to solve, let's sit down and work it out together,"[5] was said by Jay C. Hormel, representing the company, to Ralph Helstein, a Minneapolis lawyer then representing the local, now President of the International union.

The Working Agreement was submitted to a vote by the rank and file of the workers and ratified by them. It is a permanent agreement, not subject to periodic renewals. Looking back from a perspective of almost ten years, Mr. Hormel felt the permanence of the agreement was a great advantage. However, in his estimation, the basic principles regulating labor-management relations should have been separated more clearly from the

procedural questions. Yet when concluded it marked the beginning of a new era. Its importance for labor-management relations in Austin has been clearly stated in the official union paper:

> The signing of this contract with the Hormel company marks a
> new era in the relationship between the union and the company. For
> the first time the relationship is one that has its conditions in black
> and white, and for the first time, both parties will be able to determine
> more correctly what their obligations and actions must be to maintain
> efficient and orderly working conditions.[6]

The Working Agreement confirms Local 9 "as the sole and
exclusive bargaining agent"[7] and incorporates the union shop
provisions which oblige all employees except supervisory and
office personnel "to become members of the union within two
weeks from the date of their employment."[8] The Agreement does
not provide for a checkoff. The union prefers to have its members
come to the union hall for dues payment and get some personal
contact with the union officers. Since the union offices are only
a few minutes from the factory, a short visit to the union hall does
not involve any hardships. The company also prefers not to
have a checkoff "because it believes the members contribute
towards a better union by frequent visits to the headquarters
office. It feels, too, that a widespread delinquency in dues would
be the promptest and most effective protest against any union
action not approved by the rank and file."[9]
The essence of the Agreement lies in the recognition of "the
principle of collective bargaining as . . . the best medium of
establishing the most dependable employment, the most satisfactory working conditions, and the greatest and most fairly
distributed compensation."[10] The Agreement thus modified basically the traditional exchange relationship between the workers
and the company: by bargaining collectively workers *associated*
and made a kind of property claim on their jobs. They replaced their *individual* and formally free, but actually sub-
servient, relationship to the company by a contract which
brought hitherto unregulated relationships within the orbit of
joint union-management *control* and modified the *values* underlying industrial organization.

## Two Interlocking Systems of Control

The Working Agreement substituted two interlocking machineries of control—the company and the union—for the exclusive managerial control of the work process. The basic structure of the corporation remains unchanged. As the upper half of the diagram on p. 20 shows, the corporation is an outgrowth of "the world of management," that complex of values and power relationships peculiar to management. The external organization of the company relates it to this world—to the markets and to various "trade" organizations. Membership in the American Meat Institute, the Chamber of Commerce of the United States, and the National Association of Manufacturers should be mentioned in this context. The board of directors is at the borderline between the external organization and those aspects of the corporation which are internal to the factory: the managerial and the supervisory hierarchy.

The managerial hierarchy consists of the board of directors, the president, the vice-presidents, and the personnel director. The employment manager is at the borderline of the managerial and supervisory hierarchy. The latter is composed of eight superintendents who are in charge of quality, output, and new products—and supervisors who assist the superintendents and who are in charge of labor. The superintendents are directly responsible to the respective vice-president; supervisors in so far as labor is concerned are responsible to the personnel director and employment manager. There is no plant superintendent, except during the night shift. The personnel director and the employment manager are responsible for all labor problems. They give orders to the supervisors, but may also deal directly with the foreman—or with the workers.

The lower half of the diagram gives the structure of the union which penetrated the work process "from below" so to speak. Its internal organization, based on the shop steward system and the grievance machinery, is quite literally opposed to the internal organization of the company. Small groups—gangs—of workers elect their grievance man: the shop steward. Each division elects a representative in the grievance machinery, the divisional

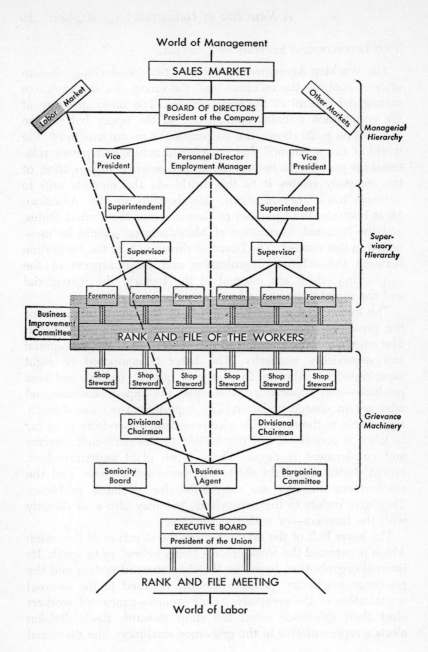

World of Management

SALES MARKET

Labor Market

BOARD OF DIRECTORS
President of the Company

Other Markets

*Managerial Hierarchy*

Vice President

Personnel Director
Employment Manager

Vice President

Superintendent

Superintendent

*Supervisory Hierarchy*

Supervisor

Supervisor

Foreman | Foreman | Foreman | Foreman | Foreman | Foreman

Business Improvement Committee

RANK AND FILE OF THE WORKERS

Shop Steward | Shop Steward | Shop Steward | Shop Steward | Shop Steward | Shop Steward

*Grievance Machinery*

Divisional Chairman

Divisional Chairman

Seniority Board

Business Agent

Bargaining Committee

EXECUTIVE BOARD
President of the Union

RANK AND FILE MEETING

World of Labor

chairman, and the rank and file as a whole elect *all* other union representatives. The ultimate control over all affairs of the union is vested in the rank-and-file meetings which take place once a month. All decisions made by the elected representatives or by any of the boards and committees are subject to approval or revision by the rank and file.

The grievance machinery and the seniority system are the avenues through which the union penetrates the work process from below. Within these systems, the union also functions as a disciplinary agent and takes part in remedying "bad workmanship and misconduct." It maintains, furthermore, a code of interpersonal relationships through its own discipline committee, which examines all actions not in agreement with the "principles of unionism."

Through the organs which it set up to deal with top management, the union is penetrating the organization of industry "from above." These organs are the executive board and the bargaining committee. The Executive Board consists of the president, the vice-president, the business agent, and five members elected at large. It transacts all business between rank-and-file meetings. The bargaining committee consists of three members besides the president and the business agent. It negotiates agreements with management, participates in the negotiations of work schedules, etc.[11] The executive board links the union to its own "world of labor," symbolized by affiliation with the State Industrial Council of the C.I.O. and membership in District 2 of the United Packinghouse Workers of America, one of the Internationals comprised in the C.I.O.

The union and the company are separate organizations, in so far as control of their own internal organizations and their relationship to their respective "outside" worlds is concerned. Yet they control jointly certain aspects of the work process—the shaded areas—linked by dotted lines—in the diagram—namely:

1. The rank and file of the workers, their relationships to the supervisory staff, and their working conditions (central area). Management prerogatives in this area are practically abolished.

2. Part of the labor market (small area to the left). Workers can only be dismissed on a fifty-two-week notice and dismissals for cause are jointly administered by the union and the company.

Among the main stipulations regulating working conditions are wages, hours, vacation and sick leave, leaves of absence, grievance procedure, arbitration, production schedules and bonuses, gang reductions and work, and working conditions in general.

### MODIFICATIONS IN WORKERS' RELATEDNESS TO THE WORK PROCESS

The Agreement stipulates that "each employee will be employed on an annual basis, and shall receive the regular weekly rate of pay provided for him in a work schedule."[12] Since the Working Agreement is not subject to periodic renewal, the company must at all times give a fifty-two-week notice before dismissing a worker. This stipulation gives to the workers a security unique in American industry. He has a guaranteed minimum weekly income which is assured to him for a year at *any* time.

Since production schedules determining the amount of output per hour of work are a matter of collective bargaining, and the speed at which workers work a matter of group decisions, the Working Agreement changed the relationship between the workers and the company radically: workers actually sell a product to the company instead of selling their services. It is true that workers produce with the help of machines either owned by the company or put at their disposal by the company. But this does not lessen the significance of the departure from the traditional organization of industry.

Equally important for the purposes of this study are the changes which the new interlocking machineries of control established by the Working Agreement have brought about in the daily administration of the work process.

Before unionization, workers were subject to the authority of the foremen without having any recourse, not to speak of a say-so, in the most vital decisions affecting their work. As we have seen, foremen had the right to hire, promote, and fire workers.

Now hiring is done by the employment manager in the front office; dismissals for cause are jointly controlled by the union and by management, while dismissals for lack of work require a fifty-two-week notice. Promotions take place on the basis of the seniority principle which is implemented by a "posting in" system giving the greatest possible freedom of movement to individual workers within a well-regulated, self-administered system of transfers and promotions.

It is true that workers have to follow "any instructions regarding the work or working conditions . . . given by . . . the appropriate person on the supervisory staff."[13] But the grievance machinery allows them to express their dissatisfaction if they feel unjustly treated. They have, furthermore, their departmental union meetings in which they determine such crucial questions as the speed at which they are working.

The foreman can give and pass on instructions, but their authority is limited since "major changes in the work or working conditions [shall be] effectuated by no less than one week's written notice"[14] to the union. A major change in anything that affects a man's life "seriously," such as an increase or decrease in the size of the gang, changes in work schedules, or a shift of work from one department to another. A change in the work shift, for example, is not considered a major change.

The new role of the foreman is that of an executor of policies which he does not formulate and which are subject to grievance procedures. The Working Agreement states: "The supervisory staff will report to the employment office any instances of bad workmanship or misconduct which cannot be satisfactorily handled informally. When in his judgment the occasion warrants, the Employment Manager will serve, through the Bargaining Committee, written first notices with respect to the individual or group concerned. . . ."[15] Note well that the employment manager who is in the front office, and not the supervisory staff, will evaluate the situation and serve notices—through the union. If a worker has received three notices for faulty workmanship within one year, he can be dismissed. If the notices are for unexcused absence, three cases within six months are sufficient. A dismissed worker may request a hearing before a joint union-management board. The decisions of this board is subject to regular grievance procedure.

The Working Agreement provides for definite steps and time limits in the processing of grievances. It stipulates "fair, reasonable and equitable conclusions"[16] as the basis for their settlement. If the union and the company cannot agree, grievances are settled through arbitration.

The nature of workers' participation in the work process opened to them in the Working Agreement is best illustrated by the nature of the grievances which arise. Most frequent are problems of adjustment in pay for conditions caused by "inadequate layout, quality of material and changes due to new products." The adjustments usually concern take-home pay on incentive schedules. Other problems arise in relation to the "determination of rates and classification of new jobs; safety problems; discharge; fault slips and notices for poor workmanship or for unexcused absences." Exceptionally, grievances are filed "in case of gang reductions and build-up; material or work process deficiencies within the jurisdiction of management and problems arising out of worker-foremen relationships."[17]

In conjunction with the departmental union meetings in which all problems affecting the work-gang are discussed, workers are thus enabled to deal with a wide variety of problems arising out of the daily life in the factory. The addition of "working conditions in general" and "over-all contract demands" makes the list even more impressive. Compared to pre-union days, workers administer a considerable section of the work process; the whole system of job assignments and transfers and the speed at which they are working are self-determined. Furthermore, they can express their dissatisfactions about anything connected with working conditions. Yet when it comes to a development of workers' initiative and their ideas in regard to most technical and most more-than-routine organizational aspects of the work, we must go beyond the grievance machinery—which does not allow workers a creative self-expression. The existing instruments which may eventually fulfill this purpose are now outside the Working Agreement; they are part of the company's master plan.

## THE MASTER PLAN

Though many of the ideas incorporated in the Working Agreement were suggested by Mr. Hormel, the Agreement as a whole must be attributed to the rise of unionism. Indeed, its onslaught was quick, unexpected, and powerful—sufficiently powerful for Jay C. Hormel to decide that "If you can't beat them, join them!"[18] But he did not become a joiner in the usual sense of the word. Realizing that he could not fight the union successfully with traditional methods and accepting the union as an instrument to settle grievances, he decided to counter its claim to power with a strategy of his own, a strategy, incidentally, which he developed in close contact with the feelings and thoughts of the workers. He has taken time from his business preoccupations to talk to the workers, to ask them questions—and to listen to what they have to say. Upon this experience and his general ideas on industrial organization, he has built a long-range master plan—a scheme which has been designed to bear fruit not in one or two, but in ten or twenty years.

To what extent the master plan would have been conceived and carried through without the formation of the union must remain an unanswerable question. But there is no doubt that we are dealing here with management's most enlightened answer to the challenge of unionism. After having lost a great deal of control over the workers through unionization and after the power position of the union had been consolidated in the Working Agreement, Mr. Hormel developed an over-all plan which put the initiative back in the hands of management. He has literally taken the ball out of labor's hands by espousing the basic objectives of the workers and carrying them far beyond the point to which labor would have been able to realize them on the basis of its newly acquired power position. Management has carried the ball to the extent of building up a system which is the avowed goal of major sectors of the American labor movement.

A genuine human interest and a desire to make workers management-oriented were the motives underlying management's actions—at least as far as Jay C. Hormel is concerned. Since I have been challenged from various sides to prove the existence of a human interest on management's side, I have systematically collected all available evidence for Mr. Hormel's attitude towards the workers before unionization. Granted that he was unaware of the conditions in the plant, all his contacts and dealings with the workers show a human interest and attitude which become no less genuine because they are expressed within the framework of the "world of management" rather than within that of the "world of labor."

## JOINT EARNINGS AND PROFIT-SHARING TRUST

The first step of management in the development of the master plan—the guaranteed wage plan—preceded unionization. And the second step—the Joint Earnings Plan of 1938—preceded the conclusion of the Working Agreement. The Joint Earnings plan provides for workers' participation in profits—the "surplus" remaining after current expenses, taxes, depreciation charges, etc., have been taken care of. Whereas the guaranteed wage is part of the Working Agreement, this Agreement only mentions the existence of the Joint Earnings Plan. It states explicitly that the union has no control over the plan.

The general philosophy underlying the plan is explained in a pamphlet under the heading, "the attitude of the company towards the general plan and towards the employees under the plan, as well as the attitudes we hope to generate among the employees towards the plan." It is stated there:

Under our system, working here means that if you earn it, you get it.

In the first place, you are on straight time so you know that your pay comes per week not per hour or per-haps.

In the second place, you have joint earnings, so you know if there is some money left over at the end of the year, you will get your share on your joint earnings check.[19]

I don't think we are dipping to the bottom of the barrel and are getting all there is there for us. You remember last year we were talking about each man saving 11¢ a day—lights, water, doors, packages, pieces of meat—you know the bets we miss.

And it's easy to leave some little job undone or badly done—or to leave some job unplanned—while taking care of your own business, or somebody else's business, but not *the* business. If a fellow has something coming, let's see that he gets it. But, add it up your own way, my guess is that the time wasted visiting, or running around, or in meetings that weren't necessary, would figure two joint earnings checks a year on a man-hour basis. It probably costs us more than that when we figure the value of business we could have done with the same energy. And of course, most of us would make money if we could sell out a year's grievances for one joint earning check. . . .[20]

This declaration strongly emphasizes the earning opportunities as the main preoccupation of management. Looked at from a somewhat broader point of view, it is part of management's attempts to give to workers a *just* share in the earnings of the company.

A significant feature of the Joint Earnings Plan is the conception of the "surplus" as *joint* earnings of the stockholders and workers. By considering "the business . . . as a joint enterprise of the stockholders as one group and the employees as the other,"[21] the plan recognizes—at least for accounting purposes—workers as partners in the enterprise. Indeed, it was the intention of the plan to overcome the limitations inherent in the guaranteed wage-group incentive system and to give to workers a real feeling of partnership. It is true that the conception of the corporation as a social organization which gives to the stockholders certain privileges to the exclusion of the workers is maintained. But the departure from the traditional concept of corporate enterprise remains no less clear.

Under the plan about 10 million dollars have been paid to the workers between 1939 and 1950 (for details see Appendix I).

The Joint Earnings Plan was complemented in 1944 by the Profit-Sharing Trust Fund, a pension fund which is maintained by company contributions exclusively. The contributions vary according to the profits realized and according to the length of time an employee has been with the company. During the first six years of operation, the trust fund yielded almost five million dollars.

### Hormel Business Improvement Project and Committee

The modifications of the traditional organization of the work process has been carried a step further in the Hormel Business Improvement Project which was instituted in 1945. Whereas the Joint Earnings Plan and the Profit-Sharing Trust make workers participate in the monetary returns, the Business Improvement Project must be considered as the first step in strengthening the bonds of partnership by allowing workers to participate in the technical and to some extent organizational aspects of the work process.

The Business Improvement Project consists in awards for proposals leading to an improvement of the work process or of the quality of the product. "A proposal may involve the reduction in waste of meat, supplies, time and effort, improve quality and uniformity of products, increase efficiency of machines and equipment, the origination of new products, the new packaging of products, or new uses for present products. . . ."[22] Here are some examples showing how the Project fosters workers' inventiveness: One worker received an award for "providing the means of using an air press to force into place the covers on the casing kits." Another worker developed a machine "for shaping the metal form to make the bottom sections of spiral chutes." A third invented "a sash cord lariat to rope around loaded lard tubs so that they won't fall off the truck."

During the first four years of its existence, the Business Improvement Project accepted 100 suggestions, rejected 131, and considered 18 as incomplete. Rejections occurred mainly because the suggestions were "found impractical" (over 50 per cent of the rejected proposals). Secondary reasons for rejections were that "no savings or advantages could be found" (over 10 per cent) and that the suggestions did not constitute "a profitable investment" (less than 10 per cent).[23]

The Hormel Business Improvement Project is complemented by the Hormel Business Improvement Committee. The latter offers a much wider basis for active participation and provides channels for creative participation in the work process.

The Committee consists of twelve members, elected for a one-year period in the following manner: The first member was a divisional chairman who chose a second member. The two chose a third member, and so on. Each member has the right to bring a guest to the meeting. Every three months, three members retire and choose their successor before leaving the Committee. Since there is a union shop, all committee members are members of the union. All members and guest members are paid for their attendance of the sessions.

Since this is strictly a management and operating function, members of the Committee, including guest members, will be paid at their regular rates for the time they spend attending Committee meetings.[24]

The Committee is not only autonomous in the election of its members, it also sets its own agenda and may take up any problem within its jurisdiction. It meets twice a month in the evening, usually at a neutral place like the city hall.

In its organization structure, the Committee is independent of both the company and the union. It lies outside the organization of the work process proper. Controlled by the workers themselves, it introduces a new conception of control into an organization whose basic control emanates from above and is checked from below. The Committee meets without management or union representatives, unless they are specifically invited to present some problem. It has a program and an investigating subcommittee whose members are chosen by the Committee. The chairman of the program committee, and a person designated by the company, establish contact between the Committee and management.

The significance which Mr. Hormel, who originated the idea, attributes to the Business Improvement Committee emerges clearly from his statement:

This marks the initiation of one additional step in our over-all program to safeguard the employment and earnings opportunities of Hormel people.

Like other parts of the program, it is merely a tool or device for us to use to make our collective effort yield us a greater return. What we get out of it will depend entirely upon what we are able to put into it.

The specific purpose of the Business Improvement Committee is to increase the number of people who give thought to the problems of managing the business. At the same time, the Business Improvement Committee is intended to bring to management problems that peculiar insight and understanding which come from being on the job itself the day a problem arises.

Good management has authority at the top. In the course of a week's work, there is many a proposal made by a vice-president and turned down by the boss. Similarly, the Business Improvement Committee will probably make proposals and recommendations which will not be accepted. . . .

On the other hand, the measure of good management is its ability to recognize a good idea and to act on it. We hope that our management is such that we will never waste a good proposal which comes from the Business Improvement Committee.

At no time should the activity of the Committee be permitted to make the slightest encroachment on collective bargaining procedures.

Similarly, the Committee should not trespass upon the Business Improvement Project program. That program is designed to reward individuals for specific ideas which they are able to promote. . . .[25]

At its bimonthly meetings, the Committee discusses problems "that have to do with quality of product, uniformity of product, safety of personnel, and reduction in waste."[26] Every member— or guest—has the right to bring up any relevant matter for discussion. If the majority desires, the suggested problems are discussed, investigated by a subcommittee, and recommendations are made to the company. The final decision about these recommendations is up to the company. Both company and union may suggest subjects for discussion, but the Committee is not obliged to take them up.

Here are some of the problems with which the Committee concerned itself: Purchase, alterations, and maintenance of equipment—such as skids, gondolas, trucks, etc.; improvements in the process of production; quality of products and introduction of new products; safety hazards; laundry and lavatory facilities; planning of new construction, etc.[27]

BUSINESS IMPROVEMENT COMMITTEE AND GRIEVANCE MACHINERY

The Business Improvement Committee constitutes one of the most significant—and promising—departures from the traditional organization of industry. In its conception, the Committee is a masterpiece of social strategy: delicately balanced between the sphere of control of the union and that of the company, management tried to solve basic issues of power and values by establishing the Committee in an area in which the role of the union and the role of the company have not yet been clearly defined. The Committee is independent of the company and encroachment on managerial control is avoided by limiting its functions to proposals. It is also independent of the union and encroachment on union control is eliminated through separation of grievances and business improvement projects.

The Committee is democratically constituted and is the outgrowth of a truly "representative system." It is also true that the Committee functions in a truly democratic manner. The meetings of the Committee which the author attended have been genuinely democratic. The problems are being investigated, workers have a real knowledge of what they are talking about, and there is a give-and-take of feeling and ideas. Yet the Committee remains a "representative system" outside the representative system workers have built up in their union: the grievance machinery. And the committee is limited in scope—and the values which it implements.

Its limitations in scope are due to its separation from the grievance machinery. Quality of product, one of the concerns of the Committee, often raises problems related to the process of production and to work requirements. Since working conditions are clearly within the scope of the grievance machinery, the Committee cannot take up such problems. A similar situation prevails in regard to "safety problems." The Committee's present limited value-basis is clearly expressed in the following statement of the company: "Like other parts of the program, it [the Committee] is merely a tool or device for us to use to make our collective effort yield us a greater return."[28]

Though major conflicts between the grievance machinery and

the Business Improvement Committee can be avoided as long as the Committee does not expand its functions, such a possibility remains a threat to the union. The union has been aware of this situation and felt uneasy about it until it requested, in the spring of 1950, abolition of the Committee—a demand which it modified later to a greater control over the Committee. Since this demand was not met, it withdrew its approval of the Committee in the spring of 1952. The union has thus raised the problems which management wanted to avoid: basic issues concerning the control of the work process, the workers' and the union's share in this control, and, last but not least, concerning the values to be expressed in the organization of industry.

As we examine the development of labor-management relations since the conclusion of the Working Agreement and the initiation of the master plan, we will get a better understanding of the significance of these problems.

## THE EMERGING PATTERN OF LABOR-MANAGEMENT RELATIONS

During the decade from 1940 to 1950 following the conclusion of the Working Agreement, labor-management relations have shown great improvements. The union and the company cooperate to assure high earning opportunities and to administer fairly the security setup and the system of rewards and punishment. The close cooperation between the union and the company in the administration of the Working Agreement is reflected in the feelings of the large majority of the workers: "We have a good union and the union and company are working things out together."

Whatever difficulties may arise are being taken care of by the grievance machinery which functions smoothly, partly because of the fixed intervals which assure prompt attention to the problems arising in the plant, and partly because of the broad basis of a "fair, reasonable, and equitable" treatment on which grievances are being settled.

These rules prevent any wrangling about the letter of the agreement and direct attention to the fairness and equity of the settlement. If he would deem it "fair, reasonable, and equitable," the arbitrator could, for example, impose a fine upon the company to be paid to the union treasury. Mr. Hormel, who suggested this stipulation, was warned by a high ranking member of management that he "is selling out the company to the union." Subsequent events have shown that this was an unfounded fear. The grievance machinery is yielding good results. It works efficiently, and evokes a mutual desire to come to fair and equitable solutions. The number of cases submitted to arbitration has declined constantly. There has been no arbitration case since 1943.

Besides settling grievances in a spirit of give and take, the company and the union have made attempts to reduce certain types of grievances. In 1944, for example, the rank and file approved an agreement authorizing four union men to take time study courses at the expense of the company. Such a participation of the union in the determination of work schedules has contributed to reduce grievances.

The cooperation between the union and the company is illustrated in the attitudes towards the postwar strikes in the packing industry. Local 9 did not take part in the January, 1946, strike. Yet it collected a considerable strike fund after the strike had been stalled by government seizure of the major plants. In August, 1946, as a result of wage demands made by the International, Local 9 filed a strike notice with the Hormel company. The rank and file authorized the Executive Board by a 2000 to 6 vote to call a strike if necessary to enforce the wage demands. A similar situation occurred in March, 1948, when an industry-wide strike materialized. In Austin, however, a walkout was avoided by a special agreement with the Hormel company: the workers were to benefit by whatever settlement the "big four" would enter into with the International. They contributed for the duration of the strike 10 per cent of their take-home pay to a strike fund—to which the Austin Chamber of Commerce and local businessmen made token contributions!

When, in the fall of 1951, the International threatened an industry-wide strike against the Wage Stabilization Board, the Hormel workers again authorized the Local to take part in the strike. Since this strike would have taken place against the government, a special agreement with the Hormel company would have been difficult, if not impossible. But the avoidance of the strike allowed Austin to maintain its reputation as a strike-free city since 1933.

Austin could avoid strikes because of the workers' and the union's willingness to do so and because the company is in a "satellite position" in the industry—a position which allows it to follow the pattern set by the "big four" and the International. Yet its dependence upon the industry exists only in regard to the standard hourly wage rate which must be set on a competitive basis. It does not exist in regard to all other aspects of the organized work process which by far excel the industry pattern, and which are responsible for the workers' and the union's desire to cooperate with management.

The nature of this cooperation can best be assessed as we realize its limitation to those areas of the work process which are jointly controlled by management and the union (see diagram p. 20). Outside this area, the struggle for power and value continues to exist. The Business Improvement Committee, is a case in point already mentioned. Unusual and, on the whole, quite untypical occurrences like the "I.M.Rumbling" column throw further light on the underlying cross-currents.

The "I.M.Rumbling" column appeared in the *Unionist,* the weekly union paper, for about three months in 1950. The column was a revival of an old "Scorpion" column of the days of aggressive unionism. Its writer attacked foremen and certain managerial attitudes.

It is significant that the union justified the "I.M.Rumbling" column partly by events totally unrelated to the work process: "One of the reasons it was started was because the Hormel company was distributing in this community the literature of the Committee for Constitutional Government." This reference to the conflict between the "world of management" and "the world of labor" highlights the influence of those areas which are most remote from the work process proper and hence outside the Working Agreement. It is indicative of an uneasiness in regard to ultimate control and the values to be realized on the industrial scene.

It would, therefore, be erroneous to assume that the Austin experiment is outside the conflict of power and values which is an inevitable legacy of the inequalities inherent in the traditional organization of industry. The Austin experiment has greatly transformed this organization in so far as the work process proper is concerned. But it has not, and could not, eliminate the underlying struggle for power. This struggle is not less prominent in Austin than it is in most other industrial centers; it is only less visible because it receded from the picket line to deeper levels where people's feelings and thoughts are molded. Beneath the calm and outward harmony of union-management relationships, an intense struggle for the loyalties of the very soul of the workers is going on—a struggle whose outcome will decide the real power of management and union as well as the degree to which workers can find a creative self-expression in their work—and their life.

# CHAPTER 3

# "You Can't Run a Place
# Like That Without a Union"

## THE UNION'S OBJECTIVES

Pending the building of a Labor Temple which will symbolize the new power of the union, Local 9 is located in a small unobtrusive building about half a mile from the plant. The visitor to the union offices first passes a window where the workers pay their dues in exchange for their union cards and for the buttons which they wear on their frocks or caps in the factory. The window is followed by a few doors leading to the small and austere offices of the business agent, the president, and the editor of the *Unionist*. At the end of the hallway is a large meeting hall which holds about 500 people. The star-spangled banner behind the rostrum is the only decoration of the simple, almost drab union hall. A few small side rooms with tables and chairs complete the union headquarters.

The geographic separation of the union headquarters from the plant—which we are most likely to take for granted—is crucial in the role which the union plays in the life of the workers. The union is not an organic part of the work process but arose from the outside, so to speak. Since the traditional organization of the industry excluded workers from any participation and reduced them to mere means, the workers—the very core of industrial organization—had to form their own organization independent of the organized work process in order to express their own needs and aspirations. It is true that the union has penetrated deeply into this process through its Working Agreement with the company, but the separation of the company and the union and the differences in their organization and their objectives are not basically altered thereby.

When the *Unionist* was first published in mimeographed form in October, 1935, it carried the following pronouncement of the policy of Local 9:

In line with the history and tradition of the Union, this paper will be radical and militant, dynamic rather than static, alive rather than asleep.

Also in line with our organization the paper will be a democratic institution. It will be responsible to the members of the organization. Committees will be charged with the administering of the affairs of the paper.

With prospects of war staring us in the face and organized drives being made on unions and especially radical unions, with the unemployed still stalking the streets and the cost of living rapidly rising, the task of the Union and this paper, its spokesman, is a tremendous one.

We are in the battle in support of all unions and especially industrial unions. We will fight for farmers and workers and will aid representatives of them in times of trouble and strife. We will fight incessantly "Law and Order Leagues," "Citizens Alliances," "Secret 500's." We will promote workers' education, forums, discussions and other activities. We recognize that we are under a system which perpetuates wage slavery. We will defend the right of free press, free speech and lawful assemblage.

All this cannot be accomplished unless by organization, education and fraternity. While we cannot hope to be successful working individually, by combining our efforts, the most beneficial results can be obtained. In union there is strength.[1]

According to Frank W. Schultz, Local 9's President since 1945, this passage can still be taken as an official pronouncement of union policy.[2]

The main emphasis of this proclamation of policy is on cementing the strength of the union through "organization, education and fraternity"; through creating a feeling of solidarity, strengthening the bonds with the labor movement, and making workers aware of major socio-economic issues. The ultimate aim of the policy is to create a "labor ideology" which directs workers' aspirations towards the labor movement—away from the philosophy of rugged individualism and toward the abolition of "wage slavery."

To what extent are these objectives reflected in the attitudes of the workers? What does the union really mean to them? Does the union provide an instrument to relate them creatively to the organized work process?

### WORKERS' FEELINGS ABOUT THE UNION

As a first step towards an understanding of the meaning of the union to the workers, we asked them: "What comes to your mind when you say 'I am a member of the U.P.W.A.'?" Their answers cover a wide range. One worker said: "Strongest militant union advanced faster than rest of industry." Such an image of a fighting organization implies a strong positive feeling about the union. The interrelationship between the images intruding into workers' mind and the meaning which the union has for them is clearly shown in the following response: "Leaves me blank, not active or anything." The blank mind—the absence of an image—is typical for any relationship which has no inner meaning. Yet for the overwhelming majority of the workers, the images or ideas evoked by union membership are positive. Typical responses are: "It is a good thing, it is what we need . . . workers need organization, same as business, everything is organized." Or: "Protection comes to my mind . . . you see, before the union was established they could hire and fire whenever they pleased . . . when you were not in with the bosses, when they did not like you, you were out." A final response: "Better working conditions, wages up, cost of living, political issues come to my mind." Only a relatively small number have mixed feelings or give such a colorless response that we may surmise absence of positive as well as negative feelings: "Not much" comes to their mind.

Whereas there were differences in the images denoting an emotional identification, workers' appreciation of the service job rendered by the union is practically unanimous. "Real good job, not only for workers, also for community"; "I think very good," and "helps working people in all different things, prestige that labor gets," may suffice as outstanding responses to the question: "From the standpoint of people in your occupation, do you think the union is on the whole doing a good service job or not?" The few workers who qualified their affirmative answers did so for reasons unrelated to the union's role in the factory: ". . . some of them unions have gone too far in destroying; I never believed in destroying other people's property. . . ." And only exceptionally did workers answer in the negative the question about the quality of the service job done by the union.

The high appreciation of the union continues to manifest itself as we asked workers: "Does being a member of the union make you feel you are a partner in doing something important?" Most workers gave an affirmative answer. Only a relatively small group gave no evidence of such feelings or their answers were so ambiguous that they seem to exclude strong feelings of partnership. One of these negative responses, however, cautions us not to attach too much significance to an isolated response: "Never got the feeling of partner . . . helping a big cause . . . like big business . . . a little bit too big for feeling of partners. . . ." This worker may feel as strongly about the union as another worker who says that he is feeling as a partner, but he has a different conception of partnership.

Partnership may, indeed, have various meanings. In its deepest sense, it implies: (1) participation in a group or movement that is experienced as a cause and, hence, implies a common goal; and (2) an emotional attachment to the partners. An illustration of the first condition can be found in all great social movements: the French Revolution, the European labor movement, the Populist movement in this country. The classic illustrations of the second condition are family ties, friendship ties, and, if we come to larger groups, the early Christian communities which were pervaded by the "compassion of brotherly love."

The meaning of partnership feelings with the union will emerge more clearly as we visualize the two kinds of relationships which the union establishes within the organized work process: (1) It relates them to their fellow workers and regulates their relationships to the supervisory and managerial hierarchy within the factory gates; and (2) it relates them to workers in other factories, other communities, and other industries. Partnership in the deepest sense of the term implies, therefore, a common goal, participation in the enterprise and outcome, and an experience of a common cause which transcends the factory gates: an awareness of a community of people and ideas—a community of work and labor.

Such an awareness is best expressed in the following statement: "If all members of packing industry in same union, would have more power and influence on legislation . . . making laws through union and bargaining committee . . . a guy would say that in union is strength . . . probably heard of I.W.W. . . . you may call it names, but it was a great organization. The radicals got upper hand, but their slogan 'injury to one is injury to all' should go down in every labor union." Similar feelings about a community of people are reflected in the following answer to the partnership question: "I think it does give some feeling of being a partner in doing something important; when we vote for something, usually for good not only yourself, but for a guy at Wilsons. . . ." Experience of the group as a common cause is also reflected in the response of a worker who said: "I feel that I am more than a member of a local."

The role of the union in relating workers to each other in the factory is well expressed in the following answers to our partnership question: "I think so. . . . Everybody pulling for each, not pulling against." Or: "Yes, for the reason that I can help my fellow-worker if he is in a little problem. If I am in difficulties, he can help." Finally: "I feel we got a setup; we have not only one behind us, we have thousands of workers behind us, all one family."

The significance of the union in relating workers to the work process emerges from the following responses: "If it would not be for a group of people, would not give you better working conditions." Or: "Being organized gives you somewhat the feeling of security, to be with your fellow workers, improve working conditions." Even stronger are the feelings of the worker who said: "I am proud of it, I would not want to be without it. They have done so much for me, security, better working conditions, more pay, put bosses in their place." Statements like these recur again and again: "Working for better contract," "More vocal ability, everybody is not equipped to go in and argue his point," or "Yes, the fact that they have raised the standard of living in this town," and "Yes, because I belong to it, I feel more safe."

Yet we must recognize the existence of a group of workers who do not have any strong feelings of partnership with the union. These workers are, as a rule, not too communicative: "Well, not necessarily in belonging to the union," "Not a member long enough" are typical responses to our question about partnership. The impact of the master plan on workers' partnership feelings with the union can be clearly seen in the following response: "Of course they have not done so much for us . . . never had to fight for anything. Hormel is willing to do everything U.P.W.A. wants. In other cases union gives security."

Usually, no specific criticism of the union is offered. Even most of the workers without strong partnership feelings have a positive appreciation of the service job done by the union. One of these workers, for example, said: "I think if it had not been for the union, I don't think we would be getting the wages we are getting. I think bosses and stuff can't run you around like they did—cussing. . . ." Another worker with similar feelings was quite emphatic in stating that "Union is security."

THE UNION'S ROLE IN THE WORK PROCESS: RIGHTS AND SECURITY

The significance of security as the main factor giving meaning to the union emerges clearly from workers' responses to the question: "What are the advantages of belonging to the union? What do you get out of belonging?" Workers were asked to list the three most important advantages. Protection, security, and seniority were on top of the list. They emphasized seniority and job security, while "protection against the boss system" was mentioned repeatedly. Many workers who listed the protective aspects of the union also mentioned wages and working conditions. Group organization, or group action, and miscellaneous advantages such as sick-leave and vacation were also mentioned by some workers. But outstanding remains the significance attributed to protection, quantitatively as well as in the manner in which most workers mentioned protection. It had a quality comparable to what free association may reveal as the outstanding quality of a dream. It is difficult to convey in any direct manner this feeling which I gained while interviewing. But there is an interesting indirect measurement, namely, the frequency with which "Rights" (that means seniority rights) have been mentioned in conversations in the cafeteria. Workers talk very rarely about what is happening inside the factory gates. Sports, recreational events, local activities, and sex are the main topics of conversation. "Rights," however, have been mentioned repeatedly.

There is, indeed, a new tradition growing up around the "system of rights" which is the direct result of union activity. It is a new order which supersedes and is in sharp contrast with the arbitrariness of the boss system. It is only natural that this new system becomes the focal point of the workers' perception of the union and of the meaning which they bestow on unionism. Security and protection are the magic words which open the gates for an understanding of unionism, more so than wages by themselves.

It is interesting that the union, and not the guaranteed wage, is for many workers the main source of their feeling of security. Asked: "What would you do if the guaranteed wage would be abolished?" many workers made their actions dependent upon what would happen to the union: "Have to get along with Rights we have. As long as Rights and union, still pretty good place, if too tough, get out. . . ." The protection through seniority rights came up repeatedly: "Well, I don't know, of course a fellow that has been there for a long time would not be affected much." Even those who would "take it," draw a line which they would not overstep: "I would stay, if it gets tough, I would go back to the farm."

Since the overwhelming majority of the workers highly appreciate the role of the union in giving security and providing a system for the self-administration of important aspects of the work process, they wholeheartedly concur with the statement of one of their fellow workers who said: "You can't run a place like that without a union." This is the best summary evaluation of the union's role. The significance of this statement is enhanced by knowing the background and experience of the worker who made it: he was told by the newspapers until he came to the factory that "unions are a racket." Many workers who came to the factory from the farms have grown up in a similar environment. It is, therefore, striking that among those who came to the factory more recently, farmers feel strongly about the services rendered by the union. First they usually resent the fact that they "have to join." It contradicts their sense of independence. But after having experienced factory life for some time, they change their attitudes, realizing that the independence they would lose without a union outweighs by far the somewhat technical independence the union shop denies them.

GROUP BELONGINGNESS AND THE WORLD OF LABOR

In spite of the appreciation of the services rendered by the union, we must recognize a certain lukewarmness in workers' feelings about the union. There is, for example, the case of an elderly worker who would really like to be independent. An emotional identification with the union is impossible for him without acknowledging that the desire to be his own boss is merely a dream, rather than the reality of his life. By leaving his feelings towards the union sufficiently cool, his dream of independence can glow affectionately. On the other hand, he is elderly and he knows that his job would be endangered without seniority. He appreciates, therefore, the services rendered by the union: "being able to meet with the company as a group and talk over our troubles and seniority." He realizes intellectually that seniority is an advantage though he feels that it is a disadvantage—"for a young or a new man." Another worker projects a great disappointment connected with his work on the union and on the company because it deals with the union.

But more fundamental than these individual constellations are the social forces determining the emotional identification with the union. It is impossible to judge today the strength of the group feelings prior to and following the formation of the union.

But there is no doubt that something existed at that time that has vanished since. It is noteworthy that a clear majority of those who express no feeling of partnership started to work in the factory after 1933. Although too much significance cannot be attributed to this numerical relationship, it indicated an important trend: a decline of emotional identification with the union and of the community experience with work and labor while the objective evaluation of the union's merits is maintained. In answer to the question: "Does being a member of the union make you feel you are a partner in doing something important?" one worker said, "Have not thought that it did . . . maybe we all take it too lightly . . . people who went in twenty-five years ago have greater appreciation." When a worker describes his feelings about the union by saying, "It's two dollars worth"—a reference to the monthly membership dues in effect at that time— then we may assume that the union has a very different meaning from the one it has for those who experienced the pre-union days and say that the union makes you feel like "a human being."

As we recall the situation fifteen years ago and compare it to the present, the declining trend becomes understandable. Then hatred of the authoritarian organization of the work process which thwarted the expression of workers' most basic needs and aspirations was dominant. Now there is a well-regulated system of checks and balances which gives workers a considerable degree of self-administration of the work process.

These changes are well illustrated in workers' attitudes towards the 1948 strike. We have seen how deeply workers were involved in the strike of 1933: it broke out spontaneously and violence was only prevented by the combined efforts of the union, the government, and management. The strike which we will examine now occurred fifteen years later. It was called by the International in March, 1948. Since at that time a secret balloting of the rank and file was necessary before a strike could legally take place, the workers of Local 9 had to indicate by voting whether they were ready to go on the picket line. They gave a remarkable evidence of their loyalty to the union by an almost unanimous vote authorizing their representatives to call a strike. But when a nation-wide strike materialized, Local 9 made a no-strike agreement with the company which gave the workers the full benefits of whatever national strike settlement would be made. The workers accepted this agreement as well as an assessment of 10 per cent of their take-home pay—to support striking workers financially—for the duration of the strike.

These events took place about three months before we asked workers: "How do you feel about the recent strike? How did you feel about the 10 per cent deduction?"

A first group of workers identified themselves strongly with the strikers. "It was a good cause"; "It was a good thing"; "Didn't get what they wanted . . . had to take what company offered them; lost, but it still showed the company that the unions had power to go ahead. . . ." Another group, though not criticizing the strike had a decidedly different emphasis: "I myself not much for people striking, here not necessary"; "According to our conditions here I see no object of striking," are typical comments for this group of workers which is akin to the group of workers who feel that "they should have settled and negotiated." Workers showed a similar variety of attitudes in regard to the 10 per cent deduction from their take-home pay. Their answers range from "wonderful thing," and "should have given more" to a rather skeptical and hesitant acceptance:

Q. Do you think the 10 per cent deduction was fair?
A. There are different points of view.
Q. What is your own point of view?
A. We all belong to the C.I.O. I guess it was all right. The strikers had to live. Somebody had to help out. As long as we belong to the C.I.O. we took the oath: "One for all and all for one."

Typical responses of the overwhelming majority of the workers who agreed with the 10 per cent deduction were: "It was fair," or "It was O.K." Only a few workers felt that "It was not fair." The following response throws some light on the attitudes of these workers: ". . . there were a few dissenters, very few, they didn't want the money to get out of town—despite assurances."

Though the number of outright dissenters was small, their attitude was symptomatic of a more widespread underlying feeling of reluctance to be drawn into an "outside" conflict.

There is no doubt that the Hormel workers would have gone on the picket line if an agreement with the company had not materialized, but they would have done so with great hesitation since the home situation rather than the conditions in the back-of-the-yard quarters in Chicago were uppermost in their mind. They were satisfied with what they had and a little bit afraid that they might lose certain benefits. "If we went out on strike with the Hormel company, we could have lost everything we got. That's why we fought so much against it. If we went out on strike, Hormel company would not have had to pay produc-tion . . . they could have cut off the trust fund." To forestall these fears the President of the union, Frank W. Schultz, emphasized in his speech preceding the strike vote that the guaranteed wage is a contractual right which cannot be taken away as a reprisal against a strike vote or a strike.

Workers' relief that they did not have to go on strike—and fear of what might have happened if it had come to a strike after all—underlay many of their responses: "I was willing on that (meaning the 10 per cent deduction). We worked every day. We could have been called out on strike  too." Or: "We did everything we could . . . it was good. . . as long as we did not have to go out on strike." Many workers considered, indeed, the 10 per cent deduction as a sort of ransom price for not having to go out on the strike. Less numerous were those who identified with the strike action out of a feeling that labor would be "chained" unless it could strike.

The interview situation revealed, furthermore, a certain lack of emotional involvement. If we compare these attitudes with those described by Sorel in his discussion of the general strike,[3] we can readily see the remoteness of workers' experience from that of an ideological identification with a struggle which creates its own "myth" (in Sorel's terms) or images (in modern psy-chological terms). Yet we do not have to go back to nineteenth-century France to get a meaningful comparison. Workers' atti-tudes during the strike of 1949 as compared to those prevailing during the 1933 strike indicate a weakening of the emotional identification with the union.

To the extent to which guaranteed wages have made a

significant contribution to the over-all changes in working conditions and to the change in social climate in the community,
they may be said to reinforce the declining trend in partnership
feelings. There are some workers for whom work became more
meaningful because guaranteed wages made them aware of the
union's potentialities as an instrument implementing ideas of
social responsibility and a community of work and labor. But
those whom the guaranteed wage does not induce to look beyond
their own welfare are more numerous, as the following response
shows: "It brings individual working men closer together. Each
man has some interest in what another man is doing because it
has a bearing on his wage." Whatever common bonds the
interdependence of earnings may create, they are not likely to
strengthen genuine feelings of partnership with the union.

PARTICIPATION IN UNION AFFAIRS

The decline in emotional identification shows itself clearly in
workers' participation in union affairs. Involvement growing out
of relatedness leads to participation, whereas apathy is always
the sign of a "broken," disrupted relationship between ourselves
and the group to which we belong or the "community" or "world"
in which we are living. To understand the meaning of the union
and the role it plays in the organized work process, we must
therefore raise questions like these: To what kind of meetings
do workers go? How often do they go?

In the early days all union meetings were general rank-and-
file meetings. There were no departmental meetings. In June,
1933, the Executive Board of the union decided to hold "separate
rank-and-file meetings of the packinghouse workers." These separate meetings developed into departmental meetings dealing
mainly with specific job problems, whereas general rank-and-
file meetings are concerned with the general conduct of union
affairs and problems concerning the labor movement.

Within less than a decade from the formation of the union,
workers' interest in the rank-and-file meetings began to decline.
In 1939 the quorum "which required 300 members present at a
rank-and-file meeting in order to do business" was abolished as
a result of poor attendance of the general meetings.[4] Ever since,

the union has tried to foster attendance. In May, 1945, it established a "door prize to stimulate attendance at meetings."[5] Various other devices have been tried to increase attendance at rank-and-file meetings.[6]

When we asked the workers in the summer of 1948 how often they attended rank-and-file meetings, and how they liked them, the overwhelming majority indicated that they go "once in a while." A small minority goes often while a few said that they never go. The majority of those who go most often are old-timers who have been with the company before 1933. Many of them did play or are now playing an active part in union affairs. Most of the workers who say that they go "once in a while" actually seldom go. Why is this so?

A considerable number of the workers have a positive attitude towards the meetings. One worker likes them "because interesting problems of labor movement come up. . . ." Another worker feels that the meetings are "very educational. You always learn something." A third said, "The way they run them here is the only way you can—rank-and-file votes on anything." A final response: "The meetings are all right, you get a better understanding of the plant."

A second group is somewhat more skeptical: "Well, that all depends upon the kind of business; if important, then it is interesting . . . it is important if it is related to something in your own division." One worker likes meetings if they deal with "anything I am interested in, anything pertaining to me personally." Others take a somewhat broader view: "Some are very interesting; they settle problems about your job, other fellows' problems in other departments."

Those who are critical do not only differ in regard to what is an interesting meeting and what is not. They also differ about what is a well-conducted meeting: "Sometimes I am disgusted . . . the same ones do all the talking; not enough different people discussing." There are many complaints about "too much arguing," "too much wrangling," "sometime guys get up and make the dandiest speeches; no head nor tail to it." Some workers feel that the meetings ". . . don't accomplish very much." "One of our troubles is few people know how to carry on a meeting. The Boy Scouts usually have better meetings."

The most critical worker said: "No, I dislike drinking, don't see fellows who have too much drinking, bicker over things which are not essential, in some meeting this has gone on until the whole room is disgusted." This comment is not typical. It refers to a period preceding the presidency of Frank W. Schultz, who would not allow such an incident to occur. It was, furthermore, made by a dissatisfied worker who has a great need to be better than his fellow workers, and who draws a sharp line between himself and "those" workers who attend union meetings. And yet there is something typical about this response: a certain dissatisfaction with the meetings—though they are well conducted, strictly following parliamentary rules and giving all workers a chance to speak.

The lack of interest in rank-and-file meetings is dramatically illustrated in workers' attendance records. During 1950, not more than one hundred out of a membership of about four thousand were present at those monthly meetings at which usual union business was discussed. The meeting at which a strike vote was taken was an exception to the rule: almost all workers attended and voted in favor of a strike. The widespread lack of involvement is further demonstrated by a certain lack of interest in union offices.

My observations of the meetings, in conjunction with many conversations inside and outside the factory, showed three main reasons for the relatively poor participation of workers in the rank-and-file meetings: (1) lack of interest in "the other fellow's problems"; (2) a feeling that large meetings do not allow real participation; (3) a feeling that union matters are being well taken care of by the union officers. The relative significance of these factors cannot be evaluated here. Suffice it to point to the interrelationship between the subjective and objective aspects of the situation. It is true that the meetings are not conducive to involving people who are not already vitally interested. But it is also true that workers could initiate changes if they had a deep concern for general problems of labor. A comparison with the vitality of the departmental meetings, in which most workers participate actively and which are very well attended, shows clearly the potentialities of involvement.

## THE MEANING OF THE UNION

It would be a grave mistake to conclude from these observations that the union is not strong or not strongly entrenched. As an organization within the factory gates giving workers security and bestowing "Rights" on them, the union is closely knit and there is an "esprit de corps" which indicates the existence of a collectivity with its own rules, symbols, and sanctions. An incident will illustrate this: I worked one morning in a department where I was not known, without wearing my union button. The workers assumed that I was a worker from another department—probably from the extra gang—and that I was assigned to their department for some time. They watched me working for a while; then, after a short discussion, the grievance man came to me and asked whether I was a union member. When I said "Yes," he informed me that I would not be able to work in the department without wearing a union button.

Other data confirm the cohesion of the union and its strength as an organization giving protection and security. The union plays, indeed, a vital role *within* the factory; hence, its life blood goes through the departmental meetings and not through the rank-and-file meetings. But as soon as we go beyond the factory gates, the situation changes; the union loses the unity of meaning which it has within the factory.

The preliminary results of a forthcoming study on "Apathy and the democratic process" substantiate these findings: they have shown that the overwhelming majority of the workers identify their *interests* with labor. Asked "With what groups do you feel you have common political interests?" they chose, in the following order (1) labor, (2) farmers, (3) small business, and (4) others. There was even an impressive minority which gave a positive response to the question, "There are 30 million workers in this country. Suppose a political party was started, made up particularly for these people, would you be willing to join in and spend your time helping to win out?" Their answers to the question, "What do you think about the Taft-Hartley Act?" gave further evidence for their identification with labor. But the "world of labor" is conceived in narrow terms and does not have the characteristics of a community experience which allows strong relatedness and active involvement. Neither the evidence, nor the reasons—nor the remedy for this situation—can be presented here. Suffice it to say that there is neither an ideological identification with labor nor a living relationship to a broader community of work and labor—a relatedness which could give meaning to work.

The absence of such an identification or relatedness is shown in a lack of symbolism in regard to the labor movement. Labor Day is a good example. The city of Austin is as quiet on Labor Day as on any Sunday morning. The union has an advertisement in the local newspaper reminding the man in the street of the occasion, but during the last few years there have been no parades, no public addresses, no flags, or any other symbolic expression of the involvement with the labor movement.

This situation is of relatively recent origin. In 1938, Governor Benson addressed a Labor Day rally. The 1940 Labor Day meeting was sponsored by Local 9 and the Chamber of Commerce. In 1942, there was a large meeting in Todd Park, and as late as 1947, Hubert Humphrey, then mayor of Minneapolis, addressed a labor rally. Since then, no Labor Day celebration has taken place.

The "old days," when workers were sufficiently involved to devote Labor Day to a symbolic expression of their feelings, are not remembered any more by many workers. They have not forgotten them but the emotional memory is lost. The situation is so different today that the memory of the past cannot be experienced any more: only if the past touches off something in us which is an emotional reality today can it be remembered in a meaningful way. Yet the past dies slowly: the situations within the plant which led to the unionization came up in many of the conversations I had in the factory. They became the folklore of the factory which, at best, touches the imagination but which for an increasing number of workers does not have enough emotional significance to lead to an inner involvement, and hence to action.

CULTURAL FORCES AND THE ROLE OF THE UNION

So far we have examined the role and meaning of the union in terms of the Austin situation. A full understanding of the development, however, requires an examination of the Austin events within a broader context of social and cultural forces.

What Max Weber called "the process of rationalization" is the most sweeping cultural force influencing the industrial scene. This process dissolved "primary emotional ties" as binding forces of the social process and rationalized all human relationships. It found its culmination in a capitalist *laissez-faire* economy— which has been called here the traditional form of socio-economic organization—which shaped man in the image of anonymous market relations. Rational self-interest of buyers and sellers rather than any kind of emotional attachment of ethical values became the dominant social force. As a result, community and partnership feelings with an ethical content arise only with difficulty. Modern organizations are, indeed, "a little bit too big for feelings like partners." Rational self-interest intruded even into the factory gates and group belongingness took a mere technical meaning typified by the "silent" or "sleeping" partner. To the member of an early Christian community such a silent partner would have been as incomprehensible as is the compassion of brotherly love to the worker who does not like to move into another community because "they don't have the brotherly love for outsiders."

The "process of rationalization" which is typical for all western civilization has found in this country strong reinforcement in the ideology of "getting ahead." Competitive individualism expressed in the values of the ambitious and self-reliant man dominates the social scene. The strength of these forces can be gauged from the prevailing conception of human nature. Workers mentioned such qualities as ego-centricity, thirst for money, disregard for human values—all the attributes of "getting ahead." Competition is "human nature," cooperation "has to be learned." To be ambitious is the central expression of normalcy. Unconscious of the most fundamental forces shaping their life, most workers experience the peculiarity of our culture and social organization as the absolute attributes of man!

The effects of the process of rationalization reinforced by the ideology of getting ahead explain to a considerable extent the nature of the partnership feelings existing in regard to the union and, as we will see later on, to the company. The union, in particular, feels its impact since, as a group organization, its strength depends largely upon the development of group feelings and the existence of an ethics of *interpersonal* relationships. Any existing feelings of partnership with the union are, therefore, not a result of the broad undercurrents of the social forces emanating from the "process of rationalization" and reinforced by the ideology of getting ahead. They grew up in spite of it. What is astonishing is not that there are relatively few genuine feelings of partnership, but that there are any at all. Religious convictions in the (not too common) sense of a real feeling for man and awe for life, and deep-seated convictions of social justice are important forces counteracting the cultural ideal of getting ahead and the "institutionalization" of rationalism.

How strongly the desire to get ahead affects union identifications is well illustrated by certain ill-feelings about unionism "because some individuals can't advance as fast," or because "one loses some ambition." These comments are particularly significant since they come from a worker who is active in the union and from another one who sincerely appreciates the services rendered by the union. They would fight for the union "if the chips are down," and yet they experience loss of ambition and of speed in getting ahead as disadvantages. Is it astonishing that many workers with a strong desire to get ahead have only slim group feelings and not much more awareness of an ethics of interpersonal relationships?

Originally, the strength of workers' aspirations to be free to get ahead was a major factor which led them to unionization. This desire had always mitigated the experience of the factory as an entity limiting one's freedom since it opened a gate leading away from factory life. Workers did not, as a rule, experience the factory as a place with four walls surrounding them. It was a place with three walls, the fourth and enclosing wall being replaced by the image of a world in which the ambitious man was free to get ahead. But the traditional organization of industry unleashed forces which created conflicts too strong to be borne. To solve these conflicts, workers formed a union, because "a man alone could not do it," could not liberate himself from the oppressive forces generated by the authoritarian organization of the factory. It would have been better if "one man alone" could have done it. But the reality of the factory made the union a necessity. It forced, so to speak, group organization on workers who grew up in an era in which the ambitious, self-reliant man was the idol of society.

The very success of the union in assuring workers a certain degree of freedom from arbitrary authority—in conjunction with the improvement in working conditions—contributed greatly to quiet the feelings which were aroused under pre-union conditions. Since the core of these feelings was hatred, they were bound to disappear as the object of the hatred was removed from the Austin scene. Past are the days when union members marched uptown smashing windows and destroying goods. Gone are the dress rehearsals of civil war when workers moved into neighboring communities to help their fellow workers repulse tear-gas attacks, or to revenge the destruction of chairs and tables in union halls by police squads. And we may safely assume that the Hormel company has destroyed the sickening tear-gas which it bought in the years immediately following the strike.[7] And with these days are disappearing the psychological mechanisms which cemented groups and created the emotional basis for union identifications based on hatred.

Today it is the service job done by the union which makes for union identifications. From a fighting organization dedicated to remove "wage slavery" the union has become an instrument administering the protective machinery established in the Working Agreement. It is more and more being taken for granted—though its services are highly appreciated just as we appreciate the services rendered by such essential instrumentalities as streetcars and other service agencies.

Whenever the objectives which are implemented by the union are at stake, workers become again aroused and involved, as the strike meeting and many other instances prove. But "unless something radical happens," workers are apathetic. This situation does not endanger the existence of the union but it leaves open the question of what the role of the union in the organized work process will eventually be. Will the union succeed in overcoming the limitations of its present operations as circumscribed by the Working Agreement and become a vital instrument in the life of the workers by relating them to a community of work and labor, or will it become more and more an agency helping to administer an organization of work which, as we will see, impedes a creative self-expression of the workers?

The problems thus raised cannot be answered without a thorough understanding of the role of the company in organizing work and the impact of industrial organization on the life of the workers.

# CHAPTER 4

# *"A Company Hard to Beat"*

## THE POLICY OF A FAIR DEAL

When the workers go to the plant, they meet a long line of cars converging on the parking areas in front and on the north side of the massive factory buildings. Most of the people move towards the various entrances of the plant; only a trickle turns to the front offices. An onlooker who would try to divide these people into "manual" and "white collar" workers on the basis of their dress and behavior would make many mistakes. Though appearance counts more for those who go towards their desks, many a worker is dressed as carefully as anybody else coming to work. Yet, the environment of the workers and that of the white collar personnel differ as they enter the plant.

For these workers, "the company" may mean various things. It is a place where they perform their daily work: the company provides a certain physical work environment. Within this environment, the company is most typically represented by the supervisory hierarchy with which the workers come in daily contact. The status system established by the company can be seen as we observe workers at their place of work. They wear grey-yellowish frocks and a simple cap with a shield, whereas the foremen, supervisors, and superintendents have bright white frocks and hats of various shapes. Management is a third rather distinct aspect of the company: from top management down to the clerk, it is marked off from the workers by the white collar. Management and the supervisory hierarchy combine in a certain organizational "setup," a system of rewards, punishment, privileges, etc. Finally, there is "the company" as it appears on the nation-wide advertising: "Hormel—Good Foods"—a firm which has established itself in the intricate web of market relations and gained an outstanding reputation.

As a first approach towards an understanding of the role of this complex entity in the organized work process, we shall examine the impact of management's policy on the workers.

The first day I worked in the factory, I concluded my observations on the Employment Office—where workers and management come into immediate contact—with the following general remarks: "There is a relaxed atmosphere. The behavior of the workers is quite free. Their relationship to the people in the office seems very friendly." After more than three years of close acquaintance with the company, these observations remain typical of management's attempts to give to the workers "a fair deal." More specifically, management is trying to create a satisfied, stable working force by giving workers the best possible earning opportunities and, as much as possible, by making them feel as "partners" in a "cooperative" enterprise. In attempting to evoke feelings of partnership, the company concentrates on emphasizing the collective effort of increasing the monetary returns and on showing workers their role in putting out a quality product with the greatest savings in cost.

## WORKERS' FEELINGS ABOUT THE COMPANY

Workers' answers to the question: "What comes to your mind when you use the words 'Hormel company'?" show that the management fair-deal policy has been successful: the overwhelming majority of the workers have positive feelings about the company. A minority is neutral, while outright negative responses or images are conspicuous by their absence.

A considerable number of the workers responding positively are reminded of the advantages and privileges they enjoy at Hormel's: "One of the finest industrial companies in the nation"; "Best setup in packinghouse"; "Spam and the Wage Plan come to my mind"; "The trademark is the annual wage." Or: "I am proud of the company because I have seen it and compared it to other companies." Another worker said, "As good a company as there is anywhere to work for." The company's reputation has been mentioned repeatedly: "I feel pretty good about telling people about it because Hormel has a good reputation, the annual wage plan. They know we do pretty well." A final response: "On the whole, I feel very proud to be employed. They have a good name, they raise labor so they can keep their chin up. . . ."

On the borderline between positive and neutral responses are the answers of these workers who mention the job itself as the first thing that comes to their mind: "I don't know, I just work there. When I am out and see the sign, that's where I work, where I get my bread and butter . . . good steady job . . . Hormel is known all over the United States. . . ." More skeptical is the following worker: "Just think it's just another job."

Clearly neutral are the so-called "product responses." Workers who referred to the company's product—meat—had neither strongly positive nor strongly negative feelings as the following conversation shows:

> Meat comes to my mind.
> Do you like it?
> I don't care. I could just as well do without it.

Job responses were at the borderline between positive and neutral feelings because "the job" is a mixture of "work" and "privileges and advantages enjoyed by being a Hormel worker." The work itself evokes as we will see negative or neutral images, while the privileges have definite positive connotations. When the latter were absent "meat" came to the worker's mind—a product which is ethically neutral because, as a use-value, it is not affected by the organization of the work process. Meat is as far removed from the organizational aspects of the company as any possible object to be found within the factory gates.

The complete absence of a negative image would be a result "too good to be true"—if it were interpreted as an absence of gripes or dissatisfaction about the company. It is impossible for there to be no dissatisfactions of some kind even in the best system and we can be fairly sure to find personal projections unfavorable to some aspects of the company even if we approximate whatever we may consider the "ideal" of industrial organization.

As we listen to some conversations with the workers we will better understand this absence of negative responses:

Does being an employee make you feel you are a partner in doing an important job?

Yes, that's right.

What about the company makes you feel this way?

Well, not your foreman. That's damn sure. It's the company. The foremen forget too easily they are working for Hormel. . . .

Another worker said: "Hormel does not care for the foremen," meaning that Mr. Hormel does not put their opinions ahead of the workers' opinions and feelings. These attitudes amount to an exoneration of top management for the action taken by its subordinates—in spite of management's direct responsibility for foremen policy. Such an exoneration is only possible if there is a strong emotional attachment to Mr. Hormel or a strong feeling of satisfaction with the setup.

Both factors are undoubtedly operative, as can be seen from the following answers to the question: "What comes to your mind when you use the words 'Hormel company'?" One worker said, "Working for best employer in the world." Another replied, "Naturally everybody is proud of the company he works for; I work for Hormel. I work for Hormel. . . . He tried to make decent working conditions for everybody." Further probed: "What do you mean he tried?" he said, "Hormel himself . . . really wants decent working conditions for everybody." Both workers have quite untypical submissive tendencies. Yet they express, in an enhanced form, generally prevailing attitudes. This is clearly demonstrated by the words of a self-reliant, radical worker, who said, "Communism would not be necessary if everybody was like Mr. Hormel."

Workers' answers to the question: "Are you satisfied that at this stage in your career your position in the company, in comparison to other people is clear and fair?" give further evidence for the success of the company's policy of a "fair deal." The overwhelming majority of the workers answered in the affirmative:

"Yes, it is fair"; "It is about as fair as they can make it." It is true that the question which elicited these responses does not directly refer to a "fair deal." However, as the answers show, the question is comprehensive enough to allow workers to project their own feelings in it. Whatever doubts may remain are dispelled by the hundreds of conversations with workers inside and outside the factory. They gave ample evidence of workers' feelings of getting a fair deal.

The existence of a widespread feeling of satisfaction among the Hormel workers is further corroborated by their responses to the question: "On the whole, do you enjoy working here? Is there any place you would rather work?" The overwhelming majority give affirmative answers such as: "On the whole, yes I do"; "Well, so many things that Hormel company offers that others don't, I enjoy that"; "As long as I got to work for somebody, I just as soon work there." Only a small group of workers answered our question in the negative. None of those who gave a negative response indicated any of the company policies as the reason why they do not enjoy working there.

### MANAGEMENT AND "THE COMPANY"

These results are all the more remarkable since work detrimentally influences workers' feelings about "the company." A good example is given by a worker who answered the question: "What comes to your mind when you use the words 'Hormel company'?" as follows: "Didn't used to think too much of it until I got on the job I liked." Workers' perception of the company is, indeed, influenced by all the aspects of "the company" mentioned above: the policy of management, the organization of the work process, the kind of work, even the joint union-management aspects of the Working Agreement influence their images and general feelings about the company.

Their answers to the question: "What advantages and privileges do you get because you are an employee of this company?" show clearly that they do not differentiate between "the company" as expressing management's policy and "the company" representing the various aspects of the social organization of the work process. Vacation was the Number one advantage mentioned.

It was followed by sick leave, guaranteed wages, and the retirement fund. These "big four" advantages are complemented by the "little two": profit-sharing and security. Only profit-sharing and the retirement fund are a result of management's policy exclusively. Vacation and sick leave are clearly a matter of collective bargaining while the guaranteed wage and security are at the borderline. The company initiated wage guarantees and follows a policy of security, yet workers do not perceive guaranteed wages as an exclusive result of company policy and they derive stronger feelings of security from union than from company identifications.

A similar lack of differentiation between the two conceptions of "the company" emerged from workers' answers to the question: "Are there any disadvantages? Anything other companies do for their employees?" The few workers who listed any disadvantages mentioned such factors as speed-up, long hours, seniority, and the kind of work to be done.

The intermingling of the various aspects of the work process in workers' minds makes it imperative to interpret carefully their responses to any direct questions about their feelings in regard to management. In some cases in which negative aspects of the work process intrude into workers' minds, their answers are not as positive as their feelings towards the company actually are. In others, they may credit the company for some aspect of the organized work process for which the union is mainly responsible. Yet it is undoubtedly true that the general fair-deal attitude of management forms a positive or at least neutral image in workers' minds. Since an image is the result of undifferentiated emotions and perceptions, it is unaffected by any analytical considerations in regard to the precise role of management, work, and the union. But it could not arise without an instinctive awareness of management's role—a strong appreciation of the privileges enjoyed by the Hormel workers.

If I had to summarize workers' feelings about the company in one sentence, I would repeat the words of a worker: "If a man is going to work for anybody else, it is hard to beat Hormel." I have heard this sentence in various forms again and again while talking to workers inside or outside the factory. It came up in interview-conversation as a reaction to different questions. Disregarding minor variations in phrasing, it was the *single most often heard expression* in any conversation about the company.

### Involvement and Feelings of Partnership

To gain a more precise knowledge of management's role in relating workers to the organized work process, we shall now examine the nature of workers' feelings of partnership with the company. The generally prevailing high estimation of the company is maintained as we listen to workers' answers to the question: "Does being an employee make you feel you are a partner in doing an important job?" The overwhelming majority of the workers responded in the affirmative.

A few workers experienced partnership as an identification with the broader goals of management. But they are a very small group, only one response pointing to a conceptual understanding of the work process as a link to the over-all process of exchange: "If you look at industry, you feel you are producing something that is on the market; you have a small part of bringing it into being."

An almost equally small group of workers conceive of their partnership in terms of their contribution to the production of use-values: "To furnish the public with food"; "When you are working in a place like that you help feed the world."

A somewhat larger group derives its feelings of partnership in doing an important job from their contribution within the factory gates. Some workers are conscious of the significance of quality production. "Well, you feel as though if you can do some good work, you can do the company some good." A group in many aspects akin to the one just mentioned emphasizes the monetary reward of quality production: "Yes, profit-sharing, the better work I do, a little bit more for me." Other workers feel as partners because of the general attitude of management towards the workers: "I don't know, just seems like cooperation between company and working man; years ago, bosses decided not to see a working man go ahead, not buy a home, keep him tied down . . . . cooperation with big officials and working man changed that. . . ."

For some workers partnership expresses more a dependency than a relatedness at an equal level: "Well, I suppose it is important for different reasons. I always figure on doing my job the right way when I did something. I'm honest about this. I want to do it right. After all, I have to make a living. If I would not do the job right, I would not have a job."

A not inconsiderable group gave—to say the least—colorless answers in spite of the fact that almost all were preceded by the affirmation that feelings of partnership in doing an important job exist: "Well, you are part of the plant, you are an employee"; or "Yes . . . because it is an agreeable company" may serve as examples. Yet only a few workers answered the question about their feelings of partnership with a flat "No." Some said "No" without further comment. One worker who said "Not much" continued after having been asked "Why not?": "Well, mostly because nothing interests me outside of making a living . . . the only reason why I didn't change are the family responsibilities."

To bring out first the positive aspects of workers' relatedness to the company: Among those who express feelings of partnership, most workers are aware of the role they play in making the operations of the company prosperous. Management has undoubtedly been successful in evoking a feeling of responsibility about the work and in fostering a sense of participation. "The better you work, the more you save. You get it at the end of the year, what profits them profits you." Not less significant is the following statement made by a worker in the course of a conversation about the strike of 1948: "Here it is different. If we don't get it in the wage, we get it in the profit-sharing. I wonder whether people understand it."

## PROFIT-SHARING AND GUARANTEED WAGES

It is interesting that profit-sharing rather than guaranteed wages becomes symbolic of workers' identifications with the company. Production under the annual wage and wage incentive system is so closely related to the workers' own group-effort as to be seen primarily in this light. The frequently heard expression, "We have a contract with the company," is an expression of this feeling of independence. The work group—the gang—and the company are visualized as two separate entities, not as parts of a whole. As a result the guaranteed-wage–group-incentive system creates general feelings of appreciation for the earning opportunities it offers; it strengthens the orientation of work towards money without leading to strong feelings of relatedness to the company as the organizer of the work process.

Profit-sharing is more conducive to make workers aware of their being part of a collective effort: "The more money I can make for the company, the more I get at the end of the year." It does, indeed, evoke a desire for a more active role in some workers. One worker said, "Should have more to say about it, this way it is just bait." Another worker felt that the "union should have voice in joint earnings. As it is, we have to take company's word, ideal setup is to be partners. . . ." Yet while a group of workers becomes more interested in the company as the social organization of the work process, another group remains passive-acquiescent: "I don't know. I regard that quite a little as a gift. I know we do earn it here and there . . . light, etc., pretty hard to put your fingers on." Joint earnings are, then, considered as evidence that "*they* are doing all right," a feeling which does not express any meaningful relatedness.

To understand these reactions, we must be aware of the dual implications of joint earnings. On the one hand, they are *given to* the workers who do not participate in any of the decisions determining their share in the profits. On the other hand, management emphasizes the role of the workers in *creating* joint earnings. Workers who do not have a conception of the potentialities of relatedness to the organized work process derive feelings of partnership bestowing meaning on work from their participation in joint earnings. But workers who do have such a conception and who really want to participate do not derive any real satisfaction from profit-sharing, although they recognize its potentialities.

These potentialities lie in a further development of the tendency to produce a quality product and to save such costs as light, refrigeration, material, etc. The already strongly developed monetary aspirations and the incipient market identification will be strengthened by such a development. But profit-sharing is unlikely to evoke feelings of partnership derived from a meaningful relatedness to the organized work process. The paucity of company identifications other than monetary ones shows clearly that workers are cut off from a larger community of work and labor. Even their consciousness of producing a quality product does not relate them to the market: they do not mention that the company could compete better, sell more at a lower price, or better satisfy human needs. They usually see only their own financial advantages, or their dependency upon the company's prosperity: "You make the company prosperous, otherwise you would soon be out of a job." There is little emotional involvement and intellectual understanding of the goals in view of which the company organizes work. Some of the workers who were on the Business Improvement Committee are a significant exception to this rule.

WORKERS' DESIRE FOR A "KNOW-HOW" AND "SAY-SO"

As we examine the nature of workers' participation in "the company," the detrimental effects of their unrelatedness to the wider goals of the organized work process on their creative self-expression will emerge more clearly. As a first step in understanding the nature of this participation we must answer these questions: How are workers related to management—that aspect of the company which mediates workers' contact with the broader organization of the work process? How are they informed about management problems? What say-so do they have?

Bulletin boards, the supervisory staff, and the monthly company paper, the *Squeal,* are the available media to inform workers about the company. Bulletin boards are of limited significance and the contacts between the supervisory staff and the workers are used more often to pass on orders rather than information which could be thought over and discussed by the workers. The company paper remains, therefore, as the most important means of information. The *Squeal* was first published in 1917. It was discontinued from 1925 to 1934. In February, 1934, publication was resumed.[1]

A content analysis of the *Squeal* has shown that the majority of the articles deal with the life of the workers outside the factory: family life and family events such as births, weddings, and deaths; home building activities, as well as recreational activities, are emphasized. A minority of the articles deal with reports on specific gangs, matters directly pertaining to the plant or to management problems. The Business Improvement Committee and awards for suggestions are examples of plant problems discussed; considerable emphasis is given to quality and sales problems. Reports on stockholder meetings, on profits, or on industry problems are examples of general management problems taken up in the *Squeal.*

The inadequacy of the present channels of information is reflected in the answers to the question: "Do you feel you should know more about management's problems?" One worker said with great emphasis, "Yes, I think we should. If we know more, sometimes we might have some ideas to help them along. I think they should study our problems and help us along." Another worker: "Yes, be great thing for me; I don't know about the others . . . that is, how we make deals . . . Hormel tells us his troubles . . . we can understand . . . it would certainly help if we had more of it. . . ." A third worker put it this way: "It may help. There would be less hard feeling between bosses and worker if we knew more about management. There would be more cooperation."

These quotations are indicative of the general feelings of the majority of those workers who express a desire to know more about management. But there are some workers in this group who are more outspoken and more articulate in their ideas: "Yes, if they have a problem, I don't see why they cannot come and tell us. No, they tell the foreman: 'I have to get this done.' . . . Often there is no logic in what they try . . . they could save a lot of money by asking us. . . ." Another worker goes further than that: "Yes, management should share problems more with you, not with individual but whole labor group; labor should be more a part . . . help figure out what's good."

Only a small group of workers express no desire to know more about management's problems: "It would not do any good"; "Rather not be bothered, I guess . . . we know they are doing all right. Otherwise, they would not give us the profit-sharing."

The existence of a—not satisfied—desire for more "know-how" is further corroborated by the rumors which originated in the plant when the joint-earning checks were distributed in October,

1949. Rumors are always due to an unsatisfied need for communication and knowledge.[2]

Whereas the great majority of the workers express a desire for a greater "know-how," only a small minority wants a greater "say-so," and a minority not much more impressive desires a say-so in the sense of suggestions.

Here are some typical responses to the question: "Do you feel you should have more say-so about management?": "If everybody had a say-so, too many conflicting ideas"; "No, I guess not; I am just employed, one cog in the wheel. I guess they have different guys in the office, the big shot conferences." Another worker said, "I don't know about that. After all, if a fellow is trained in management, he is fit to say about it." A smaller but not insubstantial group wants a say-so limited to suggestions: "I am just a working man. Management runs its own business. If I would run mine, I would not want anybody else to tell me what to do. It would be O.K. if it is a question of improvements or suggestions." Only a small group of workers want more of a say-so: "Management gets lopsided if working people don't have something to say about it."

These responses show the existence of three groups whose numerical significance declines as their interest in a say-so increases. This result is all the more astonishing since "knowing" and "doing" are closely related in the workers' mind. If we group the answers pertaining to workers' desire for more knowledge along the scale of increasing interest and compare them to those pertaining to their desire for a say-so also grouped according to a scale of increasing interest, we find a strong parallelism in the position of the workers along the two scales.

The interrelationship between knowing and doing is not only felt by those who have a social philosophy rooted in the ideas of equality of opportunity and self-expression. It can also be found in the meek, submissive type who does not reach independence of feeling or thought: "No, I wouldn't have the ability to approve them any . . . when people learn about management problems, they feel they should have more to say."

How can we explain the relatively undeveloped desire for a say-so in view of the strong interrelationship between "know-how" and "say-so"—and in spite of workers' widespread complaint that "management is only using our backs and hands but not our brains."

Part of the explanation lies in shifting frames of reference. Whereas most workers interpreted "know-how" in terms of information about the organized work process and management problems in general, they thought about the conduct of the business when answering the question about say-so. Such a shift in the frame of reference is due to workers' primary interest in the work and the work process rather than in management problems more remote from their daily experience. But there is a more important factor explaining the situation: a lack of consciousness and experience of a democratic group process which manifests itself in the conception of management as a specialized function outside the realm of possible active participation.

"I guess they have different guys in the office, the big shot conferences." Or: "If a fellow is trained in management . . ." may suffice as indications of workers' feelings that management is a specialized function. Indeed, this seems so obvious that the reader may ask why we raise this point at all. Is there anybody who would deny that management is a specialized function? Is there any doubt that management requires a great deal of thorough and specialized knowledge which the workers not only do not have but would, as a general rule, be unable to acquire?

Management is, indeed, a highly specialized function. But it is a function which may be discharged either democratically or in an authoritarian manner. It is discharged democratically if those best qualified perform it while they remain responsible to those whom they serve. And it takes on an authoritarian character if it is the privilege of a special group or class. During the middle ages, for example, the concept of a "function," which played a predominant role, was clearly a rationalization of basic inequalities between social groups.

Analysis of the data has shown that most workers have an authoritarian conception of the *discharge* of a specialized function. Can it be considered a coincidence that it is a worker with a typical authoritarian personality structure who is the mouthpiece of the group of workers who express little or no interest in a say-so? The pronouncement of this particular worker on leadership is almost identical with a slogan used by the Nazi party before coming to power: "Too many cooks spoil the soup"—a statement to which he added: "It would take a man to make decision when a decision is necessary." Is it an accident that one of the workers who does not want a say-so adds, "Wouldn't know how to get at it"?

## PARTICIPATION IN THE COMPANY

These attitudes are far from accidental. They are a reflection of a lack of consciousness and experience of a democratic group process. The management function has traditionally been discharged in such a manner that there has been no room for workers' participation. Recent efforts made by management to remedy this situation by instituting the Business Improvement Project and Business Improvement Committee have alleviated the situation. The Business Improvement Committee is, indeed, of outstanding significance in pointing the way to potential identifications with the goals underlying the organized work process. Here are a few examples of the opportunities for participation offered by the Committee: In one of its meetings, a member brought up the question of bruises on livestock. The workers pooled all their knowledge about the treatment of hogs outside and inside the plant—finding a great deal of interest in seeing their own work for the first time in a broader perspective. They decided that an experiment should be made by marking certain types of hogs, keeping track of them through the whole process of production, and then observing the results when the hams were being boned. At another meeting workers felt that certain losses occur because of deficiencies in steam jets in a department. The problem came up at several meetings and was discussed with management. It showed workers' concern for improvements which make their work more effective and save money to the company. A most significant problem which came up in this connection was the introduction of sand-blasting machines. Workers were very much aware that these machines would replace some of their fellow workers in the construction department. They debated the merits and dangers of such a precedent for a long time. Finally those won out who felt that the security of employment which they all enjoyed made it possible to advocate the introduction of labor-saving machinery. This example shows how fundamentally attitudes can change as the organization of the work process is modified.

The new interests and attitudes evoked by workers' participation in the Business Improvement Committee are well illustrated by a letter which a worker wrote to the chairman of the Committee:

Recently I suggested through your committee a plan to improve and enclose the loading dock. I would again like to use this procedure for further suggestions. Since presenting this suggestion Mr. Gray [a vice-president of the company] has contacted me about the loading dock proposal. His opinion was that my plan was very good, but emphasized that Buildings 4—2B—2—5 are in need of repair. Mr. Gray considered Buildings 4—2B—2—5 project a priority to the loading dock conditions. I am by no means contradicting Mr. Gray's point of priority, but, as a matter of suggestion, I would like to have the two projects combined as one. The following points will somewhat explain the reasons for combining the two projects as one. First of all we can say that combining the loading dock project and project of Buildings 4—2B—2—5 is a beneficial and a logical business improvement. These combined projects will improve working conditions and congestion up to 100 per cent in some instances. I believe that management as well as employees consider working conditions and congestion a major item especially where there is efficiency and productivity involved. Another point that both employees and management are greatly concerned about, is when a financial savings is involved, which simply means more profit-sharing for employees and more profit for management. By combining the two projects there will undoubtedly be a large saving due to the fact that you have everything available at one time, such as plans, manpower, machinery, materials and the possibility of not having to do some unforeseen problems over again. As an example: the present laundry which has been in use approximately a year will have to be torn down and rebuilt when plans for Buildings 4—2B—2—5 are completed.

Now let's consider long-range planning which is very essential and a very thrifty mode of business, there are a few things that should be considered. Will material be available at a later date, if so, at what prices? If the trend of prices goes anywhere near as high in the next ten years as it has in the past ten years I think that management can see the tremendous amount of savings that will be involved by combining and completing both projects in the very near future and not a plan of completing one project and then completing the other project in a span of perhaps five or ten years.

In view of these submissions and those of the original loading dock suggested plan, the personnel connected with the loading dock and myself wholeheartedly wish that the company will realize the need and necessity of the loading dock suggested plan and will combine it with the project of Buildings 4—2B—2—5.

Sincerely,

This letter—dated February 10, 1951—reproduced here in its entirety, shows clearly that workers can become much interested in what are usually considered managerial problems.[3] Another aspect of the proceedings of the Business Improvement Committee is noteworthy: the establishment of new channels of communication between management and the workers. When examining, for example, the problem of stainless steel trucks, the Committee asked management to get in touch with certain workers who were best informed about this type of equipment. A similar situation arose in regard to some rack trucks. The Committee found that these trucks—which have sealed bearings—are not satisfactory because the bearings dry out in the cookers and no way was found to grease them. Again the Committee asked management to consult with a worker before buying any additional trucks.

Whether the identifications established by the kind of interests evoked by the Business Improvement Committee are adequate for a creative self-expression of the workers will be discussed in Chapters 11 and 12. Suffice it to point here to the new horizons opened by workers' participation in the Committee and to the possibilities of growing partnership feelings with the company. These potentialities have not been realized, mainly because the Committee has not been in operation long enough, nor has it affected a large enough number of workers to change the basic attitudes of the majority of them.

It is, therefore, not astonishing that workers' partnership feelings with the company do not relate them creatively to the organized work process. Workers have a positive attitude towards the company, they are very appreciative of the setup, the privileges they enjoy, they even have more or less vague feelings of partnership. But these feelings are not deeply rooted and hence workers' involvement in the organized work process is superficial because most workers are emotionally and intellectually cut off from inner and outer participation in this process. To understand these conclusions and evaluate them in a fair manner, they must be seen within a broader frame of reference of the social and cultural forces which are operative in the industrial scene.

### CULTURAL FACTORS: CONCLUSIONS

As with the union, the relative absence of strong feelings of partnership based on emotional identifications must, at least partly, be explained by the impact of the process of rationalization. But for the company, this process has at the same time substituted goals and incentives which create new possibilities for identification. As long as the company directs its main efforts towards the strengthening of monetary values, it has the full support of the most powerful cultural forces. It can fully exploit the values of an acquisitive society, provided it succeeds in convincing workers of a harmony of interests. The nature of the partnership feelings evoked by management's policy shows that the company has been successful in this respect.

Workers' desire to be free to get ahead is another powerful cultural force affecting their feelings towards the company. Generally speaking, this desire strengthens monetary objectives. Yet, within the context of industrial organization, it lessens workers' feelings of partnership. We must recall that the sentence which best expresses the attitude of the workers towards the company starts with an "if": *"If* a man is going to work for somebody else it is hard to beat Hormel," or: *"If* you got to work for somebody else. . . ." or: "As long as you have to work for somebody else. . . ." I have never heard a worker express an unconditional acceptance of the company as an organization to work for—not because of any dissatisfaction with management, but because of the unfulfilled desire to be independent.

To the extent to which workers can get ahead within the company, they will feel more strongly related to it. But the limited possibilities of advancement do not permit widespread feelings of partnership to arise from this source. In the absence of alternative channels of participation, most workers are left with the feeling that they are "just working there." This is the price management has to pay for a like-mindedness of purpose, also growing out of workers' desire to be free to get ahead. This desire creates an atmosphere of understanding which is largely responsible for workers' acceptance of the present organization of industry as illustrated so well by a worker who said in a conversation on workers' participation in management: "If *I* would run this place, I wouldn't want anybody else to tell *me* what to do." The context in which this statement was made leaves no doubt that he visualized himself in "a small business of his own." If ever he was to achieve this objective he wanted to be really free —an understandable psychological compensation for a life spent in the factory.

Nevertheless, it is an illusion. Even if one out of every ten workers would succeed in "getting out of there"—something that would be a major achievement of "free enterprise"—nine workers would remain to spend their life in the factory. And the needs of those remaining are essentially like those who succeed in getting away: in some way or other, they want to express their feelings and thoughts freely and develop whatever their potentialities may be. *Their* dream of independence can, therefore, only be realized if they will take part in a democratic work process and thus be able to develop a democratic consciousness transcending the limitations of a purely ego-money oriented desire to get ahead. An acceptance of the present organization of work which has as its counterpart a widespread feeling "that I am just working here" is not conducive to such a relatedness to the work process and, hence, inimical to workers' self-expression.

The reasons for this situation, its implications and the problems arising out of a transformation of the presently existing organization of work will emerge clearly as we explore more systematically workers' relatedness to the work process.

## CHAPTER 5

# The Game of Work

### THE WORK ENVIRONMENT

The rectangular outlines and massive forms of the interpene-trating brick buildings may convey a sense of the simplicity and strength of modern architecture to the approaching workers. But once they enter the plant, they find themselves in a rather barren environment. The aesthetic possibilities of modern tech-nology and art are conspicuous by their absence. Few energizing colors—not to speak of paintings—break the monotony of grey-ish walls, low ceilings, and a mass of steel railings, chutes, chains, machines, tables, and various instruments which make a meaning-less if not bewildering impression. Most workers are not going to see the clouds or the sun in the sky or anything reminiscent of a human environment until they check out to have lunch in the newly built and decorated cafeteria. Unless an accident brings them to the equally new and bright medical department, they will be absorbed by the rhythm of the work process which started the moment they pulled the chain or pushed the handles open-ing the doors to their respective departments.

The conditions under which they work differ greatly. In few factories does the working environment vary as much as in a packinghouse where the working "material" is a life-product with many peculiarities. The necessity for refrigeration and cooking accounts for the wide differences in temperatures, rang-ing from 10° F. below zero to 120° F. And the variety of forms brought about by nature limits the application of machinery

74

during those initial stages of the work process which deal with the animal product as a whole. Although there are some incidental machines such as the de-hairing machine, for the most part the work is done by hand with the help of tools, mostly knives. General mechanization takes place only in the later stages of the process, particularly in canning.

Another peculiarity of the packinghouse is the specialization of labor. Practically all the work is divided into routinized minor operations. This happens even in the early stages of production where the use of tools prevails—a situation which bears out Henrik de Man's thesis that "repetitive work is by no means restricted to machine production."[1] Indeed, during these initial stages each worker usually repeats the same movement—a cut, for example—over and over again. Only during the later stages of the work process where machinery is more widely used may the functions performed by the workers become more diversified, since the use of machinery usually involves a variety of functions. An example of a machine operation which is less repetitive than the use of tools is retort-cooking in the canning division.

It is true that some knife jobs require a great deal of skill. But only a few jobs are so skilled that they could not be learned within a few weeks or months. Indeed, the company does not classify jobs according to skill level—though in many cases real mastery of the knife and of the ability to sharpen it requires several years' experience.

The same divergence of conditions existing in regard to temperature and mechanization is also found in regard to noise, lighting, ventilation, coloring of the rooms, and the general outlay of the working space. Some departments are overcrowded, some have ample space; some are somber while others are bright. Almost all work is done under artificial illumination in rooms that do not have any windows at all. The out-of-doors view is shut out even in those few rooms with windows since the glass used is not transparent.

Such is the general work environment of most Hormel workers. They get up early in the morning, rush to their place of work after a hurried breakfast, punch a time clock, and begin to work. They leave work for short, designated periods, go back to the same work, and finally again, punching the time clock, return to their homes. This "rhythm" is a predominant factor in molding their lives day in and day out, week by week, month by month, year after year. How do they experience the work process? What feelings and thoughts does it evoke in them?

### Likeness and Differences of Workdays

Workers' feelings about the repetitiveness of their work is a key to an understanding of their work experience. Their answers to the question: "Is one workday just like another to you, or is every day different?" gives us a first glimpse of their feelings. Typical responses were: "It is about the same all the way through"; "It is about the same; I do that one job." Or, "Of course, your work is practically the same. Each week repeats the same thing." There are a great variety of statements with this same theme: "With me, it seems to be about the same . . . some days are a little bit shorter"; "Sometimes it is about the same, then tough times; knife does not work, sore back." Another worker said: "They are all about the same except Friday and Saturday; Friday, you are anxious to get paid, and Saturday is short." These quotations give a good idea of how those workers feel to whom the workdays seem "pretty much the same."

Workers who feel that one workday is just like another, or that they are "more or less" alike are about as frequent as those who feel that they are different or "slightly different." In view of the reality situation, the feelings of those workers for whom the workdays are much alike need no comment. But why do about half of the workers feel that there are differences between the workdays? Some of them actually change jobs during the week or do different things on their own job. One worker, for example, who performs a variety of tasks said, "They are all different. When I go in, I wonder what is going to happen." Another worker in a similar position said, "That's what I like; each day has something different, not as monotonous as it would be on the chain." For others, the change consists in ". . . different things that happen with the people and with the material"; "The work is the same . . . but there are different things to talk about with the people." A last response which points to the importance of the human contact: "Routine conversations make enough difference." The fact that "every day is a little different because of different people" is mentioned repeatedly. Other factors which account for the feeling of differences in work days are "working conditions" and the way workers feel: "Whether the working days are just alike or whether every day is different depends on how you feel. If you have a cold, things go tough; otherwise, one day is pretty much like another day." Another worker said, "Just depends on how you feel in the morning. If grouchy, everything goes wrong."

These responses show that most workers do not experience significant differences between workdays. With the exception of the relatively small number of workers who have different work tasks most days are indeed pretty much alike, no matter whether workers say they are different or not. Only the human contacts bring a touch of variety into the monotony of the daily work—a monotony that can be felt in the very responses of most workers who say that there are some differences between the workdays. Indeed, the significance of the human contact is far greater than is indicated by the frequency with which workers mentioned it: it is generally taken for granted and not specifically mentioned. But if you talk to an old-timer who remembers "them days when the boss didn't allow us guys to talk to each other" then you know how important the human relationships on the job are. And if you speak to a worker who has been sick for some time and could not go to work, and he asks you about "the fellows in the gang"—then you realize the secret attraction which the plant has for many workers. Whether it is gossip that impels you to go to the plant ("My mother-in-law tells me you just like to go there for the gossip") or whether it is a feeling of group solidarity, or simply being with and around people, does not matter: the shop community is a major factor making the experience of work more positive.

### THE DESIRE FOR A "BREAK"

However, the human contacts cannot compensate for the monotony of the work itself, as is shown in workers' responses to the question: "Do you ever wish while you are at work 'I wish something would happen'?" Again workers are about equally divided. While a bare majority answers in the negative, a significant minority wishes that something might happen.

The most frequent wish is a breakdown: "I wish there was a breakdown . . . change has a lot to do with it . . . to break the monotony." A more drastic expression of a similar feeling is: "Well, I wish a lot of times the damn thing would break down so you could go home." No less dramatic is the answer: "I wish somebody would drop a bomb so we could get out early." To this the worker added in a resigned tone of voice, "But it never happens." Others wish that something might happen that would interrupt the monotony without there being an actual breakdown: "Something exciting, lots of times I wish just something exciting [would happen]." Or: "I want to see a good water fight—then the inspector may tie up the floor." Some workers just wish not to be at work: "I wish I was fishing"; "I wish I had a rich uncle."

These responses are proof of what repetitive, monotonous work does to people. And, as we will see now, the feelings of those who do not want anything to happen are essentially like those of the workers who have just spoken to us. The most frequent comments made by this group were: "No, I like to get out of there"; "No, I don't wish that. What they want is to get the hogs out, to get a little recreation." Or: "No, because you want to get the work done and be free to do whatever you want to do in your personal time." It is true that one worker said, "You wish that something don't happen, that nothing detains you from work." But he also said in another context that if something detains you from work "the time drags." The only worker expressing a positive attitude towards work said, "To wish that something would happen sounds like somebody who has no interest in life—though, when I smelled the flowers, I thought it was fun to go home today."

These responses show a common element in the feelings of both groups of workers; namely, the desire to get away from the repetitive, monotonous work. While some workers wish something might happen so they can get away immediately, others do not want anything to happen to interfere with their getting away soon. Personality factors, time perspective, and the objective conditions of work determine into which group the same basic forces push the workers. The identity of these underlying forces is clearly demonstrated in the responses of some workers: "When you are tired, you wish the chain would break down to get a breathing spell, but on long days only. On short days you don't wish it, because you want to get out of there." In other words, if the end is so far away that you cannot grasp it or the work is too hard, you want something to break the monotony, but if the burden is not too great and you can see the end of your exertion, you do not want anything to interfere with it.

## FATIGUE

Though the desire to get away from work is a common element among the workers who say that they do want something to happen and those who do not have such wishes, the fact remains that about half of the workers belong to the latter group. The decline in fatigue is one factor explaining this situation. As one worker said, "Those days, when we wanted something to happen, are past. I used to a long time ago when the strain was too great."

It is true that the majority of the workers feel tired after work, as is shown by their answers to the question: "Does your job make you physically tired? What about the job makes you tired? Is it monotonous?" But they are not exhausted and recover rather quickly from their fatigue.

"Using your muscles and standing in one place" are among the most frequently mentioned reasons for fatigue due to physical strain. Particularly "standing on the cement floor" or "standing and bending" account for weariness. For some workers the feet or legs get most tired, for others the arms, depending upon the kind of work they are doing. "You get tired . . . because you got to use your strength, especially on heavy hogs. At night sometimes your arm falls asleep; you hold it up in the air. You try to get circulation, you can't sleep well, and you are tired in the morning." More workers get tired from standing than from heavy use of their arm or back muscles. "To stand on one's feet up to ten hours" makes you tired.

Many workers indicated that they got more tired or only tired when they worked long hours: "Unless we work ten hours, five to six hours not overtired"; "Sometimes, if we work long hours, I get tired"; "Your job makes you tired in winter not in summer." Winter is the heavy season when the hours are very long, whereas during summer the hours are much shorter. This shows that the hours of work are an important factor influencing fatigue.

Other factors causing fatigue are the general working conditions: lighting ("Light bothers your eyes") and, in some departments, working clothes ("You have to wear a lot of clothes, rubber overshoes, etc."). For completeness' sake, let us add that the physical and mental disposition of the workers has a great deal to do with fatigue: "Sometimes the job makes you physically tired. It differs upon the kind of rest you get at night." The age of the worker naturally affects fatigue: "Ten years ago, when I first went in them doors, I did not notice it; when little older, I noticed it."

Though the overwhelming majority of the workers reported they feel tired, their fatigue does not interfere with their outside activities—except during the very heavy season when the hours of work go up to ten or, exceptionally, twelve a day. As a rule, they are tired but not worn out. This is a result of the constant increase in the mechanization of the work process which "took a great deal of the drudgery out of the work." I have observed many improvements which eased the burden of work and know that great changes have taken place during the last ten, fifteen years. The fatigue is, furthermore, in a considerable number of cases a result of the monotony of the work, rather than of the physical strain. This is well illustrated by the following conversation:

*My Question*: Does your job make you physically tired?
*Worker*: Did it make you tired when you worked over there?
*My Answer*. Yes, it did.
*Worker*: It does me.
*My Question*: What about the job makes you tired?
*Worker*: I don't quite know . . . you get used to it. You use only

one kind of muscle, but if you get on another job, you use another muscle.

*My Question*: Is it monotonous?

*Worker*: Yes and no. You get tired from loafing if you have nothing to do. You get bored and lazy.

This conversation brings out clearly what has been indicated in previous ones—that other elements than purely physical ones account for feelings of fatigue. Often it is a mixture of physical and mental strain, a kind of lack of involvement which leads to what this worker called "laziness." The impact of both factors is explicitly recognized by some workers: "Oh, yes," the job makes you tired; "it gets kind of monotonous, and it affects your feet and back." Another worker said, "Sometimes you get tired lifting boxes; other times just monotony." Or: "Sometimes monotony that makes you tired; sometimes standing around more tired." A number of workers mentioned monotony as the only factor making for fatigue. "Well, you stand on one spot all too long, just hammering along, gets kind of monotonous by 6:00 o'clock"; "I am less tired with more work because there is no loafing; loafing gives you a tired feeling."

These responses show that with the exception of relatively few jobs involving heavy muscular effort, the work is not so much a burden as it is "a grind"; its repetitiveness rather than the physical effort wears the worker down.

These conclusions are substantiated by the high incidence of injuries, particularly cuts, which do not follow the usual fatigue curve.[2] Injuries do not occur frequently when workers are most tired, but during the first hours of work when they are not yet in the rhythm of work.

BOREDOM AND THE PASSING OF TIME

In view of this situation we may expect workers to be bored on the job. However, the workers' reaction to the question: "Do you ever get bored on the job? Why do you think this is so?" does not bear out these expectations. The overwhelming majority of the workers say that they are *not* bored. There is also a lack of correspondence between the consciousness of the monotony of the work and the feeling of boredom; and there is even a lack of correspondence between consciousness of monotony and awareness of the differences between the workdays.

Typical majority views are: "It is not boring; you just make up your mind you are going to do it." Or: "No-o-o, it is not boring, it's just routine, the same routine every day." The last response is significant because it shows that those workers who feel that work is not boring do not necessarily imply that there is anything interesting about it. They merely feel that work is performed in a manner which does not make them feel the effect of the monotony.

A similar thought is expressed in this conversation: "Do you ever get bored on the job?" "Yes and no; sometimes a guy gets to thinking. . . ." Not to get bored means in this case "to take it in its stride," to adjust oneself to an uninteresting job. That this is not an isolated instance is shown in the lukewarmness, to say the least, of many answers, and the paucity of ideas as to why work is not boring. Those workers who do get bored have more to say: "Fast work and long hours, too much sameness"; "It is monotonous, nothing happens"; "Oh yes, it is bound to bore you, chain work is monotonous" are some reasons given by workers in this group.

One of the few reasons given by those who say that they are not bored is the passing of the time:

> Do you ever get bored on the job?
> I don't think so.
> Why do you think this is so?
> *The time passes.*

How could the passage of time possibly neutralize the monotony of the job? Whatever the answer may be, there is no doubt but that the time does, as a rule, pass fast. A large majority of workers, when asked: "When you are at work does the time generally pass slow or fast?" indicated that it usually passes quickly. Only a small minority feels that the time goes slowly. Many workers, however, intimated that sometimes the passage of time is slow and sometimes fast.

When queried as to what circumstances make it go slow or fast, answers typical of the majority were: "When really busy, time passes fast; when slack, it really drags"; "It goes fast when you have something on your mind like the machine, or you want *to get the stuff out*; it goes slow when everybody gets lined up."

This response shows that somehow the worker must feel "occupied" with the work, he must be busy, and he must have the desire to get the work done. Such feelings are expressed in various forms: "Well, all depends on the job you are on; very slow when something that does not take your attention; if you just take your time, slow; if something else ahead, fast." This statement is particularly interesting, because it was made by a worker who is not "on production," that is, one who is unaffected by the wage-incentive plan. He must feel that there is "something ahead" of him in order to get the feeling that the time passes fast; he must feel "pushed." When workers can set their own speed—as a gang "on production"—they always put something ahead of themselves; they are always under the incentive to make production, and this accounts largely for their feeling that generally the time passes fast.

In order to understand this attitude, we may visualize the work process as a flow going by the workers. They keep busy by servicing the flow and pushing it along. Whenever there is some interference with the flow itself, the time goes slowly: "It goes slow a day when few lines are running and you don't have much to do. . . ." It also goes slowly if there is something wrong with the material, for example, "if the bacon is bad," or "if there is a breakdown" and "you just stand around." These are factors slowing down the flow itself.

Other factors determining the speed with which time passes relate to the conditions surrounding the flow of work. If the work is not too hard—"When it is close to good speed without strain"; "When the hours are short"; and "The temperature is not too hot or too cold or humid"—then the time passes fast. It passes fast because attention is not diverted from the flow itself, and the work can be done without too much interference. Whatever brings variety into the work, or intensifies the human contacts, contributes to speeding the passage of time. It helps if you are "not standing on one place," or "if you do a variety of things," and, last but not least, "if you can visit with a guy." "Having conversation" and "being able to walk off a little bit" are among the more important factors that make the time pass fast. The importance of human contacts is clearly illustrated in the following conversations:

Is your work monotonous?
Not during the short season.
It doesn't affect you much then?
That's right; more to talk about—baseball, vacations.

Workers' attitude as to their roles in the work process is another significant factor. "When I get disgusted—on certain jobs, the time goes slow"; "It depends upon the job you have"; "If a person is not feeling good," the time passes slowly, too, because you do not feel like giving attention to the flow of work, and you do not have the energy to push it. Thus an inner disposition must be present to make the time go fast. This is why time goes slowly "if you have an outside interest and you are anxious to go home." Whenever something comes up that has more meaning for the workers than work, or something he feels strongly about, time goes slowly. For some workers time goes slowly "towards quitting time," because their desire to "get out of there" becomes greater than their desire to push the flow and "make production." But when the desire "to go out quick" is not so immediate that it makes you forget work altogether, it becomes a powerful force "to keep busy all the time."

Work, then, becomes a game which "breaks the monotony of having nothing to do." In its purest form the game becomes sheer movement for movement's sake: "If I just can keep my hands moving, then I know the time is passing fast." And as long as the time passes fast, workers do not experience their jobs as boring. On the chain, the monotony becomes overwhelming, particularly when there is heavy manual labor, little opportunity to talk, and almost no chance to visit. A short smoke in the locker room between the regular breaks is about the only time a worker can leave the place where he stands and works.

When I worked on the chain, we had an elaborate system of letting each other "out" and "carrying" the work while our fellow workers were out. At no other place in the factory did I find as strong a cohesion among work groups and it is not accidental that the union started in the hog kill—the backbone of the packing house. "Them are tough guys"—fellows whom the chain links almost literally to each other, and who have more group solidarity than other gangs. In this as in other respects the workers on the chain are more an exception than the rule. Most workers are so busily engaged in pushing the flow of work that they do not *consciously* suffer from the inherent monotony of their work. They are well adjusted, because they have reduced their level of aspirations to the rather low level of the job. They coast along, keeping busy, visiting, talking, making time go by, and getting the work done in order to get "out of there" in order to get home! A worker to whom this passage has been read commented on it as follows: "True worker brings aspirations to level of job. That's why a new man is not so good. The first six months are the toughest. I was at the verge of quitting. After a while, you get used to it."

The strength of the desire to get the work done in order to get out can be clearly seen in the conversations of workers in the cafeteria. Among the rare references that they make to work are to be found almost invariably such questions as these: "What is the work load today?" or "When do we get out today?" I have rarely taken a meal without somebody at the table raising a question of this kind. Since the time when workers can leave is determined by their work load, the faster they work the earlier they can go home. If they know the workload, they can work towards a goal; to get out at a certain time. If they do not, the goal disappears and work becomes burdensome. It is for this reason that a foreman rates higher if he tells the gang how much work is to be done. A foreman who does not inform the gang is "no good," because he makes time drag and makes workers feel the monotony of their work.

As long as the foremen do not interfere with the game of work, workers feel free, as shown in their responses to the question: "Do you have enough freedom to do your job your own way to satisfy you?" The overwhelming majority answered in the affirmative: "Yes, I do my job to satisfy myself." Other workers are somewhat more reserved: "Times you do, times you don't."

Or: "You got to consider the job has to be done." The reasons given by the workers for their feelings of freedom are: (1) You are not told what to do and (2) you have enough time to do your work. To quote: "Yes, if you can show them, you do it your way, pretty flexible, we have an awfully good foreman in. . . ." Or: "Oh yes, if you find an easier way, he lets you do it. . . . Can't learn with the boss behind me. . . ." The significance of time is brought out in the following statements: "Whenever you have an average run of hogs, you have enough time." Or: "Yes, plenty of time to do your work." Finally: "Ya, I would say I have. Because they allow us six minutes for sharpening the blade. . . ."

The remarkable speed at which workers operate makes one wonder how they can get a sense of freedom because of adequate time. Yet they do because they can set their own pace of work. They would certainly resent it if they were *told* to work as fast as they actually do. But since "they don't tell you much about your work" and its speed is self-determined, workers feel free from outside restraint.

How strongly the absence of any interference from above affects workers' feelings of freedom is well demonstrated by the rare occasions when foremen become a source of irritation. Asked: "Do you ever get impatient or angry on the job? Remember the last time?" many workers mentioned the work process and/or the people in the gang, but only a few workers mentioned the foremen. One worker gets mad "If the boss discriminates," another "If the boss accuses me of something I did not do . . . then I get angry like hell." But he does not suppress his anger: "Boss accused me of three different things, making a miscut, cutting a hide I did not cut, missing a cut which I should have made. I parked my knife, followed him . . . and told him what I thought, which was not very commendable, but it cured him for a month."

Though the freedom from outside pressure which allows workers to indulge freely in the game of work minimizes their experience of the monotony of their work, a certain artificiality in the passing of the time remains. You always "have to keep busy and shoot the bull" to be sure that time passes really fast. As one worker said: "It is never monotonous; if it is so, I *make* something happen." Time does not flow by while you are part of it, because the flow of work does not go *through* you; it *passes by you*. The moment the product moves on to the next man, it has ceased to exist: it has lost its meaning. While they work, workers' minds are already on the next thing to be done and the next cut to be made. They push the work sufficiently ahead of themselves to be completely absorbed in what comes next, without following any one piece from the beginning to the end.

Work in itself does not seem to be an experience which touches you, nor does time carry you. You push it, you keep it at a safe distance, always running a little bit ahead of it. Woe if you meet it: if you meet it in the factory, its "weight" will crush you, because it will stare at you with the ugly face of emptiness. "As long as your fingers move," everything is all right. But when the machine stops, and your fingers do not move any more feeding it, then you become restless, and the monotony becomes overwhelming. "The work drags after you."

## FACTORS GIVING MEANING TO WORK

In view of this situation, it is not astonishing that the overwhelming majority of the workers derive their greatest satisfaction from the money they earn rather than from the work they do.

"Another day, another dollar, like they always say" is almost a classic rhyme expressing the feelings of most workers. Asked "What makes you feel that your job and how you do it is important?" workers felt almost unanimously that money makes the job important. Typical responses are: "I suppose you could put it that way: we all work for the dollar." Or: "I imagine that most are working to make a living. That seems to be the important thing in life."

Since money is of such central importance, it is fortunate that most workers "are pretty well satisfied with the amount of pay they are now getting." A typical answer was: "Good pay, you can't kick on the pay." The degree of workers' satisfaction depends upon their standard of comparison. Those who were aware of the tough times they had gone through in earlier years were most satisfied. "Well, I accomplished quite a bit on the side, getting somewhere in the world, not just being a misnomer, an overlooked cog in the wheel . . . can remember last depression, socially, financially as well as spiritually." At the other extreme are those workers who are conscious of the difference of the earning opportunities in various departments—and of the rising prices.

But we must not conclude from this general emphasis on "the dollar" that money is always an adequate factor giving meaning to work. As a result most workers would like to have a skilled job. It is true that workers' desire for a skilled job must, in many cases, at least partly be explained as a desire to have more prestige and/or to make more money. Skilled jobs usually pay more (except for the machine shop), and always carry more prestige. To have a skilled knife job means to be in the upper part of the job hierarchy.

The top of the hierarchy is defined by three attributes of the job: a good-paying job, a knife job, and a clean job. As any one of these three factors is missing, one descends in the job hierarchy in the factory.

But we have, in the case of this plant, an interesting situation which allows us to compare the relative significance of money and skill as factors giving meaning to work. There is a group of highly skilled workers—in the mechanical department—who are not on "production," i.e., who are not under the wage-incentive system, and whose weekly pay checks are considerably lower than those of many workers in the plant. In other words, their skill level is inversely related to their income, whereas the two are usually positively correlated. Yet, these workers do not, at a rule, resent the fact that they get less money for a higher skill, because they are aware of the difference in the kind of work they are doing. Indeed, many workers in the machine shop could post out and get higher paying jobs in the plant, yet they do not use this opportunity. One reason why they do not post out is a certain difference in the working environment and the speed with which the work is done. Another is the satisfaction derived from doing skilled work. I was one day standing in front of the bulletin board where jobs are posted to the workers. Next to me stood a machine shop worker whom I knew. I asked him: "Why don't you bid for that job? You have enough rights to do so." He answered: "A mechanic is a mechanic because he likes that kind of work."

A similar feeling was expressed by a worker who said "money" makes his job important—as the following conversation shows:

Did you ever do anything in your life which gave you a feeling of satisfaction besides the money you made?
Yes, I have such a feeling if I fix my car.
Did you ever have a similar feeling at work?
When I worked in the butcher shop, I liked it, because it requires from beginning to the end a little skill.

The significance of factors other than money is furthermore illustrated by the emphasis on doing the job well—the nearest substitute to doing a job which allows one to use one's abilities. In this way workers can at least give *something* of themselves. Frequent are responses like these: "Yes, sir, I am well satisfied. I feel I have given the company a day's work, and I feel that they have paid me a day's wages"; "Yes, I am satisfied because I believe I have given them an honest day's work for an honest day's pay." Somewhat less enthusiastic is the following response: "Oh, I feel that I am doing a day's work. Good pay for what I am doing." In some cases satisfaction derived from having the work well done is mentioned quite independently of the pay check—and application seems to give a positive content to work. "Having done a day's work," or "having a job well done" are mentioned repeatedly. Most articulate is the following response: "Yes, I am satisfied the *way* it was done, done to the best of our ability."

The "knowledge of a job well done" may be strong or weak, it may give content to the work or merely give a feeling of security. But it is remarkable how consistently this thought returns in spite of the dislike of the work done. "I am satisfied because I feel I did my job well, but I am not satisfied with the work I do." More than one worker explained in the group sessions that they get their "feelings of accomplishment" because of the way in which they do their job, rather than because of the skill required. But whenever the nature of the work involves some responsibility, workers emphasize it rather than money:

"If job is not done right, it holds up the whole gang." Or: "If I don't do my job right, the whole department is out of work."

However, there are relatively few workers in the packinghouse whose job requires responsibility, initiative, or workmanship. "You can't put interest first . . . you just can't put it first" —simply because there is little interesting about the job. Exceptional are, therefore, feelings of accomplishment as expressed in the following conversation:

What makes you feel that your job and how you do it is important?
Did you ever shine a car? When you got done, didn't you feel proud it shone?
Yes, I did.
Maybe it's personal. Others don't care. I like to see a smooth, nice piece of work. That's what the company pays you the wages for.

This was said by a worker who has one of the highest skilled jobs in the plant! The best most workers can say is: "There is always a certain amount of satisfaction to get into a good run, sometimes a thousand hogs, top all previous records."

The absence of any qualitative content of the game of work leaves something important in workers unsatisfied. This is well illustrated by workers' answers to the question: "What abilities do you have that you want to use but can't use on the job?" The majority of the workers stated that they have unused abilities—though the same workers indicated that they feel "free" on the job! Typical responses are: "Everybody has abilities he does not use on his own job, it is specialized, it would be different with a craft." Or: "I would like to drive a car. . . ." And: "Rather be working at some place where more mechanically inclined . . . fix things. . . ."

As a rule workers assume that abilities not used in the performance of the work proper can only be used by members of the supervisory staff—a result of their unfamiliarity with a democratic work process. Hence, the not infrequent comment in connection with a statement of lack of abilities: "I like to be boss in. . . ." Or: "There is nothing like being your own boss." A similar thought occurs among the small number of workers who do not mention any abilities which they would like to use on the job. They "do not know of any other way to do their jobs" and accept "a job as a job." The most articulate expression of this feeling is found in the following response: "I haven't tried to use any abilities on that job of mine. I do the work just as it come to me. To use abilities you have to be boss or straw boss."

It is, therefore, understandable that most workers were luke-warm and manifested a lack of involvement when asked: "How do you feel after the work has been done? Satisfied?" Most of them gave an affirmative answer. Only a small number quali-fied their affirmative reaction, and a still smaller group ex-pressed outright dissatisfaction. Yet their behavior and gestures betrayed their words and gave them a somewhat fictitious char-acter. The level of satisfaction is, indeed, so low that it amounts in many cases to little more than an absence of dissatisfaction: "Day's work done, not scared to come back next day." Workers who share these feelings are usually satisfied because it is all over: "Well, you are glad the day's work is done; when you are tired, you want to sit down some place"; "I am glad that the work is done; I can go home, I hurry home." Some workers are so anxious to get through that they assume everybody in the world feels the same way: "I am happy that it's over with, just as you feel when you get through with the interview."

A good summary statement of the ultimate meaning of the game of work is contained in workers' answers to the question: "Does your job lead to anything you very much desire?" Typical majority responses are: "No, because I just have that job, and that is all to it." Or: "It's just a job; I am making a living. Out-side of that, it does not mean nothing to me; anybody could do it." Among the minority who answer the question in the affirma-tive, we find such responses as: "It leads to future security." Or: "It leads to old age security." Others just mention money. Maybe one worker who was puzzled about the question expressed best the general opinion: "I don't know what the desire is. A job is not an answer to a desire. A person would like to do better, have a better position, to command more pay; that's only a natural tendency."

## THE EXPERIENCE OF THE GAME OF WORK

Workers' answers to the question: "What do you first think of when you think of work?" allows us to refine these general impressions and to discern certain trends in workers' experience of the game of work.

The monotony of work, the "grind," the physical fatigue, and the lack of a feeling of accomplishment combine to create a feeling that work is burdensome; hence, the tendency to look upon the work process itself as something negative. One worker said, "When I first think of work, I think of labor—never of a job that requires much brain." Another: "Just think of more work."

These responses bear out Henrik de Man's observation that "in every language, the word 'work,' or its equivalent contains etymological constituents whose emotional coloration implies the action of an evil, a vexation, a humiliation."[3] These feelings are well summarized in the response of one worker who answered the question as to what he first thinks of when he thinks of work by saying: "Damn it!"

Those workers whose job involves a great deal of physical labor or repetitiveness emphasize the hard labor aspects. When the physical strain or the monotony cease to be outstanding the primary orientation is towards the reward for work. Money is the most often mentioned factor among those who have a positive attitude towards work. "I think of money"; "I think how much I am going to make"; "I think of what you are going to get for what you are doing." But even those who think of the reward cannot entirely forget the painful aspects of work: "I think of something that *has to be done* in order to keep a family going." The relationship between the "utility and disutility" of work is shown in a more calculating manner in the following answer: "I think how much physical effort—and compare it to the compensation."

Another secondary force accounting for the positive responses is the desire to do creative and good work. "Getting at something, getting it done," is a significant response with twofold implications. "To get at something" expresses a language flowing from an image of molding, creating something. In the words "to get it done" appear more the reality of the work process and the forces emanating from it. They imply that if it is impossible to find any inner meaning in the work, the very best one can do is "to get it done." One worker carried this thought to its logical conclusion when he said in answer to the question: "What do you first think of when you think of work?" "I think of getting it done . . . get home again." We meet here an important force influencing the attitude towards work; the desire to get through with it—"to get out of there."

The "game of work" in which workers engage offers the workers an escape from two powerful forces: One pulls them away from the work process towards money—an end which is psychologically outside this process since it is in another sphere of relatedness. The other directs thought towards the painful—monotonous—aspects of the work process. Workers who are not overwhelmed by one or the other of these two forces usually give a neutral response to the question: "What do you first think of when you think of work?" But the very colorlessness of their responses indicated a delicate balance of forces and the difficulty of positive forces connected with the work process itself to arise. In the extreme case work not only loses all its meaning but any thought about it is repressed. This is well illustrated by a worker who, when asked: "What do you first think of when you think of work?" laughed and said, "My goodness, such a question—nothing!"

Fortunately, the majority of the workers do not have such extreme feelings. They do not consciously experience work as an oppressive force because they have lowered their level of aspirations to the emptiness of the job. They do not expect anything else than what the work process offers and they direct their energies towards money and activities outside the factory. Does this mean that work has a neutral effect on their life? Or does the work process generate forces in the unconscious which the free indulgence into the game of work hides from the eye? With these questions in mind we will now examine the main forces activated by the present organization of the work process.

# CHAPTER 6

# The Flight from and to Work

## WORK AND OFF-WORK ACTIVITIES

People who walk in the neat streets of the city of Austin may not notice the shrill whistle signaling the end of a shift. But the workers in the plant react to it instantly. The hour they waited for, or in anticipation of which they worked hard, has come: they are off work. Most workers rush out of their department to the locker rooms or to the clock where they punch their time cards. The behavior of these workers testifies vividly how anxious they are to get out. In one of the departments in which the foreman gives a sign when the time has come to leave, the time interval between the sign being given and the room being empty is so short that I did not realize at first how and why twenty people disappeared in an arrowlike fashion within a few seconds. No less vivid is the testimony given by those workers who are already standing at the time clock in order not to lose a minute when "quitting time" comes. They assemble in a line several minutes before their time is over, waiting for the clock to strike the hour and to punch out. Holding their time card ready, they watch the clock. If a look could move the hand of a clock, there is no doubt that it would jump a few minutes ahead.

Having punched out, the workers converge to the nearest exit. During the summer time, particularly when the sun is lighting up the blue sky, the daylight will blind their eyes, now adjusted to the artificial illumination of their work place. During winter it is as dark when they leave the plant as it was when they walked through the gate in the morning: they may not see daylight except on weekends. But even more abrupt than the outer change in atmosphere is the inner change from work to being off work. When the workers pick up their cars on the vast parking lot surrounding the factory, they are in the twilight of work and leisure: still dazed by the work, they begin to look forward to the free hours ahead of them.

Their first impulse is to get some rest or to do something that will "break the grind" of work. "I am looking forward to relax"; "I want to play lazy" are typical responses to the question: "What do you look forward to after work?" It is not difficult to intuit the feelings of a worker who looks forward to "coming indoors and kicking my shoes off." Before doing this many a worker has already stopped at a bar for a drink. They felt a need of "doing something like that after work." Some did not know why, others were quite articulate about it: "You just need a beer to break the grind."

Whether they stopped at a bar or went home directly, almost all workers are looking forward to their family. "To go home" or "to go home to the family" have been mentioned repeatedly. "I am looking forward to meeting my husband"; "I am looking forward to my wife" were words said with deep feeling.

It is, indeed, impossible to understand the meaning of work without having spent some time in the homes of the workers and having seen them with their families. Family life is not just something that compensates for the work: it bestows a specific meaning on it. Asked: "How long do you expect to continue working anyway?" a worker said, "I have a long way up. I want education for the children. That's about the only purpose in life, so that they do not have to work as hard as I did in my life." This is by no means an isolated goal: education of the children as a means to a "better life" is one of the most important aspirations of the workers.

The role of the home and of family life is well illustrated by a worker who said in response to the question: "What makes your job important?" "It gives me a decent living, a roof over the house, you can live the way you like, money doesn't do everything." This is the answer of an unsophisticated soul who is fond of the home he has built himself and who enjoys his family. The following story may give an even better idea of the significance of family life as a factor giving meaning to work. A worker mentioned in a group session how his interests increased because his children ask him so many questions. While talking about this, he said: "They don't even want to go to bed. Then I tell them I don't want to go to work either, but I have to, to make a living for them." Even if we cannot hear the humor of the reply, "But Daddy, we don't make no money going to bed!" it might be possible to visualize the situation and to realize that it might not be too much of a burden to make money in order to have such a family life.

After having rested and spent some time with the family, workers have their supper, or lunch, as many of them call the evening meal following old farm tradition. Many things occupy them then: gardening, maybe farming and keeping up their cars. Some read, listen to the radio, and go out for meetings, to sport events or see friends—unless taking care of all the many things which have to be done in the house keep them at home.

Hobbies and creative activities may play an important role in their life. A creative worker, who needs a real feeling of accomplishment, answered the question: "What do you look forward to after work?" as follows: "One of the biggest things, to go home, to play with the kids, to get that out of my system, see how they are . . . then my interests, *try to accomplish something for that day. . . .*" Note: this worker tries to accomplish something for that day—after the day's work has been done.

Whether they are with their family or their friends, rare are the occasions when workers feel like talking about their work. In response to the question: "Do you talk with your friends about the work you are doing?" only a very small number indicated that they do talk with their friends—or their wife—about their work. Quite a few said that they "only" talk with their friends "if they ask me," or that they talk "sometimes" or "seldom." Some workers are outspoken in saying that they do not like to talk about their work: "If we get out of there, we are through with that to the next day." Another worker said, "When I leave down there, I am through down there. I like to talk about something else." He adds to this with some astonishment:

"Railroadmen always want to talk about their work." Other workers express the same thought in different language: "Usually, when out of there, we talk about more worldly things, unless something funny happens."

## "Separation" of Work and Life

The general dislike to talk about the work seems to indicate a strong separation of their life off the job from their work—an impression which is substantiated by their answers to the question: "Do you find that your experience in working is useful to you personally, I mean can you use this experience to your benefit off the job?"

The great majority of the workers feels that work has no meaning for their life off the job. And the reasons given by the few who indicated that work is useful to them personally show how limited the usefulness of their work experience actually is. One worker, for example, feels that work is "financially useful." Only exceptionally do workers point to the knowledge of material which they get, or the skill they acquire. It is useful in "buying meats"; "in keeping the knife sharp or helping other people to butcher." For some of the workers who also farm, the skill they acquire is useful "in butchering" or similar work. A few workers point to the human contact on the job as something useful for their life off the job. "You get to know different people and opinions."

Only two ideas of general significance really relate work and life. One worker—a mechanic—said, "Yes, mechanical instinct that you keep picking up is useful, tinkering here and there, helping somebody." Another worker feels that work "makes you responsible." Or, as a third worker put it: "The routine keeps your mind well grounded . . . and makes you a stable citizen." This was said by a worker whose creative life outside the work is so well developed that he can accept work as giving him a certain stability. However, these three workers are the exception which confirms the rule: for the overwhelming majority of the workers, the work experience has no meaning for their lives. The situation is well illustrated by a worker who talked about the time off the job as his "personal time." The work process is so de-personalized that it is not considered as something that belongs to the person!

The separation of work and life is further highlighted by the overwhelmingly negative responses to the question: "Do you ever do anything off the job which helps you in your work in any way?" Only a few workers do something during their free time that gives meaning to their work. A worker with a strong desire to become a foreman said, "Yes, in this case . . . self-improvement. I like to give myself more background and knowledge in packing industry." A mechanic who is interested in engineering pointed out that he "reads technical articles, etc." A worker-farmer related the question to his farm work: "If you go to auction sales, you talk to different farmers, learn to judge their experience . . . you keep your farm papers, etc."

If it were possible to departmentalize ourselves into separate spheres, then we could dismiss any further thought on the absence of meaningful identifications with the organized work process and be satisfied with the mere observation that family life and outside activities are the most important factors giving meaning to work. But the human psyche is a unity which is striving to develop a unified harmonious pattern of relationships: there is a tendency towards integration in us. This tendency manifests itself in an attempt to minimize conflicts resulting from discrepancies between contradictory types of relationships. It may lead to growth or to decay: we may try to solve a conflict by moving to a higher plane (where we meet new conflicts which will further stimulate our growth), or we may try to solve conflicts by adjusting at a lower level where we may stagnate or be pushed further down.[1]

No matter what the precise nature of man's desire for integration, its mere existence highlights an intimate relationship between work and life. Work and life may be sharply separated spheres only in the sense that the work experience has no meaning for the life of the worker. But work and life cannot be separated in the sense that work has no impact on the life of the worker. Indeed, work is one of the most essential factors in determining the level at which integration takes place, as well as the degree of integration which can take place.

As we become familiar with workers' life off the job we will see how the experience of work affects their life and how the forces emanating from the organized work process create conflicts which render the process of integration more difficult.

FIRST TENDENCY: THE DESIRE "TO GET AWAY FROM IT ALL"

The desire to get away from work comes out most strongly when workers are off work: during their weekends and vacations.

Two ideas recur again and again in their answers to the question: "How does the weekend differ from the days you work?" and "What do you most like about weekends?" These ideas are: "It makes you feel as though you are free to do what you want," and "it is a time for rest and recreation." Here are some variations of this theme: "I like most that I *don't have* to get up so early"; "You can relax, you know"; "Yes, more relaxing, stay up late and sleep late"; "You have a little bit longer to do something for yourself, to visit more of your own." Similar responses are: "Don't have to work, don't have to get up, visit our folks"; "Oh, I look forward to Sunday rest, recreation and enjoy the Sabbath day"; "More time, sleep later in the morning, read papers, visit."

A variety of factors account for the difference in emphasis on these aspects of the weekend. As we would expect, older workers feel keenly about "getting a chance to get rested," whereas younger workers see in it more "a chance to roam around, be a little bit free with your time," though they rarely forget to add: "and an opportunity to relax." The kind of work done, the degree of physical exertion it involves, as well as family conditions, are other factors which account for the difference in attitude towards the weekend. But the desire to get away from work permeates all the answers. It manifests itself not only in certain activities; even more strongly, it is expressed in the mental attitudes of most workers: "What I like best about weekends is to *forget* you have to work, really relax"; "You are away from work, mentally and physically." What is significant is that this worker wants first of all to *forget* about the work, get rid of this thought, rather than relax from the strain of the work. She wants to get work out of her mind, rather than out of her bones and muscles.

Only one worker said that she likes most "the satisfaction of the work done . . . start in another week." The general feeling about the weekend is perhaps best expressed in the statement: "It gets you away." That there are many workers who would like to get away for more than a weekend is shown in their reaction to those workers who studied under the G. I. program and worked in the plant during the summer months to supplement their income. One of these G.I. student-workers said to me: "What makes me mad . . . they kid me about school. They say: "You don't have to worry, you don't have to stand here and do the job.' Many told me: 'I am glad *somebody can get out of here. . . .*'"

There are many instances which show that physical fatigue is not the main factor in workers' desire to get away from work. I spent many weekends with some of the workers, and we were all much more worn out on Monday morning than before or after any other workday. And yet, rest and relaxation comes first to their mind when they think about the weekend! The following conversation is relevant to this point: "How does your weekend differ from the days you work?" "Oh, you rest up more." "Or get more tired!" the wife of the worker interjected. Both the wife and the worker were right. Just looking at his weekend activity, he must have gotten more tired, but he did not *feel* it as much, because it was a different activity more in agreement with his own way of life than the activity in the factory. It was an activity which had both rhythm and freedom. Naturally, you get tired from working, but the physical tiredness does not pervade the weekend as much as does the psychological fatigue.

The voices of the workers who echo this psychological fatigue and the implicit desire "to get away from it all" rise to a crescendo when they answered the question: "What do you like best about vacations?" Freedom from work is the outstanding factor mentioned by the vast majority of the workers: "Sleep late, not worrying about being at work, *forget* your working problems . . ."; "I completely *forget* work and anything connected with it"; "Gets your *mind off work* you have been doing all year." "To get away and *forget*" may be considered as a summary statement of the feelings of many workers.

The fact that vacations were listed as the Number one advantage derived from working for the company should be recalled in this context. Probed as to why vacations are so appreciated, workers' responses ranged from "You can do something" to the strong pronouncement: "It gives you the feeling that you don't have to slave every day of the year to make a living. You can see the country and get away from the job." All responses center around the same theme: "Boy, something to look forward to, gives you a relief if steady day-by-day job is a necessary thing."

It is natural that workers want to get away from work. But— *c'est le ton qui fait la musique* and the often compulsive desire to forget expresses much more than the need for a change and for new impressions: it is an attempt to escape the oppressive grind of work. As one of the workers said so clearly: "What I like best about vacations is to fish . . . you are not on a certain schedule, you don't *have to* get up early, you get up earlier, but you don't *have to,* so you don't get tired." Could there be a better example for what we called "psychological fatigue" than the feeling of this worker that you don't get tired if you get up early for fishing because you don't *have to* get up early? Workers' attempts to overcome the feelings of constraint created by work gives to their desire "to do what they want" during their vacations its peculiar emotional overtone.

SECOND TENDENCY: CARRY-OVER OF WORK ATTITUDES INTO THE LEISURE TIME

However, the desire to forget by "getting away from it all" is not enough. Unfortunately it is not so easy to change from the strenuous game of work to an inner relaxation, since the attitudes acquired during work become so deeply ingrained that they are often carried into the life off the job. This dilemma emerged from workers' responses to the question: "How do you feel about your working life as against your life off the job? Do you enjoy working more or less than anything else you do?"

The most striking result is what may be called "a need to have something to do." Here are a whole series of interesting responses: "You don't live to work, but awful tired when no work"; "If all would be off-time, I would be nervous"; "I wouldn't want to be without work, because it would be terribly monotonous— for my notion"; "It passes the time away faster . . . better for you mentally, too"; "Yes, I like to work; I couldn't be idle, always glad to be back after vacations." A somewhat neutral summary of these feelings is given by a worker who is an ideal type of the average, because he has completely "internalized external necessities." He said, "Well, a person has got something to occupy their time. Got to have something to do."

In the extreme case, this tendency becomes a compulsion which, like the gold of Midas, spoils everything that it comes in contact with, as the following conversation shows:

*Question*: How do you feel about your working life as against your life off the job? Do you enjoy working less or more than anything else you do?

*Worker*: I don't know. I wouldn't want to work more than I've to.

*Wife*: Don't say you wouldn't want to work, because everything you do ends up in work.

Asked what he does during his vacations, and what he likes best about them, he answered: "I don't go much, work around here . . . get started and keep going until all done. . . . I like best the chance to meet other people. . . ." Once you get started, you keep going, and when you are "all done" you start all over again. The repetitive movements of the work become part of the vacation. As a result, you "would get crazy if not working."

Since we want to illustrate a tendency rather than evaluate a situation, extreme cases are most significant because they show this tendency in its purest form. And this worker continues to illustrate vividly how work attitudes may affect the life off the job. Asked: "How does your weekend differ from the days you work?" he said, "There is not a hell of a lot of difference . . . it is a day of rest if a fellow wants to take it. . . ." Actually he works outside the plant during his vacations. And what he likes best about vacations is the opportunity "to go out and earn a few extra nickels." The question: "If you inherited some money and had enough to live on without working, would you want to work anyway?" he answered as follows:

*Worker*: I tell you if I would not work, I would get nuts.
*Question*: Why do you say that?

*Worker*: Just sitting around, I would get nuts. If I sit around for two days I am in everybody's road.

*Question*: Do you ever read or . . .?

*Worker*: No.

[At this point of the conversation, his wife breaks in:]

*Wife*: He just does not know what to do with himself; he can't relax, it's his nerves.

*Worker*: I don't have any.

*Wife*: I found that out many times, we all do.

*Worker*: I haven't been really home for a long time. I was. . . . I can't be without doing something.

*Question*: Would you want to do what you are now doing?

*Worker*: No, I wouldn't be working in a packinghouse.

*Question*: Where would you want to work?

*Worker*: I would like to have a popcorn wagon, get out in the air and sunshine.

This worker who "has no nerves" has shown in his relationship to me that he is a sensitive person, and yet he suppressed his feelings strongly. When asked, "What do you first think of when you think of work?" he said, "Skip it."! Like the British soldiers at Gallipoli,[2] being both sensitive and suppressed, the impact of work on his unconscious is stronger, and he must follow the inner compulsion more blindly than workers with a greater consciousness about their work. Deep down in him, he would like very much "to take the rest" which the weekend affords, and when he was asked, "What is the best kind of vacation you could possibly have?" he—who works all the time—answered, "Go to the coast, do nothing, just loaf, take my time. . . ." But he cannot do it; he must always do something, because he is unconsciously compelled to carry his work attitude into his whole life.

In this worker the forces generated by the modern organization of work have found their purest expression: the chain on which he works is the medium through which they affect him. Is it an accidental result that the chain symbolizes also his psychological situation? It is true that the forces emanating from work are enhanced here to such a degree as to be almost a caricature of a neurotic. But let us not forget that the caricature gives a true picture of the real forces which affect all workers. And there are others who "dislike most the inactivity," or who say, "Well, I couldn't quit working; I just couldn't. The day is too long if I don't have something to do. I have to do so much work." This was said by a worker who drowns his conflicts in alcohol, and whose compulsive need to "have a drink" equals his compulsion to work.

The lack of experience of a clear-cut difference between work and weekends may serve as additional evidence for the impact of work on the life of the workers. A substantial minority answered the question: "How does your weekend differ from the days you work?" by responses such as: "Oh well, it is about the same thing, I most generally work." Or: "There is not much difference." And the extreme: "There is not a bit of difference." These statements are symptomatic of a tendency which pervades even the answers of many other workers who feel that there is a difference between the weekend and the days they work: namely, to carry work attitudes on into the weekend in spite of a strong psychological fatigue and desire to get away from work, and from everything work stands for.

### Third Tendency: The Desire for Creative Activities

While a compulsive activity which carries the on-the-job work attitude straight into the life of the workers is one extreme delineating the off-the-job attitudes of the workers, a creative activity delineates the other extreme. Many workers have a hobby which allows them to express their desire for a creative activity. The following conversation shows this clearly:

What would you really like to do if you could do what you wanted to do?

It is hard telling. I would have my hobby shop in the line of engineering.

Would you like to invent things? [This worker has mentioned this interest in a previous conversation.]

I could stay there from five o'clock in the morning until midnight and enjoy it.

It is obvious that an occupation in which one wants to engage from five o'clock in the morning until midnight is more than a hobby in the ordinary sense of the word. And yet, for most workers, creative work is in some way connected with the idea of a hobby or play. Hence, the significant concept of the "play-worker" which is closely related to the feeling of accomplishment or creative activity—as the following conversation shows:

If you inherited some money and had enough to live on without working, would you want to work anyway?

Suppose would be one of those play-workers, would not work here, could not accomplish anything, invest it in a farm.

Another conversation shows the same tendency to relate creative activity to a play or hobby:

*Question*: What would you like to do if you wouldn't have to work?
*Worker*: Oh, pick up a hobby.
*Question*: What hobby?
*Wife*: Fishing or carving is a hobby.
*Worker*: Carving.
*Question*: You like to create something?
*Worker*: Yes.
*Question*: Did you ever carve?
*Worker*: Yes, when in school.
*Question*: What did you like about it?
*Worker*: Something that comes natural to me.

The expression "something that comes natural to me" symbolizes a free, spontaneous, creative activity. The same element can be discerned in the following statement:

I don't like work as much as work on a farm. I spend there the best part of the afternoon and the evening. The work you do there you don't have to do; it seems better . . . you are *cooperating with nature, watching things grow*, close to nature; one trouble with job is the mechanical noise, artificial lights. . . .

I believe that the reader can intuit the quality of a feeling arising out of "cooperating with nature" and "watching things grow."

As an outstanding example of a worker expressing a need for a creative expression, I like to mention a worker who has a series of "hobbies" which he follows with such an interest and devotion that they express a deep search to perfect an idea. For this worker the weekend becomes "a spiritual upliftment." The Webster dictionary does not list a word "upliftment." It was a word made up for the occasion, as is shown by the fact that he added: "I don't know how you could call it." It expresses beautifully a feeling of positive satisfaction and elevation beyond the level of the week's work. A similar feeling is expressed in regard to the vacation: "They give you something to look forward to, a period of time to *accomplish* something, rest, fresh air and sunshine!" Rest is mentioned, too, by this worker. But how different is the context within which it is mentioned: it stands between accomplishment and sunshine, the latter being almost as rare in a packinghouse as the former!

We have thus met another force—a desire for a creative expression which is directly opposed to the routine and the monotony of the work. It is interesting that in this case the routine of the work does not interfere with the creativity of the worker, because work becomes relegated to a sphere of the personality where it becomes the handmaiden of the creative self, rather than suppressing it.[3]

The need for a creative activity—and the inability to satisfy it in the work process—has far-reaching consequences. We observed, for example, that work does not evoke the same tendencies among those workers who do farming besides working in a factory, or who have strong outside interests. For them work has a much more positive meaning than for those who do not have similar outlets. Although these conclusions need further study, there is ample evidence to show that the feeling of work being something imposed, forced upon the workers, is only partly due to the "laboring aspects" of the job; partly it is a result of the impossibility to express one's creativity in the work process.

THE NEED TO BE OCCUPIED

The interplay between the desire "to get away from it all," the compulsion to carry work attitudes into the whole life, and the need for a creative self-expression has results as varied as the workers in the factory. Some typical constellations will be discussed in Chapters 8 through 10. In this context we must limit ourselves to show the most common effects of these tendencies.

Fortunately, not many workers experience them as powerful,

opposing forces. The majority neither experience anything approaching an "upliftment," nor are they dragged down to the level of automatic mechanical activity: the forces are not felt as extreme moods, because they cancel out and form an average:

How does your weekend differ from the days you work?
I go to church or I go fishing.
How do you feel about it?
I would say average.

Maybe we can list also the following response among the average experiences of life. "What I like most about weekends is something to look forward to during the week, day of relaxation." But when it comes: "Well, outside from going to church, they don't differ too much from the days you work . . . you take a Sunday trip, read, cut the lawn, etc. . . ." This is certainly an activity very different from that of the weekdays, and yet this worker does not *feel* too differently about it, for life has reached the steady level of the average. It is a relatively low level, since the desire for a creative experience is weaker than those powerful forces emanating from the work process which create the tendency towards repetitive compulsiveness and automatic activity.

But this drift towards an average level must not prevent us from recognizing the impact of all three forces on the life of the workers. Even for those who have an average experience of their work and life, the tension between the conflicting tendencies growing out of the organization of the work process exists—and grows as their distance from their work increases. What has been experienced as freedom from outside interference within the factory gates is replaced by a feeling of restraint—at least for those who cannot find a positive creative way of expression. They are tied to their work with an invisible, but not less effective, *rubber band*, whose pull is the stronger, the faster and further they try to get away from it. This rubber band breaks only if workers "break the grind of the work" and the compulsiveness it creates.

Since it is almost impossible to work eight hours intensively and switch over suddenly to a new, creative way of life, workers are pushed into some kind of activity which keeps them occupied without reminding them of their work. "To be busy, to have something to do, to keep occupied" thus becomes the most typical experience of life. As the most often heard statements in regard to the life *on and off* the job, they are indicative of the real psychological values connected with working, and of the impact of work on the whole life of the workers.

This need to be busy-occupied comes out most clearly in workers' response to the question: "If you inherited some money and had enough to live on without working, would you want to work anyway? Why?" The overwhelming majority answered in the affirmative, pointing to the "need to be occupied." Here are a few typical responses: "You have to be active and keep your mind occupied"; "It keeps your mind occupied. You can't be idle too much." Or just: "It keeps you occupied." Even those who would not want to work would want "to be occupied" somehow: "I would want to travel, have a farm in lake region, just to have a place to go and take care of it, a few books, keep you occupied."

This need to be occupied is the common denominator between the life on the job and the life off the job. In it, all three tendencies discussed above merge: "If I wouldn't have to work, I would buy a farm . . . live . . . raise *what I wanted* to raise. . . . I would want to *keep myself occupied* raising things, learn about them, *find out what makes them grow*." This response contains a mixture of two elements: the desire for a free activity, and a curiosity about the meaning of life. They combine in a desire to be occupied. In other cases the same desire expresses less a creative urge and more a tendency to carry work attitudes into the life. The interplay of all these forces is best illustrated by the role fishing plays in the life of the workers.

Fishing, traveling, and "going someplace" are the favorite vacation pastimes of the workers. Fishing has a slight edge over the other two. If we compare what workers actually do during their vacation to what they would like to do (as revealed in their answers to the question: "What is the best kind of vacation you could possibly have?"), we find an approximately equal distribution between "going someplace" or traveling, and fishing. If we include the weekends into their pastime activities, fishing becomes *undoubtedly* the *most important relaxation* that workers have. It is true that the beautiful lake country of Minnesota invites fishing. But it invites equally swimming, rowing, sailing, or riding in a motor boat. The lakes are even tempting just to relax, lie on the shores, and bathe in water and sunshine. Why do most workers fish rather than indulge in any alternative "activity"?

Fishing does not necessarily exclude the enjoyment of the other possibilities offered by the lake country. This is shown in workers' answers to the question: "What is the best kind of vacation you could possibly have?" One worker said, "Going out fishing and laying around a little." Another: "Going north, fishing and rest." These responses show that fishing is connected with resting and relaxing. But it remains significant that fishing is mentioned first: as a rule, workers get more rest and relaxation from fishing than they would from just relaxing.

The following answer gives a clue to the understanding of this situation: "Well, I like fishing trips, fishing, just loaf around a little—but it gets tiresome if not doing anything; time passes slow, therefore fishing . . . catch big ones." This is a most revealing statement, because it shows that one of the most important aspects of fishing is "to be occupied." I once talked to a worker whose compulsive need for activity for activities' sake was so strong that he could literally not sit still. He was permeated by restlessness. But he loved fishing!

Indeed, fishing is the ideal relaxation, because it allows a unique combination of attitudes: Fishing gives the illusion of doing something while actually doing nothing—and enjoying the beauty of life. You sit and do nothing, you wait, but since something might happen any moment, time does not drag. Fishing has an element of surprise which is so conspicuously absent from the work process. It thus becomes the ideal pastime, because the tendency "to be occupied" can be combined with the desire "to get away from it all." Fishing has elements which are just the opposite of the work process: It is relaxing; it is outdoors; you can feel the sunshine and the wind; you are surrounded by water and woods ("you are in the neck of the woods"); last but not least, you are free. You could not be farther "away from it all" than in the northern lake country.

And yet, it has elements akin to the work process: It does

not require any initiative or attention and, most of all, it allows the psychological mechanisms of busy-ness to go on. It makes it possible to carry an essential attitude growing out of the work process into the leisure time without making its experience in any way similar to the experience of work. It thus reconciles conflicting tendencies and resolves a conflict temporarily without touching the forces creating it. It does not, therefore, solve anything. This may be considered a drawback. From the point of view of a pastime activity, however, it is a further advantage, since it eliminates the necessity of a basic change in attitude, of effort and attention.

We must add to this already amazing list of qualities two further attributes of fishing: It has a competitive element—"to catch big fish." it is, incidentally, a competition which does not require exertion. This competitive element is closely connected with important status symbols—the size and amount of fish caught. It is not only nice to fish, it is also nice to find one's picture with a handful of big fish in the monthly Company paper.

To conclude: The most important attributes of fishing are the harmonization of the tendency to get away from work and to carry work attitudes on into life. It is the ideal form of relaxation for people who have to relax while doing nothing and still being occupied. Its unique way of reconciling these two conflicting tendencies allows the third tendency, the desire for a creative experience of life to make itself felt. By resolving the conflict between the desire to make time pass fast and enjoy it at the same time, it makes possible an experience of the "eternity" of time. The hours spent fishing thus become the genuinely happy times in the life of the workers—times they talk about a great deal during the year, in order, as one worker so beautifully put it, to "relive" them. Contrast this with the dislike to talk about the work, and you have a deeper understanding of what work does to their life. Indeed, fishing is an activity which becomes symbolic of the forces determining the impact of work on the life of the workers.

The degree to which workers carry over into their life what they experience in fishing varies according to the manner in which the personality structure of the workers allows the work experience to intrude in their whole life. To the extent to which work intrudes in their life, it drags it down to an empty busyness which kills the monotony of time. Only as the "rubber band" is being cut and this intrusion broken, can the creative forces in the workers come into play—and the desire to get away, to be free, can find positive expression. The crucial point is: How and where is the compulsiveness of the grind broken? If it is broken soon and in a positive way, then its damage is limited. If it is allowed to work its way into the unconscious—as it always does to some extent—and if there is nothing to counteract it, then it breaks the worker rather than the worker breaking it. Those workers who succeed in giving to their life a creative orientation deserve the admiration of all those who do not have to subject their daily existence to the forces generated by the work process. Not too many workers are successful—most of them must be satisfied with those interspersed moments which allow them to be free from work.

# CHAPTER 7

# Alienation from Work

## TECHNICAL AND SOCIAL DIVISION OF LABOR

When the workers return to their work after a weekend or vacation of fishing they are still imbued by the beauty of the Minnesota lake country: its blue water, its dark-green woods, and its crisp air. They feel better because they could forget for a fleeting moment that it is their fate to work in a factory. But as they drive to the plant they know that they have escaped the forces generated by work for a short time only. And before they fully realize it, they are again playing the game of work: again trying to kill the monotony of an empty work performance, again attempting to break the grind, and again being caught in a conflict which seems beyond their control.

This game and the forces which work generates in workers' life must be partly explained by the repetitive, minutely divided work process. But the concrete technical aspects of work explain only part of the story. The division of labor is, after all, not only a technical problem, but also a social one: it is determined by the social organization of industry as well as by certain technical requirements. And workers do not only contribute to the production of something with certain mechanical, physical, and chemical qualities: they also produce use- and exchange-values.

Since work is basically a social process, the absence of any meaning derived from the concrete technical aspects of the work process in no way excludes workers from playing a meaningful role in the social process of production. The thoughts which can-

not be expressed on the job itself could find an outlet in participation in those spheres of the work process into which the division of labor has delegated the process of decision-making. Nor
does the absence of a feeling of accomplishment derived from the
exercise of skill exclude consciousness of a meaningful contribution to society. The energy which is cut off from identification
with the product-workmanship could be expressed in identifications with the purposes or uses which the product serves.

There are, indeed, as many possibilities of meaningful identification as there are values and goals connected with the organized work process. Workers could derive meaning from identification with the various spheres of the company. Partnership feelings could give meaning to work; so could implementation of the
immediate goals in view of which work is organized: productive
efficiency. In addition, there could be a consciousness of more
remote goals: competition on the market and profit maximization
could bestow meaning on work. Union identification is no less
significant: conciousness of the general role of labor in the over-
all work process could relate workers to a community of people
and ideas.

PRODUCTIVENESS

Workers' answers to the question: "What does it mean to you
to be a producer?" are a good starting point for examining their
consciousness of the role which they play in the social process of
production—and of the meaning they derive from it. This query
was intentionally phrased in this general, comprehensive manner in order to get at all the shades of meaning associated by
workers with "productiveness," as the best expression of a meaningful relatedness to the process of production. The question has,
indeed, strong positive implications and was asked—both in tone
and gesture—in such a way as to direct feelings and thoughts
towards the positive, creative aspects of the work process. Usually
I moved my arm and hand in a way suggesting a formative, creative process.

The company was frequently mentioned in answering this
question. Typical responses are: "I don't know how to answer
that. I want to be a producer as long as I am working. I want

to satisfy the people I am working for." Or: "Well, you have to be a producer on the job, or you would not be there long." The first response has a positive element, the second expresses a mere necessity: unless you produce, you will get fired for bad workmanship. Whereas we may assume that the first worker who spoke to us has a natural fondness of the company, the second worker gives only evidence of a symbiotic identification with management: the meaning of being a producer is reduced to a desire not to be rejected by the person or institution one is working for. The paucity of responses showing more than a feeling of dependency confirms our previous finding that company identifications based predominantly on money are not conducive to relate workers to the social process of production—no matter how positive they may be.

Workers' relatedness to the supervisory staff gives part of the explanation for this situation. Under the present organization of work, the role of the supervisory staff is, on the whole, one of nonintervention: neither positive nor negative. It is not negative because the supervisory staff does not act as an enforcement agent of management, as it did prior to unionization. And it is not positive because the supervisory staff is neither a medium enabling workers to express their initiative and ideas nor an organ allowing them to take part in the decisions affecting their daily work. As a result, workers are cut off from a possible human relatedness and from positive identifications with the organization of the work in so far as it affects their jobs. The Business Improvement Committee and the grievance machinery do not, as we will see later on, sufficiently compensate these shortcomings.

The neutral role of the supervisory staff—in conjunction with the impact of the guaranteed-wage–wage-incentive system—is of crucial significance for an understanding of workers' experience of their work: The security of employment and the absence of authoritarian work discipline allow workers to engage freely into the game of work. In playing this game workers *accept* the goal of productive efficiency. But their acceptance of this goal is either unconscious or it is experienced as a concession rather than as a new orientation which gives meaning to work. The difficulties which management still has in regard to time study illustrate the absence of positive identifications with the most important immediate goal in view of which work is organized. It is significant that the only comment which linked me in a detrimental way with the company was that I was "the Jew who does time study for the company." That this was said by a worker who was drunk in an up-town bar is insignificant. Nor does it matter that none of my activities in the plant could have given reason for any well-founded suspicion along these lines. On the contrary, it is the fantastic nature of the charge which gives it a great symbolic significance. It expresses deep-seated fears: fear of becoming part of a still more inhuman machinery; of being an even smaller cog in a machine which turns around still faster.

Projections of these fears on the Jew are revealing. The image of the Jew is for most workers closely related to money. As a worker said in a group meeting: "My wife tells me I should be more of a Jew than an Irishman. . . . I would make more money." Usually the image is less positive in content and more the receptacle of all the unresolved conflicts and repressed guilt feelings of the anti-Semite. A situation which makes one value—money—supreme and reduces men to cogs in a machine is indeed conducive to arouse projections which link the goal of productive efficiency to money as the only value embodied in the social organization of the company.

These limitations of money identifications could be overcome, at least partly, if they were accompanied by a relatedness to the over-all market organization—as the "highest" expression of exchange-value. Yet company identification of this kind is quite exceptional. In view of the remoteness of the workers from the market, it is quite understandable that they do not perceive in the process of buying and selling any objects for identification. But there is a much more important factor explaining the situation: workers' unconsciousness of any purpose transcending the factory. They are not only unrelated to exchange-value, they are also unaware of producing use-values satisfying human needs.

### MONEY-SERVICE ORIENTATION

The whole problem of service-money orientation of industrial organization is put into sharp focus by the answer of a worker to the question: "Does being an employee make you feel you are a partner in doing an important job?" She said: "It is not important, just doing something; in war time I felt it was important, now it is just a job." The creative urge of the worker who expressed these feelings is strong. It expresses itself in poetry and a desire to give meaning to work—not merely by making it a means to make money, but an inner meaning growing out of relatedness to a goal with which she can identify. During the war, she could bestow meaning on her work because it was part of a common effort. But when it ceased to be service-oriented, it became again "just a job." These feelings are particularly significant since they come from a worker whose general orientation is towards management, not towards the union.

The following conversations further illustrate the absence of a service orientation in industry and the resulting separation of "work" and "rendering a service":

> If you inherited some money and had enough to live on without working, would you want to work anyway?
> Never given it a thought, probably do some good.
> Would you work?
> Probably not.

Another worker when asked whether he would want to work at what he is now doing if he had money, answered:

> I can't see any disadvantage. I seem to be getting along okay in this world [he pauses and adds] there is a lot of things better.
> For example?
> A business of your own or serving the public.
> Note: "serving the public" is conceived outside the work process, not within it.

The absence of any service orientation—or, to put it differently, any use-value identifications—explains why the production of food was mentioned relatively rarely as giving a feeling of "partnership in doing an important job." In a factory processing food

I would have expected workers to mention their product more often than they did. Food satisfies one of the basic human needs and a participation in the process of producing food is certainly something that could give meaning to work. Yet even in answer to the question: "What does it mean to you to be a producer?" food was mentioned relatively rarely. The most direct response was: "I am putting out food for the people." Other workers mentioned food only after some rather direct probing:

> What does it mean to you to be a producer?
> Well, it benefits the people.
> Do you have a feeling of being a producer?
> Oh yes; you produce things to eat, food.

In a third conversation, consciousness of producing a use-value came out even more indirectly:

> Oh yes, you feel as a producer.
> In which way?
> You are making a product that we try to make good, that I eat myself.

Besides the lack of directness in response we must note a lack of involvement when the question came up in the interview. A similar aloofness became evident in workers' answers to the question, what makes the job important for the worker, for the community, and for the country. Food was mentioned more·often in connection with the country as a whole than with the experience of the work itself.

### Work—a "General Good"

The deeper implications of the absence of a positive relatedness to the social process of production become clearer as we examine what may be called workers' "projected work process identifications." A large number of workers try to give meaning to their work by projecting some vague idea of a "general good" on their work—usually on an area bordering the organized work process. A purely mechanical count of frequencies of responses to the question: "What does it mean to you to be a producer?" gives *first* place to such projections. And if we realize that many of the product-identification responses denote more a feeling for the ultimate use of the product than for the workmanship connected with the process of production, the significance of the "general good" responses emerges even more strongly.

Asked what it means to be a producer, one worker said: "It means a lot; I think I am doing some good in the world, I see ten carloads of Spam. . . ." Other more general expressions are: "Yes, I feel that I am doing somebody some good." Or: "It makes you feel good that you are helping somebody else." A similar, rather dim but clearly positive feeling is expressed in the following conversations:

> What does it mean to you to be a producer?
> You mean a worker? I like it, everybody should!
> And what does it mean to you?
> Progress; if you produce, you go ahead; if you don't, you go behind.

Since workers are unable to give meaning to work by identification with the organized work process, they search for it in the vague realm of "progress," of "doing somebody some good," of "helping somebody else."

Interesting in this connection is the answer of a worker to our question about the meaning of being a producer. He said: "We are all producers . . . consumers . . . idea of contributing . . . people over here . . . great psychic value from being producer just like a carpenter building a home." This is an intellectualization of something that is not felt to exist but felt as something that should exist. The comparison is with an activity completely unrelated to the kind of work done in a packinghouse. It is put, furthermore, in the form of an idea, rather than expressed as a real experience. A similar projection is contained in the following response of a worker: "Producing" feels "like making something, even if there is really nothing to make."

It is significant that a conscious direction of workers' feelings and thoughts towards the positive content of work brought forward a vague feeling of some general good. The frequency of the "projected work identification" responses highlights the deep need to bestow meaning on human activity. And the difficulties —if not the impossibility—to do so under the present organization of work explain why the central experience of the factory also becomes a mechanical one. In the absence of any consciousness of the values connected with the organized work process as a whole, the organization of work becomes an overpowering machine, a tremendous wheel in which the workers are only a relatively small cog.

MECHANICAL EXPERIENCE OF WORK

The following conversation illustrates the situation well:

What does it mean to you to be a producer?
Something you can give to help . . . but in my case, it is just labor.
What makes you feel that way?
You contribute in an awful small way, but if you get a whole bunch of little cogs, you can probably make a pretty good sized wheel.

What an astonishing mixture of feeling and thought which cannot meet, but move on different planes! A feeling of work being "just labor," of being "a little cog in the wheel," but an awareness (in which feeling and thought merge) that being a producer includes a creative orientation towards life—"give to help." And a thought that "a whole bunch of little cogs *probably* [sic!] make a pretty good sized wheel." The worker did not emphasize the word "probably," but his tone of voice was pervaded by an air of skepticism which found its verbal expression in the word "probably." This skepticism results from a lack of feeling of accomplishment, and from the absence of relatedness to a larger unit—a situation which relegates "giving to help" to a thought-out possibility rather than to an experienced feeling.

Many other conversations indicate how the lack of consciousness of a role in the social process of production makes "being a cog of a big wheel" such a crucial experience. To quote:

Do you have the feeling of being a producer?
If I make a fair living, yes.
Do you have the feeling of contributing to something?
I have the feeling of being a cog of a big wheel.

Asked "What makes you feel that your job and how you did it is important?" another worker answered, "Well, it's just a cog in a wheel; in other words, if you are not on the job, and the hog gets dirty, you are just beating yourself out of money." This response illustrates how the lack of identifications with any of the goals and values of the organizad work process—and not only the inability to bestow workmanship on the product—gives to money such a great significance. It also shows how little money really contributes to relate workers to the social process of production.

The frequency with which workers use idioms like "to be a cog in a wheel" or "to be a small wheel" in their conversations shows that they *experience* the factory as a mechanical unit and therefore conceive their role in mechanical terms devoid of emotion and unaffected by the ultimate goals served by the machine. The mechanical image even intruded into workers' feelings of partnership with the company. Asked "Does being an employee of the company make you feel you are a partner in doing an important job?" a worker who is farming part-time said, "You are cogs in the machine and you are feeding people, that's important." Before mentioning "feeding people," he said, "You are cogs in the machine," a situation of which he is more conscious than the average worker because he experiences almost daily an organization of work entirely different from the factory. But other workers gave similar responses to our question about partnership.

The mechanical experience of the social process of production is undoubtedly influenced by the low skill level and the divided work process, as the following conversation shows:

What does it mean to you to be a producer?
It depends.
[In order to find out upon what it depends, I talked to this worker about the work he does in the factory and the work he does on the farm. In the course of this conversation he said]:
You feel more as a producer on the farm.
Why?
Because you can see what work you have done, how much you have produced.

But it does not follow that workers could not perceive with their minds what they cannot see with their eyes: goals and values which give meaning to the organized work process. The following comment of a worker in connection with our question about partnership feelings with the company shows, indeed, that consciousness of workers' role in the social process of production allows them "to see what work [they] have done": "I think what makes me feel like a partner are the contacts I had, the student course I took. I could see how much a share the worker has; I could see what contribution workers could make." There could be no better illustration of the importance of a consciousness of sharing in the organized work process.

## PRODUCTION FOR WHAT?

Since the present role of workers in the social process of production does not relate them meaningfully to this process, they do not produce for *somebody* whom they know or to whom they are personally related; neither do they produce *something* which they can follow in their mind through the various stages of the process of production. They do not even produce for some *purpose*, some goal which is, in any way, related to the work process.

The company has been aware of this situation, as shown in its attempts to create a service orientation by building up a consciousness of a "meat-team" consisting of the farmer, the processor, and the retailer of meat. The community feelings and identifications thus created are better than nothing, but they fall far short of giving real meaning to work.

The union does not seem to deal with the problem at all. Its separation from the organized work process explains its aloofness partly. As a result relatedness to the union has been mentioned even less frequently than relatedness to the company as a factor giving meaning to work. Asked: "Does being a member of the union make you feel you are a partner in doing something important?" only one worker revealed union identifications giving meaning to work. He said, "Well, it makes you feel more free and feel more like working, because you have something to work for." This response shows clearly the great untapped potentialities of giving meaning to work while strengthening the union's role as an organization satisfying deeper human needs.

Until both the union and the company have fully developed

the potentialities of meaningful relatedness to the organized work process, workers will be alienated from their work, cut off from a larger community of people and ideas. Their alienation from the product of their work is highlighted by the fact that the *only* worker who mentioned the product as a source of satisfaction mentioned Spam—a product which is produced in an entirely different department from the one he is in. It is, furthermore, a highly advertised product which became famous —or infamous—among the G.I.'s during the war. However, the sincerity with which he expressed his feelings illustrates the significance of the more remote areas of the organized work process as potential sources of meaningful identification.

Until these potentialities are realized, the development of any ethics of work will be thwarted and the "moral impulse to work," the need to give meaning to the work activity, will lead a subliminal existence, vaguely projected but without possibilities of concrete expression.

# CHAPTER 8

# *"A Christian Gentleman"*

As we followed workers on their daily journey through the plant to their weekends and vacations, we tried to recognize average-typical attitudes and the forces shaping these attitudes. Now we shall mingle again with the workers but this time we are not interested in what work attitudes various groups of workers have in common, or what we find most frequently. We try to get acquainted with workers who are typical in the sense of having a "heightened" consciousness—or unconsciousness— of certain aspects of the organized work process. As we listen to what some "outstanding" representatives of different points of view have to say about their work, their union, and their company, we will get a better understanding of the variety of existing attitudes, and of the forces shaping them.

First we meet an older worker who grew up in a rural community among ten sisters and brothers. His parents were farmers. He went to a rural and then to an agricultural school. For over fifteen years he was an independent farmer. He had to give up his farm in the late twenties because of the drought and the depression. Before coming to the Hormel company he had traded in mechanical equipment for a year. He is married, has four grown-up children.

## The Game of Work

He has been on his present job during most of the time he spent in the plant. His work involves a variety of operations, as indicated in his answer to the question: "Is one work day just

123

like another, or is every day different?" He said, "Our work days are different. Two days a week we take meat to the cooler . . . on other days we cut the meat. . . ." Asked: "When you think about your place of work, what comes to your mind?" he answered, "It is cold and wet, and there is artificial light. You work under electric light, in winter you don't see the sun at all." The work is physically tiring, "not so much" because of the monotony of the job, but because "you have to wear a lot of clothes, rubber overshoes, etc." While at work, he talks "most all the time, about practically everything. We talk about baseball games, after ball games, we talk about fishing, hunting, of the war experience of the army fellows."

But in spite of these conversations and in spite of the differences in the work done, he feels bored on the job: "It is just natural, I guess everybody does sometimes." We are, therefore, not surprised to hear that the time does not pass too fast: "Kind of slow. If you don't see the sun, there is only one thing that helps to make the time go fast—you want to get out so much production. You are always working against time. One of the big advantages of the straight time-incentive pay is that it takes lots of drudgery out of the job, and gives you so much interest instead of being just a hired hand. You are in business for yourself."

The game of work—"to get out so much production"—is played so well that he gets the feeling of "always working against time"! The wage-incentive system, based on the guaranteed wage, is given a central place in making the game possible. Indeed, it is credited with giving a sense of independence and thus bestowing more meaning on work. You are "in business for yourself" because you make your own decision about the amount of production—above the contract basis—which you will turn out that day. "If you feel good, you make yourself and the gang a little extra money. If a fellow does not feel too good, the gang carries him. If it's not chronic, it's O.K."

THE COMPANY AND THE DESIRE FOR INDEPENDENCE

The same theme of independence and ability to control one's own work recur again and again as the crucial factors determining his attitude towards the company and the union. Asked: "Now we want to discuss what comes to your mind when you use the word 'Hormel company'?" he said, "We think we are about the best off of any worker in the packing industry. We have the straight-time, the incentive pay, and a pretty shrewd employer who makes every use of advertising and public relations to build up on his treatment of workers and union. . . ." The significance attributed to the guaranteed wage comes out even more clearly as he lists the advantages derived from working for the Hormel company: "The annual wage and incentive pay . . . that is important. That also makes you feel that you are working for yourself rather than for somebody else's whim . . . vacations are important too . . . you can do something if you have a month. . . ."

The emphasis on guaranteed wages and the wage-incentive system rather than on profit-sharing and the trust fund is striking. It is partly due to the fact that the guaranteed wage, though management-initiated, has been drawn into the sphere of workers' participation. He himself had, furthermore, a personal interest in the guaranteed wage. In his discussion of "straight time," he underlines the differences between the system in existence before unionization and the present plan:

Yes, straight time and incentive pay did not come overnight. Straight time was first proposed considerably different. It was his [Mr. Hormel's] idea to transfer you any place. It is his story that they did not understand straight time . . . the first work schedules were yearly schedules. Now, we get the gain each week . . . there is a tendency to increase production because they [the workers] felt more secure, that they would get paid for extra effort.

I believe that the line he draws between the old and new scheme is somewhat too dogmatic: a natural result of his emotional orientation towards the union and the union-influenced aspects of the work process rather than towards management.

This interpretation is substantiated by his answer to the question: "Does being an employee make you feel you are a partner in doing an important job?" He thought for a while and then replied, "Well . . . yes, it does. We have a union shop, and then you feel that you have something to say about the conditions you work under. . . ." The union shop gives a sense of partnership—with the company!—because it gives a feeling of independence and relegates the foreman to a secondary place. "We have a contract. If we work more, it is to our benefit. You get not only a percentage of extra work, you get the full benefit. We do not depend upon the foreman for anything except to keep the work records and get us supplies." Far from depending upon the foreman, workers "may keep nudging him to do his work more than he does." Any attempt to run the gang would only have deplorable effect. When the company put a foreman in charge to "run the gang . . . the gang took the attitude: if this fellow comes in and is going to run the gang, he is going to run it. So they have done just what they were told and *nothing more*." As a result "things got so balled up" that they had to get another foreman.

The guaranteed-wage–wage-incentive system has—as we will see later on—a great share in making workers exercise their own work discipline and work as hard as they can—or want. No wonder this worker comments: "Oh Lord, all the silly things," when he reads that as a result of the guaranteed wage "workers lose interest in their jobs and would not produce." The significance of workers' ability to set their own pace of work is clearly demonstrated by his answer to the question: "Do you have enough freedom to do your job your own way to satisfy you?" He said, "Yes, I think so; some days we do not see the foreman. Sometimes we go home, he don't know."

However, the role of the foreman is, at best, neutral. This worker gets mad because of "the way they walk through the department . . . the way they stand around, look wise . . . and I know they don't know a damned thing about what we are doing." Speaking about an incident when "the gang took too much time on the clean-up," he added: "I thought the boss was coming down and look around as if we could not do the job. I thought it was none of his darn business. He could go home for all we cared." Since no feelings are lost between this worker and his foreman, we are not surprised to hear that "never, thank God," do they praise him. "I would not consider their praise was worth very much, I would doubt the sincerity of it." If he gets blamed "he won't pay much attention to it" since praise or blame are "not a bit" important to him. All that may happen is that he gets "sometimes peeved" about poor material and "irked" when he wonders "why they could not have provided for it."

## THE UNION AND THE NEED TO BE FREE

The sense of freedom derived from the absence of authoritarian control does not, unfortunately, mean freedom for expressing one's abilities. "I always like to keep records and things like that. There is no chance there." His real sense of freedom is derived from the union because "you feel you have something to say about the conditions you work under. J. C. [Jay C. Hormel] asked me what difference does it make belonging to a union? What have you got there? I answered: The morning when I put on the union button, I felt like a man when I walked through the gate; before I felt like a dog. I could be transferred or fired. The boss could fire you if he did not like the way you parted your hair, or if he didn't like that you have no hair."

Interestingly enough—and not too astonishing in view of his background—he had first been skeptical about the union: "The way I joined the union down here in Sutton Park is a story. We lived up the street here. In those days I made eight to ten to twelve dollars a week. When we were through work, I went out in the country to cut wood and haul it in. I had a little orchard. My wife worked in a store. She said they would go down and take part in the organization of the union. I did not pay much attention but she mentioned it again, and she said I better go. I wasn't interested. Her dad was a railroad man and knew something about unions. She said I owe it to her and the kids to go. I went. I took no money with me, because I heard about organizers, the way they grabbed money. I came back to the house to get a buck and became a charter member of the union. . . ."

He, who did not dare to take a dollar along for fear the union organizers would grab it, acquired one of the strongest union identifications when the union began to modify the organization of work. Asked: "What comes to your mind when you say: 'I am a member of the UPWA,'" he said: "Well, the first thing that you belong to an organization that is industry-wide . . . we are the most representative workers in the industry and have a responsibility to broaden that organization." He "certainly" feels that he is a partner. He is quite emphatic in saying this and in pointing out that the main advantages of belonging to the union are that "it makes you feel that you are a *human being*; from that all the rest of them come. . . ."

To this worker, the union is not merely an instrumentality to further his own ends. He recognizes a responsibility to bring to others the benefits of unionism and he is even willing to give up individual advantages for the sake of the group—as the following conversation shows:

Are there any disadvantages of belonging to the union?

Yes, I suppose there are. There are times when you have to give up some individual advantage that you might gain for the general good. In the long run, I don't know whether this is a disadvantage. I could never figure it out.

What do you mean by giving up individual advantages?

You could maneuver yourself in a softer job if you have no respect for seniority.

There is a true feeling of solidarity and an experience of the labor movement as a common cause which gives meaning and direction to life. Though he realizes the intricacies of the Taft-Hartley Act, he takes nevertheless a clear-cut position in response to the question: "What do you think about the Taft-Hartley Act?": "Well, the Taft-Hartley Act is so long and complicated, it is hard for the ordinary labor man to comment on it. Senator Ball says labor is criticizing the Taft-Hartley Act and don't understand it. That goes for Senator Ball, too. He don't understand it. In 1946 Ball said: I am going to do something to take power away from labor unions. Now he says that no legitimate power is taken away. But there are so many petty annoyances . . . it is the same about the closed shop. I could say much more if I knew better. Ball said it did not hurt any individual labor man, although it may have clipped the wings of labor organization. You can't do that without hurting individual labor men. More than that, you hurt the non-union men, even the scabs, individually and collectively, because it gives a man a liberty that is not worth preserving."

Such an attitude does not only express a strong labor ideology and group feeling. Even more important than that: it reaches into the realm of human values by giving to the union an ethical content and by elevating the relationships between workers beyond the swamps of rugged individualism.

### SATISFACTIONS DERIVED FROM WORK

A worker who finds such a deep meaning in the union is naturally cut off from strong management identifications. He had considerable contact with top management and took an active part in recent negotiations. Though he esteems Mr. Jay C. Hormel as a "shrewd employer," he cannot suppress a certain skepticism: "J. C. . . . would substitute a company union in a minute if he could get away without unfavorable publicity and efficiency . . . he is the kind of man who would run not only the plant but the union and the employees too."

The lack of relatedness which is part of such a skepticism is clearly expressed in his negative response to the inquiry: "On the whole, do you enjoy working here?" He stated emphatically: "I don't enjoy working here. The thing I like best is the noon hour. I can lie down and take a nap." It is noteworthy that the work process itself came to his mind rather than management's role in its organization. This shows a dislike of the work stronger than his feelings about the company, an inference which is clearly borne out by his response to the question: "Are there any disadvantages of working for this company? Anything other companies do for their employees?" Again he thought for awhile and said:

There is a disadvantage about the annual wage. At times there are long hours to make up for short hours. The type of work in a packinghouse is always a disadvantage. I wonder sometimes why anybody works in a packing house.

Why do you think people work there?

Because there is employment close to your home. I doubt whether anybody likes it. . . . It is bad . . . this is one reason why the packinghouse workers as a class are hard "livers" and why they do a lot of drinking in their free time. They also do fishing and hunting. Before, when I lived on the farm, I wondered about hunting. Now I do it. A man would go crazy if he did not do something like that. He would get so nervous and upset. . . .

There is, indeed, not too much about the work that gives real satisfaction—though he answered our question: "How do you feel after the work has been done? Satisfied?" by saying that he feels satisfied "most of the time." Actually, "the pay check" makes the work important. "It is not a very . . . it is a hard, dirty job, nothing that anyone would do except that there is a pay check connected with it. When I went to work in the packinghouse, I went to work in the . . . because they worked longer hours. When the banks closed up, I didn't have a dime."

Since the pay check is the important thing, it is good that this worker is "pretty well satisfied with the amount of pay" he is getting. "I would say *pretty* well satisfied. A packinghouse is the poorest paid major industry. The packers are probably in a better financial position than any one industry. That is perhaps *the* reason why I am dissatisfied. Wages are low when packers are in a position to pay." To take industry's ability to pay as a standard of comparison is quite unusual and points to an enhanced consciousness of the organized work process. The dissatisfaction such a comparison creates still leaves him "pretty well" satisfied on the whole—as far as the pay is concerned. But there is nothing of yourself you could give in doing the work and hence, there is no feeling of accomplishment; "lots of people could do his job."

## MEANINGLESS WORK—AND A CREATIVE LIFE

Fortunately, there is something to compensate for the absence of meaning in work:

What do you look forward to after work?
Well, I guess that's important. That's why you want to get your work done and get out of there. I have a lot, a garden. I go out there . . . sometimes I even go when it is hot . . . people wonder about it . . . but some people, when they get through work play golf. I work in the garden. I am still a farmer at heart. Back in the good old days we rented land and raised fruit . . . my wife picks them and sells them. I just raise them. Selling is not the important thing. I would raise them if the birds ate them. . . .

When did you have your orchard?

From 1935 to 1938.

What did you mean by "good old days"?

It was sarcasm, I meant the time before the union.

The strength of his feelings about raising things comes out in a story told in another context. "I saw Mr. X the other day. He showed me his rose garden which was well tended by his gardener. He took pride in it . . . I told him: 'I don't have a big garden, but I have a little rosebush in front of my house. I planted it, and it blooms every year. I get more enjoyment out of this little rosebush of which I take care myself, than you do of your whole garden, for which you hire a gardener. . . .'"

These conversations show how strong the creative urge of this worker is. He would enjoy raising things, even if the birds ate them, an attitude reflected in his answer to the question: "What does it mean to you to be a producer?" He said: "A creator of wealth." But he cannot "create wealth" while working in the plant. No wonder that he doesn't want to think about his work "when out of there." Asked: "Do you ever do anything off the job which helps you in your work in any way?" he answered: "No, I don't know what I would do that helps me." Human contacts during the work are the only bond between the work and life. Work becomes a personally useful experience because "a better understanding of people" is of benefit off the job. But this positive element is not strong enough to compensate for the time spent on the job, which contributes to make you "feel lonely"— "because you dream about something you can't do." It makes you feel lonely, since you know deep down in yourself that the dream will not come true. So you must accept the fact that you will work "at least until sixty-five, until you can cash in some social security."

We can now understand why this worker thinks "Damn it!" when he first thinks about work—and why weekends and vacation are experienced as a relief from not having to work:

How does your weekend differ from the days you work?

Well, usually we go out on Saturday nights, or have friends in or play bridge or go to movies.

What do you most like about weekends?

That you don't have to go to work. . . .

What did you do on your last vacation?

This year I have not taken a vacation. I have taken a couple of days usually to do some personal business.

What do you like best about vacations?

The freedom from going to work.

[His general feelings about his work are well expressed in the following conversation]:

How do you feel about your working life as against your life off the job?

I don't feel like working at all. [He laughs and continues]: I might as well be honest. Other people won't admit it, but the only difference is that I admit I am lazy.

But you like farming.

Yes, it is a better life, although my wife might not agree. . . .

If you had enough money to do what you wanted to do, what would you do?

Then I would work. I would have a farm, breed livestock, and monkey around.

A man who gets lazy when he thinks about his work, would start working if he had enough money to buy a farm! The fact that work, then, is conceived of as a free activity is shown in the addition "and monkey around." There is not too much time to monkey around if you raise livestock, but you don't *have to* do it, and you can take it in a rhythm of your own. You don't punch time clocks, and you can take a little bit of time off when you want to. Hence, you monkey around! You are a "play-worker," as another worker put it.

This worker's need for a self-expression is so poignant and finds such a variety of outlets in his life off the job, that the latter and not the job itself becomes the decisive factor determining his life. The tendencies evoked by the organization of the work process are, therefore, of secondary importance to him and do not set the tone for his life. Consequently, they are limited to the time spent on the job. This limitation is made easier by the conscious recognition of their existence (work: "Damn it!"), by the acceptance of work as a necessity "to feed a family," and last but not least, by an acceptance of manual labor as something that should command respect—no matter what the prevailing preference for "white collar" jobs and no matter what the reputation of the packinghouse.

## FOR A MORE DEMOCRATIC ORGANIZATION OF WORK

In none of the responses quoted so far could we find any traces of relatedness to the organization of the work process. The explanation of this absence of identification is not difficult to find: The goals in view of which work is organized now are rejected as incompatible with a "satisfied working class." Instead of being dependent upon management, workers must "share in ownership, management, and profits." The following conversations reveal how fundamentally he disagrees with the present organization of industry:

What groups do you feel have political interests against you?

Should I say economic royalists? The people that own the means of production and want to keep control of the means of production. Which groups have most power now?

The man with the biggest pocketbook because he is the man that controls the means of production. When my dad was a kid, you could hardly stop a man from making his living. A butcher started with a couple of knives. The blacksmith just needed tools. Usually he could go to the local banker if he was a good citizen and could borrow the money. Now to produce an automobile, you use a hydraulic process. The man who owns the machines can say, Mister you can't use those tools. Mister, you can't make a living for yourself and your family. If Henry Ford says tomorrow: "I don't want to produce more automobiles," the guys can't do it on their own. For no reason he can say it. That is why labor should share in ownership, management, and profits. . . .

In a conversation on religion, he said:

You should always remember: "Thou shalt love thy neighbor as thyself." God created the earth. He put man there. Everyone is entitled to enough of the fruit of this earth if he works . . . he should have a reasonable standard of life. Social justice is simply giving the people the opportunity to make use of the products of the earth. . . . The ownership of wealth is not wrong but the misuse of that ownership is wrong. Society does not owe anybody a living but the opportunity to make a living . . .

He feels so strongly about these objectives that he would be willing to join a labor party and "spend his time helping to win out"—provided such a party would espouse his ideas on labor-management relationships. Pending such an opportunity, he is trying to make the work process more democratic than it is at present. He welcomed the idea of the Business Improvement Committee because he saw in it a possible way of overcoming the present shortcomings in workers' "know-how" and "say-so" about management problems. His ideas on this score are well expressed in the following conversation:

How are you informed about management problems?
We are not informed.
What about the *Squeal*?
I have no confidence in the information in the *Squeal*. It is propaganda. . . .
Do you feel you should know more about management's problems?
Yes, I think the workers could help them a lot. They are so damn jealous of that end of it. There is a small chance that labor will get to know more about their problems.
Do you feel you should have more say-so about it?
Absolutely!
Why?
Because you never have a satisfied working class in this country until labor shares in profit, management, and ownership. Notice I said *share* in it.

His initial hope that the Business Improvement Committee will make it possible eventually to achieve these objectives has been dashed by his fears that it is being used to weaken the union and to build a rival company organization: "It seems to go haywire . . . they get it mixed up with the union . . . take up things that should be settled through the union. . . ."

His emphasis on sharing has a double meaning: he wants to bring out that labor as an organized group should share in the formulation of policies. But he does not want to give the impression that he wants to "take over." Strongly rooted in the world of labor and deeply influenced by the social philosophy of the Roman Catholic Church, he wants an organization of the work process which is based on real partnership between labor and management—a partnership which is founded on a cooperative, genuinely democratic organization of industry. The strike is only "a last resort" in this struggle to achieve these objectives, "although I would strike and strike hard if the necessity arose."

These attitudes express a fundamental disagreement with the values underlying the present organization of industry. They imply a rejection of the ideology of "getting ahead" and of "rugged individualism" which means that "the biggest and the strongest and the most inconsiderate and ruthless get the biggest pork chops, and the guy who has the least respect for the right of his fellow-man as a man." A feeling for human values growing out of a deep religious experience leads to an ethics of interpersonal relationships which makes "the liberty to do injustice to your fellow worker" a freedom not worth while preserving. Ultimately, he rejects the present-day organization of industry because "there is not a bit of Christianity in it." "Our present economic system is not compatible with religion, it is not compatible with Christianity." Since "you can't be a Christian on Sunday and forget about it if you go into the factory on Monday," you must work to bring about social justice. In doing so, "you prepare yourself for death—for eternal life."

Such a depth of commitment leads to strong participation in union and community affairs. "He doesn't go for pleasure" to union meetings, but he goes out of a sense of responsibility and because he is involved with the labor movement. "If the wage guarantee would be abolished *and* the union would be destroyed" he would quit Hormel: "I would get a hold of a piece of ground and get enough to live on." Even in the normal course of events he hopes some day to live on "a little place across the road from a country church so that I can go to Mass every morning." Then he could have an existence denied to him by the present-day organization of the work process: he could be "a good honest-to-God Christian gentleman."

# CHAPTER 9

# *Victim of a Foe Unseen*

THE EXPERIENCE OF WORK

The worker with whom we are getting acquainted now also spent his youth on the farm. He had three sisters and brothers. He went to rural school and then to high school in a nearby town. Without finishing high school he went into farming during the early twenties. He "liked it good and got along dandy until the drought and the low prices." He lost everything and then had, for sixteen years, a variety of temporary insecure jobs in construction, carpentry, canning. "During summer there was plenty of work, during winter nothing." During the depression he was unemployed for one year, then had a WPA job followed by various other ones. Asked whether he still remembers those days when people were—as he said—"five cents a dozen," he answered: "You ain't kidding."

He came to the company in the early forties. With the exception of the first six months, he has been processing specialty meat ever since. His work days "vary" because of "different kind of work." He does not feel bored on the job. The time goes "fast if you are busy; if there is not much to do, the time drags." He never wishes while he is at work that something would happen, nor does he ever get impatient or angry on the job: "I always try to keep my head level. If boss asks you, say nothing, go ahead and do it." Probed by the question: "And if you don't like it?" he responded: "Do it anyway. I came over there, asked for a job . . . if other fellows can do it, I can do it. . . ."

Though he indicates that "he likes to work around meat," his answers lead to a presumption that he accepts rather passively his working environment. He came and *asked for* a job! Since it feels good to "get" a job in a world in which jobs are scarce, how much better does it feel to have found, after much struggling, shifting, and unemployment, a really good and secure job! The gratitude is transformed into submissiveness. Before us does not stand a man who feels that a *free* man in a free society has the *right* for a job opportunity; before us stands a man broken by the misfortunes of his life—"you ain't kidding." As a result he clings to the job and becomes completely identified with it, as is well illustrated in his answer to the question: "What do you first think of when you think of work?" He said: "Do the job and do it well."

He is so absorbed in doing his job well that he becomes oblivious of the real nature of his work—as the following conversation shows:

Does your job make you physically tired?
Well, sometimes . . . I was most tired when I first worked in the. . . .
What about the job makes you tired? Is it monotonous?
Well, if you stay up too late at night, go to work again. Never been monotonous to me.

It is certainly true that you feel tired on the job if you stay up late at night. But to give this as the only reason for fatigue after work is more indicative of a desire to "whitewash" the job, than of the actual fatigue connected with the job. I worked with this worker for several days, and his was by no means an easy job. It involved a great deal of walking around, lifting, bending, etc. Indeed, it was so fatiguing that he had to go to the locker room several times during the day in order to be able to stand the strain. Yet, while the fatigue penetrated his muscles, he built up a strong enough defense mechanism to prevent it from penetrating his consciousness.

This worker had no hesitation in talking to me. Indeed, we became good friends. His answers are not due to an attempt to impress me in any way. They are rather a result of the necessity to see his job in the best possible light in order to be able to be fully grateful for the job. There is a proverb saying "Never look a gift-horse in the mouth" because otherwise one might have rather mixed feelings—and maybe conflicts—about the gift! And a job out of unemployment and unsteady work is indeed a precious gift!

The pattern of acquiescence and gratitude is followed consistently in the answer to the question: "Do you have enough freedom to do your job your own way to satisfy you?" His answer is: "Yes, sir, plenty." But when it comes to the question: "What abilities do you have that you want to use but can't use on this job?" the objective reality becomes overwhelming, and the pattern of gratitude is broken, without in the least being shattered. It is broken, since the response to the question is a clear: "No, I have not." But it is not shattered, because the blame is put on himself: "If I had to do it over again, I would take a knife job in the hog-cut." As we listen to the reasons given for wanting the hypothetical change, the reality of the job becomes clearer. If you have a knife job on the hog-cut, "the temperature is even, there is not the heavy work, there is no lifting (cf. the feeling of fatigue!). You get to be a good knife man, for example a hand-boner, you draw the money. It is skilled work."

We may note the explicit admission that the work is heavy, and the implicit admission that there is not too much satisfaction in an unskilled job—except for the money it draws. What is most striking, however, is the strange—and psychologically significant—mixture of freedom of choice and force of circumstances. Looking back now, he feels there *might* have been a choice while in actuality there was no real choice for a new employee to *take* a knife job, a privilege granted only to those who have quite a bit of seniority. A bid for the knife job is available *now* when he has accumulated seniority. But now he cannot face the situation realistically—because this would imply a conscious admission that his job is not as rosy as he makes himself believe. Hence, his answer to the question: "How do you feel about your working life as against your life off the job?": "I like it just the way it is." This, in spite of the fact that if he could do it all over again, he would want an entirely different job, and that his real longings and aspirations are completely unfulfilled—and so repressed that they are not intruding into the consciousness, unless a (hypothetical) situation arises in which the defense mechanism supporting the submissive acceptance of the existing conditions ceases to function momentarily.

## THE MEANING OF THE UNION AND THE COMPANY

These underlying attitudes are expressed in his company identifications. Asked: "What comes to your mind when you use the words 'Hormel company'?" he said, "Like my job, satisfied with it, glad I got it. Not young any more would be difficult to get other job." Further questioned: "Does being an employee make you feel you are a partner in doing an important job?" he responded, "Well, it does, *kind of*. . . ." "What about the company makes you feel that way?" "They are paying you wages, that is your bread and butter," he answered. Partnership based on such feelings takes on a peculiar meaning: it is not relatedness on the same level, but dependence. To this worker the company becomes in the true sense of the word "the provider": it provides him with bread and butter.

To make sure that nobody can take the bread and butter away, he looks toward the union. The main advantages of belonging to the union are: "Protects your job, company can't fire you unless awful, awful good excuse. Eight holidays with pay." The protective features are indeed uppermost in his mind when he thinks of himself as a member of the UPWA: "You got the protection of your job and your rate and your hours. Union also fought for extra hours on holiday, eight holidays. If working conditions are not satisfactory, you can run to the union." His expression "you can run to the union" betrays somewhat his statement about his feelings of partnership: "It makes you feel you got some responsibility, you are one of the gang . . . you will stick together. If you was not a union member—no dice." There is a genuine feeling of group-belongingness, but it expresses more a need than an active orientation. Observation during work has shown that his expectation of being treated as a member of a group is greater than his own orientation towards his gang. He caters to the foreman, not to his fellow workers. He "likes his foreman" and bends his head to his orders. However, looked at through the prism of values of the foreman, the break straightens out into the attitude of the "ideal" worker who "really appreciates his job"!

Indeed, after the day's work has been done, he feels "well satisfied. I feel that my day's work is done—well done. I added another day to my paycheck . . . lots of fellows come in in the morning and ask: 'When do we get out of here today?' I don't feel that way. He pays us for every hour." The only reservation in regard to the satisfaction derived from the pay is: "Of course, if prices keep going up, we can't make ends meet." In another context, he added to this: "The merchants up town raised prices before you got the raise . . . that's a hell of an attitude toward the working man." But the satisfaction derived from "having a job well done" is less spontaneous; it is experienced more as a duty in order to keep the job and earn the wages. Asked: "What makes you feel that your job and how you do it is important?" he said, "Wages—sure. Next thing to do something for the company, to make them wages. If there is a light burning, I put it out. A fellow says, 'Why in hell are you doing that, you are not paying the light bill.' I say, 'If you save, you get more profit-sharing.' Didn't he know? Yes, he will holler most when check not big. I save every ounce of meat."

At best, work can give a vague feeling of doing something good. Asked: "What does it mean to you to be a producer?" he said, "It means to me that I am producing something for the world—for the people who have to eat." More concrete do his satisfactions become only as we return to profit-sharing which he lists among the main advantages derived from being an employee of the company. He first mentioned (1) sick leave, then (2) profit sharing, and finally (3) paid vacation. Probed, he stated that these advantages are "more important than straight time." We may surmise that the listing of sick leave as the first item betrays some anxiety. His comment on profit sharing, that he considers it "a little Christmas money," is indicative of a passive-grateful feeling rather than of a real consciousness of having earned it, as his earlier statement about profit-sharing may have induced us to believe. The importance attached to vacations—"a very nice thing"—shows a basic orientation away from work. It is in line with his double emphasis on "eight holidays with pay" as one of the main advantages derived from being a member of the union! His feelings that there are "no disadvantages" connected with being an employee of the company and that "on the whole" he enjoys working there must be interpreted in the light of his strong identification with work and his job—an identification which does not allow him to let the negative aspects of the work come to his consciousness.

Though "it would be nice" to know more about management, he is essentially satisfied with the present organization of the work process. He even identifies with certain aspects of the market: "competition" makes his job important to the country, "salesmen have to sell the product." This is an unusual—and quite abstract—relatedness which does not have any counterpart in a strong desire for active participation in the work process. Asked whether he feels that he should have more say-so, he answered: "In some cases yes . . . lots of times . . . too many people in the day-room—could spare a man—lots of times the foreman can't see everything either, they have their hands full . . . meeting with big boys in office." He visualizes a "say-so" pretty much in terms of a consultation and suggestions in regard to problems which come up in connection with his work.

While his identification with the world of management remains abstract, he is not really rooted in the world of labor. But his experience of the depression filled him with so much anxiety that he identifies strongly with labor as an interest group—as his attitudes towards the Taft-Hartley Act and a labor party show:

What do you think about the Taft-Hartley Act?
I don't think a thing of it. I don't like it.
Why don't you like it?
Because they are labor-haters—both of them.

He emphasized "I don't like it" in a way which left no doubt about the strength of his feelings. He does not have more knowledge of the law than other workers do, but he knows what it means to be pushed around, not to find a job, and not to have the protection of the union.

Questioned about the desirability of a labor party, he responded:

Yes, yes, sir; if they stick together; if they do, they get it; they got it in a nutshell . . . and get out and vote . . . the trouble is most forget to vote—they should vote.
What do you think the aims of such a party should be?
Good working conditions, good standard of living, living wage.

His strong feelings for labor—without evidence of a real labor ideology—are also expressed in the following conversation:

With what groups do you feel you have common political interests?
Labor and farmers.
What are these interests?
Farmers produce everything, if it wasn't for city men, farmers would starve, one buys from the other.
What groups have political interests against you?
Business district would be opposed to you because of the union, business get their people into office.

Fear as a strong undercurrent of his general motivation comes again to the surface in his attitude towards the 1948 strike:

How do you feel about the recent strike?
I was not for it. I don't like strikes. I hate 'em.
How did you feel about the 10 per cent deduction?
It was fair, a good deal, a drop in the bucket for other, justified, give a little for poor devils who did not have anything.

These responses give evidence of a mixture of compassion and of relief that there was no strike. The relief was expressed very emotionally—since the conflict, dissension, and fighting which accompany a strike aroused a great deal of anxiety in him.

WORK INTERFERING WITH LIFE

Gratitude for having a job, satisfaction with the existing industrial organization, and espousal of labor as an interest group are, unfortunately, not enough to give to life any meaning. They do not contribute to a more democratic way of life since work attitudes affect the whole life—unconsciously but not less effectively.

It is true that life for this worker, as for practically all the workers, is almost completely separated from work. His answer to the question: "Do you ever do anything off the job which helps you in your work in any way?" is: "I don't." And asked: "Do you find that your experience in working is useful to you personally, I mean can you use this experience to your benefit off the job?" he said, "Yes—suppose that I want to make sausage." Quite typically, he prefers to mention an unreal and hypothetical benefit rather than facing the reality of the situation. Even if he did "make sausage" such a home activity would certainly not establish any central relationship between the work and the life off the job. How peripheral this relatedness is, can be seen from the fact that he does not usually talk to his friends about the work: "Well, not very much."

But the separation of work and life does not diminish the influence of work on his life. Indeed, this influence is particularly strong since he has so completely "internalized external necessities," and is so strongly identified with the work that the tendencies created by the work process have their full impact on his unconscious. As we follow him from the plant to his home, we shall notice quickly what forces direct his existence.

Right after work, he has "a couple of beers" to break the impact of the work. He is looking forward "to come home, work in the garden, putter around in my new home." One does not get much of a feeling of relaxation from listening to these things. The expression "*work* in the garden" rather than gardening is not insignificant; it shows how strongly work preoccupies this worker. And the "puttering around" expresses in this context an inner unrest which comes out in the open when he answers the question: "If you inherited some money and had enough to live on without working, would you want to work anyway?" as follows: "I would still work. I am one of those fellows. I can't sit still."

How strongly the identification with the work process affects his life becomes even clearer in his response to the question: "How does your weekend differ from the days you work?" He said, "There is not much difference; weekends I don't do nothing . . . sometime a little vacation . . . see my daughter . . . go fishing

or rest . . . enjoy watching things grow, grain threshed. . . ."
This is a long list of activities which are entirely and completely
different from the days of work! And yet the first reaction of the
worker was: "There is not much difference." The contradiction
is, however, only at the level of appearances. It is not a contradiction at the deeper level of feelings. It simply means that the
experience of the weekend is—to start with—not much different
from the experience of work because, psychologically speaking,
routinized and mechanical activity and "I don't do nothing" non-
activity are very close to each other. *"Les extrèmes se touchent"*
—because they are equidistant from a meaningful activity! Only
after the compulsive tendencies created by the work process
have lost some of their strength, only then can he enjoy what
he likes best about the weekend: to have "a rest, a little recreation."

Besides the human contact—seeing his daughter—fishing is
the only activity mentioned which resolves the vicious circle
created by the attempt "to get away from it all" and the compulsion to carry work attitudes into the whole life so to speak, into
the center of the circle. But since the circle still surrounds you in-
visibly but none the less inexorably, you do not want to move while
you are fishing at one of the lakes: you know instinctively that you
move right back in the tensions of the vicious circle. While
you are in the center, you are in the kind of mood which makes
you "enjoy watching things grow," but it must remain a fleeting
mood just as the clouds in the sky are, because tomorrow you are
back in a situation where you feel that you "can't sit still." Indeed,
you forget how well you could sit still yesterday while fishing. No,
you did not really forget, but it was a different world, a world
which is remote from you when you "do your job and do it well"
—and yet it is right in you.

His real desires come again into the open when asked: "Would
you want to do what you are now doing—if you inherited some
money and had enough to live on?" Certainly not: "I would like
a big garden or a small chicken ranch." This is a thought far
removed from everyday work. Even during vacation—which is
about as far as one can really get away from the work—the conflict created by the work persists. "What do you like best about

vacations?" "I don't really know how to answer it . . . it peps you up . . . you get lonesome for places, after that you feel like going back to gang and work." It may "pep you up," but it leads you right to where you came from: the "rubber band" had its effects. If you start out to be lonesome and hence, lonesome for some place, you naturally end up being just as lonesome because the lonesomeness is in you—and then it is good to come back to the gang and to the work which keeps you occupied. The ideal of vacation, however, would be different. The best kind of vacation would be "to go north fishing . . . I have not been able to take that yet. . . ."

A comparison of these attitudes with those of the first worker brings their meaning into sharper focus. The two workers have a similar background and similar experiences: both were farmers and both had to give up their farms because of the drought and the depression. And yet, they are on opposite poles in their experience of their work and their life. One is acquiescent and submissive, the other upright and self-reliant. One has a symbiotic identification with management and its foremen, the other keeps the distance he believes to be necessary to make him feel free. How different is the meaning which the union and work have in their life! For the first worker the protection which the "setup" and primarily the union gave were used as a shield to go into battle for basic human values; it freed energy for constructive purposes. For the second worker protection is used as a shield which alleviates fears and anxieties: it is a passive protection. The first worker is fully conscious of the nature of his work without allowing it to inundate his creative life outside the factory gates. The second worker identifies with the work process and is therefore unable to realize his creative potentialities. While tragedy lies in being defeated by an enemy against whom all forces are marshalled, there is even deeper tragedy to succumbing to a foe unseen.

# CHAPTER 10

# A Would-Be Salesman

A GOOD JOB OR "THE SAME OLD RUT"?

After having become acquainted with two workers whose reaction to factory life led them into diametrically opposite directions, we shall now meet a worker who does not touch their depth of inner triumph or defeat, but who brings into sharp focus the hopes, disappointments, and problems of the vast majority of the workers.

He is a young man, a real Austinite, born and raised in the community where he has lived all his life, with the exception of a few years in his early childhood. He attended high school, almost but not quite graduating from there. Three of his brothers work at the Hormel company where his mother and his father earned their livelihood, too. Only two brothers and two sisters are not connected with the company—a not uncommon pattern of family-company relationship. He is married and has two small children.

Not counting a few part-time jobs while he was at school and during the summer, he knows only one place of work: the Hormel company. He started to work there about ten years ago, spent two years in the army, and returned to the company at the end of the war. Most of the time, he has been in a department handling meat. His job is not exhausting, whether it makes him physically tired or not depending more upon his outside life than upon the work performance itself: "It differs according to the kind of rest you get at night. On hot days or when the baby cries or when I

146

dream I don't get enough rest." Only when he has to do the "same work on the job"—only then does he get tired because of the monotony of the work. "If I am so long on one machine, the job gets monotonous."

When he thinks about his place of work, "lots of women, some of them pretty," come to his mind. He also mentions the product he is working on; the material may make him angry: "Christ—a lot of times you remember that situation which slowed us down" is his answer to the question: "Do you ever get impatient or angry on the job?" But "usually" the human contacts and the game of work make "the time . . . pass fast." It goes fast "because you work steady and you talk. It used to go slow on payday for you were anxious to get out and spend the check which burnt a hole in your pocket, you wanted to drink and dance."

Yet the passing of the time is artificial as can be seen from his response to the question: "Do you ever wish while you are at work, I wish something would happen?" He said: "I wish somebody would drop a bomb so we could get out early." How little content the game of work has becomes manifest when he is asked: "Is one workday just like another to you or is every day different?" He replied, "One workday is always closer to payday." His wife, who happened to be in the room at that time interjected: "He is happier on Sunday. Workdays are different because they are closer to Sunday."

There is not only the emptiness of the work process which rested heavily on the young fellow who wanted to get out and enjoy his life. There are also the ambitions of the growing man who make him painfully aware of the work he is doing. Asked: "Do you ever get bored on the job?" he replied, "Yes and no, sometimes a guy gets to thinking . . . things that a guy should do, like selling. Other days you just take it in its stride without thinking." To achieve what many attitude studies call "satisfaction with the job," this worker has to "take it in its stride without thinking." When he starts reflecting, his real ambitions come to the light: to sell. He is, indeed, talking for the great majority of his fellow workers when he answers the question: "Outside of getting a better wage, do you ever use the words 'getting ahead'? If so, what do you mean by it?" He said: "Yes, I mean getting a business. My buddy and I thought about it, but when I got out of the service I got in the *same old rut again.* I didn't know quite what to do. I had thought of it, to be independent, often thought about being independent. Sometimes it gets on my nerves taking orders from somebody else." He thought of "liquor business" or "a clothing store" as possible business ventures. But most of all, he wants to sell. "Everybody who is selling" is among his friends.

Unfortunately, he did not have "the little luck, the little pull and the education" which he lists as the most important things in getting ahead. The "common sense," which he mentions as the fourth most important factor, did not help alone. He is sorry he did not use the opportunities offered by the G.I. Bill of Rights. "I wish I had gone on to college like him," is a remark he made about his brother at the very beginning of our first conversation. However, as he told me later, army life "just muddled them all up. It was worse for me; a bigger span of ideas as to what a person could do, but did not know what to do. . . ." His wife could not help him to get a clearer orientation. She has no illusions about the work in the plant. Having worked there herself she still remembers the dreams she had right after she began to work there: "Bacon was coming and coming and coming toward me—in an endless row, always, always the same bacon." If he really wants to become a salesman, she would not object. But she does prefer to have her husband around—on a good paying, steady, reliable job. And this is exactly what he has. He is glad about it, but he is not sure that this is the place where he should be.

## THE COMPANY: GOOD EARNING OPPORTUNITIES

The ambivalence of his feelings about the job emerges immediately after he is told: "Now we want to discuss what comes to your mind when you use the word 'Hormel company.'" The emotionally and ethically neutral "meat-packers" comes to his mind. Probed "Is it nice?" he continues: "In my estimation this is one of the best meat-packing plants." His appreciation is genuine but somewhat subdued by his negative feelings of working in a meat-packing plant. "Jesus Christ," being an employee "does . . . in a way" make you feel you are a partner in doing an important job. "If I do my job the way it should be done, if better than other companies, then we've accomplished something very good."

Since the Hormel company is undoubtedly better than other companies, he does, on the whole, enjoy working there. "We have our problems but all companies have." What makes the job really important is money: "Any job you do is important . . . to make a living." The "most important advantages and privileges he gets because he is an employee of this company" are, therefore, the annual wage and production. In another context he said, "The annual wage gives us one of the best setups in the meat-packing industry." He likes it and "it's all right as long as production is involved." Like many other workers he considers the guaranteed wage and the wage-incentive system as a unit: together they give the good earning opportunities the Hormel workers enjoy. After he had mentioned the annual wage and production, his wife brought up profit-sharing. He repeats it, then his wife mentions the trust fund. He agrees and adds: "vacation and sick leave." She reminds him of insurance and he has a final comment: "The annual wage, that brought everything to a head." It is significant that he, spontaneously, mentioned only those aspects of the organized work process which give him his earning opportunities—and those which lead him away from work.

His answer to the question: "Are you pretty well satisfied with the amount of pay you now get?" is in the affirmative: "Compared to pay in the country—but not compared to some other departments. Other departments make twice as much. Some departments make 100 per cent. All should be equalized. That is why I never did like production." Asked what would be better, he said, "An annual wage with bonus." His previous statements and many conversations show that he does not mean literally what he says when stating that he never liked production. He does not like the present inequality in earning opportunities between different departments. The percentages which he quotes refer to the amount of production—and hence earnings—above the contract base. Since he has been working for a long time in a department in which earning opportunities in comparison to other departments were not too good, he felt very strongly about it—until he had an opportunity to "post out" and work in another department with higher earning opportunities.

Now his ambitions—as far as his job is concerned—are "a higher rate or a cleaner job." That is all to hope for since the job itself is uninteresting and has to be done in a certain way. Asked: "Do you have enough freedom to do your job your own way to satisfy you?" he said, "Nobody has that freedom. Lots of times I want to do it my own way." When queried, "What abilities do you have that you want to use but can't use on this job?" he does not even think in terms of his factory job. His thoughts wander back to his hopes and doubts of getting away from the plant. He says: "Work outside. I can't state exactly what I would do. In the Service I have picked up ulcers." Since there is nothing even potentially interesting about the job, it is not astonishing that he feels "anybody who has any common sense can do the job."

His relationships to his foreman are, at best, neutral. "More or less," he thinks they want to help him to get along in his work because "the more we work the better rating they get with the company." But "lots of times" they do something that makes him mad: "The way they jump you, eat your ass out, the way they talk to you, they could talk reasonably, reason with you. . . ." Probed: "Did you talk with them about it?" he said, "I tried it once and I got into a big argument. Everybody in the department heard it. He got mad; then I did. He says he is still foreman and what he says has to go. He was irritated. We all know it but not that tone of voice." He shows independence and accepts the existing setup, though he does not have too much respect for the foremen—they do not know as well as he does "how the actual work" should be done. He resents the way "they throw the authority around without talking it over" and feels that they are quick in blaming and slow in praising: "They seldom praise you. But if you do not do good work, they let you know about it." Asked whether they should praise you a little more, he responded, "I well think they should. People would work better. Praise gets you a long ways always."

### THE UNION AND THE LABOR MOVEMENT

No matter how long a way praise may get a worker, it is unlikely to contribute to the development of democratic attitudes. The chances are greater that it will lead to "apple-polishing." The union is apprehensive of that possibility and accepts, therefore, the present setup. It uses its grievance machinery to hold the foremen in check without giving workers an opportunity for a strong participation in the work process. As a result many workers who came to the company after the working agreement had been concluded do not have any strong emotional identifications with the union. This worker's feelings about the union illustrate clearly what price the union has to pay for its failure to develop a conception of a democratic group process.

Asked "What comes to your mind when you say 'I am a member of the UPWA'?" he gives a rather lukewarm response: "I am a union member in local such and such, and I work in the meat-packing industry." His working in the meat-packing industry plays again—as it did in his attitudes toward the company—a crucial role. He decided to join because "you couldn't do otherwise." Asked if he would have joined if he could have done otherwise, he answered: "It is hard telling. My parents worked then, if they had been union members I might have joined." Again lukewarm in tone, though more positive in content, is his response to the question: "Does being a member make you feel you are a partner in doing something important?" He "thinks so." Further inquiry as to "What about the union makes you feel that way?" led to the answer: "We are holding the common people together, better wages, better contract setup." He becomes very positive when stating that the main advantages of belonging to the union are: "Organization, you can see the problems of both sides, management and fellow workers, find out what other unions are doing." There are no disadvantages and the union is, on the whole, doing a good service job: "I think our union is for the common working people, we are democratic. I don't think we are communistic."

He attends "some of the" union meetings, some he "don't"; he likes "a well-conducted meeting," believes that the union is "not a place to argue," and feels that "the good meetings outclass the bad." He made "a lot of friends by belonging to the union," and got more interested in political affairs because of the union: "Yes, I have, I have got interested in finding out what our town is doing, city affairs, national affairs." He has been active in union affairs, being a grievance man for a year. Though he was glad that he did not have to take part in the big strike of 1948, he "thinks it was a good cause." He again espouses labor's point of view without showing any strong involvement when answering the question: "What do you think about the Taft-Hartley Act?" He does not "think it is too good. Laboring class is tied up. Does not say anything about businessmen. Just the union has to abide by it."

There is no question about his loyalty to the union and his identification with labor as an interest group. "Labor" is the group with which he has common political interests. They are: "Wages, hours, earnings, your home, insurance policies, insurance of holding a job." He "could not say" what groups have political interests against him. But he "always feels that big business is working against us. They should not because we help earn their living too, but it seems they control everything." In another context, he said: "Labor should have something to say with big business. We are producing. We are the majority of the people. The majority is supposed to rule. Big business should not have its say alone." He would therefore welcome a "party made up particularly for the working men." It would be "a very good thing, they should get out and talk with everybody, and get people interested in politics. They should not just form a party and let it go at that. . . ."

His wholehearted espousal of a labor party has to be taken with a grain of salt. He is carried away easily and does not always follow his words with deeds. It is symptomatic of his general orientation but it does not take any concrete expression in his ideas about the organization of the work process. Asked: "Do you feel you should know more about management's problems?" he says with great emphasis: "Yes, I think we should. If we know more, sometimes we might have some ideas to help them along. I think they should study our problems and help us along." The *Squeal* gives "lots" of information but "it is not sufficient. I look at the pictures, like to read it. I know so many fellows. Nice to read about the organization you are working for." Though he would like to have more "know-how" he expresses neither a labor ideology nor a democratic consciousness when it comes to a "say-so": "No, I don't think we should [have more of a say-so]. Not any more than talking things over once in a while."

## WHAT WAY OUT?

The lack of experience of a democratic group process combined with the emptiness of the game of work lead to a lack of relatedness to the organized work process which makes the experience of work a burden. Asked: "What do you first think of when you think of 'work'?" he says, "Pushing gondolas," then laughs and adds: "I think of something hard." No feeling of a valuable contribution, of productiveness, can arise. "Being a producer" means to him "raising a family." While saying it, he laughs in a way which indicates that the immediate connotation of "producing" children was in the back of his mind. Then he goes on: "Putting out products, putting stuff on the market for buying purposes." Starting with an almost primitive down-to-earth act of productivity he ends up high in the realm of abstraction: the market stripped of all concrete aspects, pure form, pure exchange value. Carried from one extreme to another, he is not really related to the work process at all. Indeed, all he expects, as far as his job is concerned, is "to retire at reasonable age."

No wonder work has no meaning. Asked: "How do you feel about your working life as against your life off the job? Do you enjoy working less or more than anything else you do?" he said, "Nobody likes to work," laughed and added, "Everybody has to work in order to live . . . you can't be a bum." During the relaxed atmosphere of a Sunday morning visit, he talked again about work and being a bum. Away from the work, in Sunday dress and with his little son, he expressed an awareness of the potential creative aspects of work—it became evidence of an "interest in life." He even gave to the bum the benefit of the doubt: "A bum may have an interest in life too, but he doesn't express it in work."

Unfortunately for him, this was one of the few moments when he felt that work may be productive and express an interest in life. Actually "his experience in working is not useful to him personally" with the exception of "buying meats." And "on the job on which [he is] now" he never does anything off the job which helps him in his work in any way. Yet the separation of work and life does not leave him free to be his own after work. He is nervous, restless, "lost if not working: I have to do something, would go crazy if not working." These feelings account partly for his having another job besides his job in the plant—though there is nothing he wants more than to get away from it all. Partly it must be explained out of the necessity to meet the bills which accumulate so quickly if one wants to have "a nice car, a nice house," and all the other things other people have—or would like to have.

Asked "How does your weekend differ from the days you work?" he thinks for a while and then says, "We go to dances if we get away." He becomes more spontaneous when asked "What do you most like about weekends?" His response is: "Day of rest for one thing, a little bit longer to do something for yourself, to visit more on your own." Though these activities differ a great deal from the days of work, the weekend is too close to the work to be fully experienced as something of one's own. The vacations give more of an opportunity to get away. During the last vacation he helped his brother "building a house" but "before I was married I went fishing and visiting relatives. I slept later, not worrying about being at work, forget your working problems."

If forgetting would be as simple as that, *Death of a Salesman* would never have been written. What Willy Loman had to forget was different from what this would-be salesman has to get out of his mind. Willy Loman was caught in a conflict between a desire to be himself and the necessity to sell himself on the basis of the generally accepted market values. He had to forget that being a salesman may mean death of oneself. This worker is caught in a conflict between a meaningless existence in a factory and an illusory aspiration to be on his own. He has to forget that a place in the sun seems to be limited to people with "more money, more education, and more training." After having mentioned these factors as characteristic of people who are socially above him, he wondered: "This may not be true, there are guys who have college education and work with me, but they have no chance to get ahead . . . maybe not guts enough to go ahead to try it." It may be that neither Willy Loman nor this worker had quite enough "guts" to get out of the vicious circles in which they are caught. This is a fate they share with most people—a fate which does not minimize but enhances their respective dilemmas. And if it is true—as it undoubtedly is—that *Death of a Salesman* is the most searching dramatic criticism of certain values of our culture, then we may wonder whether our would-be salesman is not caught in a conflict greater than his manifest problem shows. It may be that the realization of his dream is impossible until human values have penetrated into the organization of industry.

Until then the would-be salesman will find some satisfaction with a company which gives him good earning opportunities and with a union which protects him against the potential arbitrariness of an essentially authoritarian supervisory hierarchy. He will find all the satisfactions that money can buy—and hope that his children will not have the same fate. But any deeper satisfactions are likely to be outside his reach and the happiness for which he is longing will remain as elusive as his striving to get ahead. The *New Yorker* had some time ago a cartoon showing two neighbors, one saying to the other: "You mean that all these years we have been trying to keep up with you, you've been trying to keep up with us?!"[1] I do not know a better illustration of the enervating meaninglessness of the game of keeping up with the Joneses—a game which is complemented by an even more meaningless game of work. Our would-be salesman must, therefore, remain "in the same old rut"—as he said himself. Something deep in him may arise from time to time: he "will get to thinking"; but the organization of work will not foster this process. It will slowly extinguish his thoughts until he is so accustomed to the existing conditions as to take work "in its stride." He will show high "morale scores" and equally high productive efficiency. Yet he may never become aware that a democratically organized work process—which contributes to the realization of a meaningful life—is a possible alternative to the present work organization.

# CHAPTER 11

# The Meaning
# of the Austin Experience

## AUSTIN'S ACHIEVEMENTS

In spite of reactions as diverse as those of the "Christian Gentleman," the "Would-be Salesman," and the worker defeated by a foe unseen, we can discern several common trends among these workers: (1) A high level of satisfaction with working conditions in general and with the pay and security setup in particular; (2) acceptance of the union for self-protection if not for self-expression; (3) full implementation of the goal of productive efficiency and a genuine appreciation of those aspects of the company which give workers high earning opportunities and a greater range of freedom.

These attitudes are in sharp contrast with those prevailing during the pre-union, pre-guaranteed-wage days, when hatred of "the bosses" and passive resistance to the company's attempt to implement productive efficiency were the order of the day.

The outward changes occurring during the fifteen-odd years separating this investigation from the strike of 1933—which marked the turning point in the history of Austin—are clearly reflected in the general increase in the well-being of the workers. In 1951 the average Hormel worker earned $4,590.00, while the average worker in the packing industry made only $3,460.00.[1] The security of employment and the high living standards are

157

reflected in the high percentage of homeownership. Over 75 per cent of the workers own their own homes—houses which are well equipped with washing machines, refrigerators, even deep freezes. And practically all workers have their own car—as a rule not old cars but new ones. The "jalopies" have disappeared from the streets of Austin. The answer of a worker to the question: "How can you tell the big shots?" is typical. He said: "Not any more by their cars."

Though social status differentiations remain clear-cut in Austin, the prestige of the workers has been raised greatly. As a result of the security of employment and the increases in the earnings, workers became respected members of the community. As one worker said: "This was a slaughterhouse town. People did not like their daughter to marry a slaughterhouse man . . . he was a packinghouse rat. There was work during the winter months and not during the summer. Now it is a year-round proposition."

Significant as these advances in general well-being may be, even more important for an understanding of the Austin experiment are the changes within the factory which brought about these results: Work performed over and above the standard work requirements averaged 60 per cent in 1950. In some departments it averaged well over 100 per cent.[2] As a rule standard work requirements correspond to industry-wide performance. The figures showing wage costs per unit of output give conclusive evidence that the high production gains are not due to low standards: unit labor costs are no higher for the Hormel company than for the rest of the industry.

But the amount of work done by the Hormel workers is approximately equivalent to that of a comparable firm employing about 30 per cent more workers.[3] And the earnings of the average Hormel workers are, as we have seen, well over 30 per cent higher than the average earnings in the industry. The Hormel workers have the same base pay, yet they produced and hence earned, well over 30 per cent more while they put in almost 20 per cent less time than other workers in the packing industry: the average Hormelite worked 34.4 hours in 1951, the average packinghouse worker 41.5 hours!

## The Underlying Causes

These accomplishments are concrete expressions of deep-seated changes in workers' attitudes towards the company and towards work. The situation prevailing before the guaranteed wage–group-incentive system was introduced and the subsequent modifications are clearly indicated by a worker who said: "When we were on an hourly rate, we had to *make wages by stretching hours* . . . we had to make a ten-hour job out of a five-hour job. Now we don't have to . . . we want to get out of there . . . and we want to make as much as we can. . . ." We can easily recognize here the essential elements of the game of work which can only be played effectively if workers are and feel free to set their own pace of work and if they are neither afraid of a speed-up nor of losing their jobs. Any attempt to stretch work would, under these conditions, only increase the burden of work by bringing out the monotony of the slowly passing time—and lower the monetary reward.

Many Hormel workers are already so accustomed to the security of employment that the fear of losing the job has practically disappeared, as the following conversation shows:

Does straight time affect your attitude towards work?
No.
Would you make as much production without straight time?
Yes.
Would you make as much production if you would work yourself out of a job by doing so?
Hell no, I see what you mean!

The very unconsciousness of what "straight time" stands for—and the implicit matter-of-fact acceptance of job security—make it a powerful force in making workers accept the goal of productive efficiency.

The abolition of the authoritarian boss system is a precondition for the full implementation of this goal. As one worker said about the pre-union, pre-guaranteed wages days: "Times I didn't work unless boss looked at you. You were whipped. They browbeat you. They got a bonus for themselves. I felt injury was done, and I tried to get away with the least I could. Now it is different. . . ." The differences are well illustrated by the following statement of a foreman: "Formerly you had to run your ass off to get them guys to work. Now you can just stand and watch." In the "old days" the bosses "pushed the workers around," now the workers push themselves around. The foreman's function is to see to it that workers receive the necessary material, take care of the records, and watch the quality of the product—an important task. But they do not enforce any work discipline. Nor does the union have to set any work standards limiting workers' freedom to produce as much as they want. Indeed, workers produce as fast, or faster, than compatible with the quality standards set by management.

These changes in workers' attitudes towards work cannot be credited to company or union policy by themselves. They are mainly due to the interplay of four factors: (1) the guaranteed annual wage, (2) the peculiarities of the group-incentive system, (3) the self-administration of the guaranteed-wage–group-incentive system through the union (and the self-determination of work schedules), and (4) labor-management cooperation.

The cooperation between labor and management and the self-administration of the security system by the workers have created a general atmosphere of trust, and neutralized the authoritarian boss system. Of particular relevance are the following stipulations of the Working Agreement: (1) Work production schedules are determined by collective bargaining and are subject to the grievance machinery; (2) production above the standard is paid in full, not according to a sliding percentage; (3) in case of changes in machinery, old earning opportunities are guaranteed; (4) the seniority principle is used for transfers; and (5) dismissals for cause are administered jointly by the union and the company.

These stipulations eliminate the anomaly of limiting the union-management contract to the pay while leaving "completely undefined the amount or quality of work expected in return for an agreed rate of pay."[4] They have created, moreover, a machinery which allows workers to determine their own pace of work and which safeguards them against any reductions in earnings in case of technological changes. As a result, the fear of a speed-up has been disappearing, while the security given by the guaranteed wage has been a major factor in eliminating the fear of losing one's job.

The respective roles of the guaranteed wage and the group-incentive system in bringing about high rates of production and earnings may be formulated as follows: wage guarantees create the possibilities for the increase in productivity, while the group-incentive system transforms them into actuality. Without the group-incentive plan, whereby production above standard is paid in full, the potentialities of wage guarantees would not have been tapped as much as they are now. But without the guarantee, the incentive earnings would be smaller and productive efficiency would be lower because workers would be afraid of working themselves out of a job if production over standard was too high.

## DEMOCRATIZATION OF THE WORK PROCESS

To have shown a way of eliminating the fear of losing one's job and the fear of a speed-up—these are major achievements of the Austin experiment. The security system which is based on guaranteed wages must, therefore, be considered an essential aspect of a democratization of the work process. Fear of losing one's job is incompatible with a creative self-expression and fear of speed-up is a sign of an undemocratic organization of work— it results from a lack of self-determination of the work performance. The increases in productivity which the elimination of these fears makes possible are, as we shall see in the next chapter, of great significance for an integration of work into a meaningful life pattern because they make it possible to reduce working hours—and thus minimize the detrimental effect of repetitive work on the life of the workers. Guaranteed wages are, therefore, in a real sense "a promise of security and a stimulus to freedom."[5]

Yet the contribution which the Austin experiment has made in pointing the way to a democratization of the work process goes beyond the establishment of a unique system of security. By establishing channels for workers' participation in the work process—particularly the Business Improvement Committee—

problems which are at the very core of a democratic organization of industry are being posed.

Mr. Hormel has, indeed, developed a new and challenging conception of a democratic work process and of workers' participation in such a process. Management has given up the authoritarian approach and recognizes the individual worker as a human being rather than as a cog in a wheel. It has, furthermore, sincerely tried to accept the union as a necessary instrument in the administration of the work process, an attitude which is expressed in the establishment of the union shop, which has given the union the security essential for constructive labor-management relations. The union, in turn, has created the very basis for a democratization of the work process by giving the workers a group organization—a prerequisite for any democracy in industry. Instead of being merely in a market-exchange relationship, the union relates the workers through a collective bond to the company. Such a relatedness is essential if workers are eventually to become real partners in the company.

## The Austin Experiment and the Traditional Organization of Industry

What is the significance of these achievements in terms of the broader stream of industrial developments?

A comparison of the traditional pattern of industrial organization with the main features of the organized work process in Austin will bring the meaning of the Austin achievements into sharp focus. Traditionally, the organization of industry has been—and still is—predominantly authoritarian. In Worthy's words: "Many businesses closely resemble the authoritarian state in the sense that all direction, all thinking, all authority tends to flow from the top down."[6] Indeed, workers were not related to the firm as associates or partners; they were in an individual "exchange" relationship. Only those who shared the control of the corporation were associates. They organized the factory in view of the maintenance and increase of capital values.

Since workers were variable costs to the enterprise, they found themselves subordinated to the machines, which were overhead costs. Putting the machines to optimum use and thus maximizing returns from the original investment rather than implementing human values were the main objectives of the traditional organization of industry. Mechanical productive efficiency was its God; the time study and efficiency experts were its prophets.

A most significant counterpart of such an organization of industry was the traditional conception of work incentives. The following story is typical:

> The superintendent of a large coal mine located several miles from a town in southern Illinois was asked: "When you don't need men, why don't you put up a sign: 'No men wanted'?" He replied: "Don't you know why those men are walking out there? We want the men going to work to see how many men are after their jobs."[7]

Fear of losing one's job was the big "stick" to induce workers to do their job. It was complemented by the not so outstanding "carrot" of monetary gain and advancement.

The very conception of "the stick and the carrot" is typical of the frame of reference of the traditional organization of industry. It corresponds exactly to the position of the worker in such an organization: he is a means to be manipulated in view of the best possible realization of exchange values. Instead of appealing to "the instinct of workmanship" or to any positive identification with the involvement in the organized work process, monetary incentives were emphasized and the worker—and his family— were menaced with hunger and poverty or lured into the desire for wealth. Work as a "calling," as something that had meaning and could give meaning to life was reserved for those who were in command of industry.

Workers' traditional reaction to such a treatment was the formation of informal groups whose main goal was job preservation: through passive resistance they thwarted the implementation of the formal goal underlying the organization of industry. In denying any human values and forcing workers to find a minimum of security and decency by opposing the only value underlying the organization of industry, the traditional organization of industry has thus in fact undermined what it propagated with unusual singlemindedness of purpose: productive efficiency.

As we have just seen, the Austin experiment has fundamentally changed this pattern. The typical Austin worker accepts the goal of productive efficiency because he is neither afraid of losing his job nor warding off a speed-up. He has at his disposal an effective system of self-administration of the work process, since, through the introduction of the guaranteed wage and through unionization, he has ceased to be a mere means in the organized work process. The Austin workers control the speed at which they work and they have demonstrated their willingness to use this right in order *to step up* rather than to lower production.

### The General Significance of the Austin Experiment

Are there any reasons to assume that the change of attitude of the Austin workers is due to a unique combination of circumstances, or can similar changes be expected in other firms and industries as the security of workers increases and organs for the self-administration of the work process are being created? There is no question that similar results can be obtained in other communities and industries. Yet a few words of clarification must be added in regard to the introduction of guaranteed wages.

The elimination of the fear of losing one's job through successful introduction of wage guarantees may, under certain circumstances, leave workers' desire to implement the goal of productive efficiency just about as strong as it was before introduction of security schemes. In extreme cases, it may even lessen it because, under circumstances usually prevailing in industry, work is meaningless and workers become "bored and lazy." They do not become so because of any laziness which nature has implanted in them while sparing the managerial class of similar natural traits; they develop a "laziness" growing out of a lack of involvement and a lack of active participation typical of the traditional organization of industry. The carrot of monetary incentives is in many cases too tiny and shriveled up to counteract the powerful forces making for apathy which the organization of work engenders in the soul of the workers.

The introduction of guaranteed wages does not, therefore,

automatically increase productivity. A real experience of employment security, establishment of organs for the self-administration of the work process, and an activation of positive work incentives are necessary. The nature of the work, the skill level, the nature of the existing labor-management relations, and other aspects of the organized work process determine the kind of measures to be taken in each specific situation and the kind of work incentives that will be most effective.

Lest anybody conclude from the above that guaranteed wages have a neutral effect, or even a negative one that has to be counteracted by such schemes as incentive plans, we hasten to add that this is a basically wrong interpretation of our findings. The real effect of guaranteed wages is this: To the extent that they eliminate the fear of losing the job, they create the precondition for much *greater* increases in productivity than would be possible as long as that fear exists.

The Hormel experience repudiates indeed all those arguments against guaranteed wages which are based on the "necessity" of workers' fear of losing their job as an incentive to "make" them work. It does not matter whether these arguments are brought forward in their simplest form of the "necessity to counteract workers' natural laziness," or whether more sophisticated prescriptions are offered against the guarantee of wages and employment: all these arguments are based on a wrong conception of the nature of work incentives.

Far from threatening productive efficiency, guaranteed wages play a strategic role in implementing the goal of productive efficiency because, as labor becomes an overhead cost—and thus an element to be taken into account in the formal implementation of the goal of productive efficiency—the *necessity* of a conflict between human values (such as job preservation and a certain degree of security) and the main values underlying the organization of the work process disappears. This is the unique contribution of guaranteed wages: to have eliminated the obstacles in the way of implementing the goal of productive efficiency and to have cleared the way for a development which gives to human values a more and more central significance. Being essentially a development of the idea of unionization—

the first and basic step in making workers more than means in the process of production—guaranteed wages have broadened the basis for a new synthesis of human values and the rational organization of industry. This potential constitutes the most significant implication of the Austin experiment from the point of view of a democratization of the work process.

UNSOLVED PROBLEMS

In order to realize this potential, important problems remain to be solved: Austin is in the vanguard on the road to a democratic work process, but it is still far from having covered the whole distance.

As we have shown, the Austin experiment activated incentives other than the fear of losing one's job; the carrot of monetary incentives has become the outstanding work incentive in the Austin scene. As a result, workers play the game of work freely and effectively. The high incentive earnings prove the extent to which Hormel workers have accepted monetary incentives. Workers are willing to implement fully the goal of productive efficiency, provided the direct increases in productivity due to increased effort accrue fully to them and only indirect savings in cost such as savings in fixed capital, lighting, supervision, and savings due to technological improvements accrue to the company. Yet their acceptance of this goal is incidental to the game of work. It is not a consciously chosen identification. As a result the only meaning of this play is money. The democratization of the work process has not yet reached a stage in which workers are meaningfully related to any alternative goals or values which are—actually or potentially—part of the organized work process. Such a relatedness creates conflicts which indicate the nature of the problems that remain to be discussed.

Typical of this conflict situation is, for example, the case of a worker who got impatient for having been asked twice in a row a question about the importance of the work, and protested: "Too many questions. Naturally, we are working there for a living; all the rest important . . . how you do your job. . . ." This worker was asked more than 200 questions and only once did he get impatient. His impatience suggests that he does not quite like to admit something that nevertheless remains true: the fact that money is the only satisfaction which work can possibly give.

I was struck by the frequency of unsolicited statements like these: "We *all* work for the dollar," emphasizing that it is "the same for anybody else," or that "everybody does it." These are nothing but attempts to justify a situation which is somehow felt to be wrong. The justifications, which were not asked for, are in the nature of rationalizations and stem, like all rationalizations, from a need to resolve the tensions of a conflict whose underlying causes are beyond one's reach.

While the workers try to find a practical solution for this dilemma by following the words of an old musical: "When the one whom I love is not near me, I love the one who is near me," the theoreticians speak about a confusion of money as a means and as an end. There is no doubt that such a confusion exists. But the nature of this confusion can only be understood if we realize the difficulties of making money "merely" a means to ends "higher" than money. It is true that everything that gives meaning to the life off the job weighs the balance towards money as a means rather than as an end. But the odds against such an experience are great indeed. It is impossible to spend over one-half of one's waking life under conditions which make money the *only* really significant aspect of life, without being deeply affected by such a concentration on money values.

Money acquires therefore a strong "sublimated" significance, since it symbolizes the freedom which the actual work—and life—process denies to the workers. Evidence obtained from interviews and observations, and eventually to be tested by projective techniques, leads to the presumption that the need to "splurge" is greater among those workers who are more caught in the conflicts created by the meaninglessness of work. And the emotional overtone with which workers listed vacations as the Number one advantage derived from working for the company is indicative of a restraining, limiting work experience: "It gives you the feeling that you don't have to slave every day of the year to make a living."

Such a feeling highlights the inability of the Austin security setup to allow workers a creative self-expression in their work. As a result, their desire to get away from an activity without meaning is not lessened, it is only diverted— for the duration of the game of work—into positive channels. The "man in the locker room" is the marginal, not the typical Austin worker. Typical, in the sense of frequency, is the worker who plays the game of work in such a way as to fully implement the goal of productive efficiency.

Yet there is something typical, in the sense of showing underlying tendencies, about the man in the locker room: Escaping from a meaningless activity which does not allow a human involvement, workers who sit in the locker rooms are worn out without being tired. Something is broken in them—an intangible link which relates them to a larger community of people and ideas. As one worker said when asked whether the job makes him tired because it is monotonous. "Yes and no. You get tired from loafing if you have nothing to do. You get bored and lazy." What he really says is this: something happens in you which breaks your impulse to work and you feel unrelated. Since nothing becomes activated through the game of work, you become as dead inside as the game is void of content. In his sculptures Henry Moore has given a vivid expression of what goes on in these men: the holes in their body are the result of "the grind of work"—a routinized activity without meaning.

MANAGEMENT AND THE UNION'S ROLE IN SOLVING THESE PROBLEMS

A reorganization of industry *per se* does not solve these problems. But neither can these issues be solved without further democratization of the work process, because only such a democratization can relate workers meaningfully to the organized work process. Alienation from work in a culture which gives work a central place in the life of the people means alienation from life, and from the very core of workers' personalities— their real selves. It means unrelatedness to the inner sources of creative living, inability to feel free in the sense of freedom *to* express oneself. It creates conflicts and deep-seated anxieties. Ultimately, it is destructive of all human values.

These are the basic reasons for the indequacy of the presently existing organization of the work process. The general problems of reorganization of this process (in conjunction with a reorientation of the role of work in the life of the workers) will be examined in the following chapter. As we will see then, everything that increases workers' relatedness to the work process contributes to the overcoming of apathy. As far as management and union policy are concerned, increased channels of workers' participation are of crucial significance to allow workers a meaningful relatedness to the organized work process.

We have seen management's outstanding contribution to the development of workers' channels for participation. But the kind of machinery established by the Business Improvement Project, which is based on written suggestions from individual workers, obviously does not provide an adequate outlet for workers' initiative and thought. The main orientation of the Business Improvement Project is, furthermore, towards "profitable investment," which does not offer a broad enough value basis for a democratic self-expression of the workers. The Hormel Business Improvement Committee is a much more significant and valuable instrument for workers' participation in the organized work process. Yet even this Committee is too limited in scope and value basis, and is artificially separated from the grievance machinery. This machinery, which is at present the core of workers' opportunity for self-administering significant aspects of the work process and for expressing freely their dissatisfaction, is a most significant contribution to the democratic reorganization of industry. But the grievance machinery does not give workers adequate channels for active participation in the life of the factory, and therefore falls short of allowing them creative self-expression. Indeed the union has failed to develop a conception of a democratic work process providing for expanding channels for workers' participation in the work process. It has no awareness of the necessity of a meaningful relatedness to the work process, and the concept of joy in work is alien to it.

It is true—and must be emphasized—that in Austin both management and the union have gone a long way in modifying the work process. But neither management nor the union have found a mutually acceptable approach to continue the reorganization of the work process by really allowing the workers to participate in the organized work process. As we have seen, the union is afraid that the Business Improvement Committee—which has been the most advanced instrument of participation—may encroach upon the grievance machinery and endanger the union's role in the organized work process. And the company is afraid of union control which may either stifle the Committee or affect management's control of the work process. Fears of this kind, which are typical of anxieties generally prevailing in industry, are bound to linger on as long as the underlying problems of power and values are not solved or, at least, as long as no constructive approach to their solution has been found.

By having developed labor-management relations to the point where really basic issues of a democratization of the work process arise, the Austin experiment highlights fundamental problems with which management and labor all over the country must eventually come to grips—once they have solved the more elementary problems of living and working together for the welfare of the workers.

As far as the union is concerned, the main question is what role the union will eventually play in the organized work process. Will it try to develop workers' potentialities of self-expression and of a democratic consciousness? Will it relate them to a community of people and ideas and thus give meaning to their work and life? Or will the union become more and more an instrumentality for administering the Working Agreement and thus strengthen the old values underlying the existing industrial organization?

At present, the union is to a considerable degree a victim of its own success—and of the positive approach of management towards the workers. It cannot rely any more on the hatred which prevailed in pre-union days and was carried over into the years following unionization. And it has not yet found an approach to developing the creative potential of the workers and thereby creating strong union-identifications. Hence its acute problem of participation. The necessity to activate this creative potential in order to involve workers "positively" in the union is again a problem of nation-wide significance.

Management's problems are equally relevant for the national scene. The question as to its ability to fully implement the goal of productive efficiency has been answered in Austin. The gains in production are so remarkable that national output would be affected if similar results were achieved in those wide sectors of industry where comparable conditions prevail. The real problem to be solved in Austin is a deeper lying one: Will management find a method acceptable to the union, an approach which will allow it to further develop the channels for workers' participation in the organized work process? Or will there be a conflict of power which leaves workers cut off from the organized work process, participating only sporadically in a limited sphere?

At present management's efforts are almost exclusively oriented towards the implementation of monetary values. To have given the workers unique earning opportunities is an achievement which is in no way minimized by this criticism. And it may be true that solution of market problems is the proper managerial function. But ways and means must be found to reorganize the work process in such a way as to give human values a central place and to allow workers a creative expression.

Success or failure in this difficult undertaking will give the answer to Max Weber's anxious question: "No one knows yet whether there will be a great rebirth of old ideas and ideals or whether the modern industrial system will lead to mechanized petrification—to a new species of man: minds without spirit enjoying themselves without heart."[8]

## CHAPTER 12

# Creative Self-Expression
# In a Democratic Work Process

### DEMOCRATIC VALUES—OBJECTIVITY AND NEUTRALITY

How to organize the work process in such a way as to give to human values a central significance—this is the essence of the problem of industrial democracy. Yet it is not possible to approach this question without knowing what values were central to the workers whose experience I was studying. How are these values affected by and how do they affect their life in the plant? Are values and experience of work of such a different order that only the trained philosopher can sense their relationship? Are those caught in the existing organization of work doomed to push ahead blindly and automatically on routine occupations essential to physical life while vaguely sensing that their whole personality has no complete expression and not knowing how to relate the values they would like to live by to the work experience they have to live with? Or are there central values which are shared and which can become part of a new organization of the work process?

The usual techniques of scientific research do not yield answers to such questions. Some will, therefore, feel it appropriate for the scientist to cease his efforts at this point and leave the rest to the philosopher or social reformer. Without any quarrel with those who conceive their role in such terms, I personally, having

172

lived closely with these workers and sensing the importance of such matters in their lives, could not break off my study at such a point. I decided, therefore, to examine with the workers the problem of values and explore the possibilities of a reorganization of the work process in view of a full realization of human democratic values.

The procedure used was as follows: I called all the workers who were previously interviewed to a meeting in the city hall. We discussed the progress of the research and I explained my desire to explore with them the new problems which arise in connection with a democratic reorganization of the work process. I suggested to them to meet in smaller groups but left it up to them to determine the size of the group, the number of times we were to meet, etc. In order to find out their ideas about these things, a questionnaire was distributed. On the basis of the answers given I decided that two small groups of five workers, one group meeting weekly, the other bimonthly, would be most appropriate. These groups met for practically a full year. The meetings were in the nature of group discussions initiated by the reading of my analysis of the attitudes of individuals or groups of workers towards certain aspects of the work process. Workers were not only asked to comment on the accuracy and adequacy of my report. They were also encouraged to state what they felt was right and wrong, what they liked and what they did not like—and how they felt the situation could be remedied.

The group discussions may be considered to be at the borderline of the diagnostic and therapeutic phase of an action research project and the insights gained by them must, therefore, be evaluated in terms of the problems and limitations of this approach. Only one of the most important problems of action research can be mentioned here: that of the functions of the scientist and its value implications. My dual role as a fellow worker and as a scientist posed these problems in a quite concrete and at the same time most general way. Can a scientist possibly abstain from value judgments? Does the scientific demand for objectivity impel him to forgo any advocacy of specific values?

All scientific endeavors are contingent upon certain values. The belief in free inquiry and objective procedures are part of democratic values. It is also accepted more and more that the scientific analysis proper takes place within a—usually implicit—frame of social and personal values. Max Weber, the greatest proponent of objectivity in social science, has shown the inter-relationship between values and scientific analysis most clearly.[1] He speaks about a line of "hairbreadth" which separates the scientific analysis of a situation in terms of certain values from the advocacy of a specific value system. Actually there is no sharp delineation between scientific analysis in terms of certain values and belief or disbelief in these values. The two are inter-related since a scientist most frequently chooses the kind of value-frame of reference which he believes—consciously or uncon-sciously—to be humanly significant. Yet somewhere we transcend this line explicitly and become the proponents of certain values.

In the preceding chapters we have confined ourselves to the analysis of a given situation in terms of certain values. In this chapter, and in the Epilogue, we go a step further by advocating the realization of a democratic society and by exploring the implications of such an ideal in the industrial scene. Such a position does not conflict with the demand for the greatest pos-sible degree of objectivity in social research. Objectivity means "respect"[2] and ability to use scientific techniques. It does not mean absence of value judgments. To look at human fate with the eyes of the "disinterested" bystander is not a prerequisite of objectivity: it implies as many value judgments as the alternative stand taken in this study, which is based on an explicit interest in fostering the democratic process and a conscious advocacy of social change. Nor does such an approach imply any imposition of values on other people. Indeed, in my actual contact with workers I tried to be as open to alternative values as possible. When I decided after a series of completely "permissive" experi-mental group meetings that we needed a framework to integrate our discussion, I chose a framework which was broad enough to encompass various points of view and yet sufficiently concrete to allow us to explore what the application of democratic ideals to the work process really means. Even then I was keenly aware that a democratic consciousness has to be developed democratically—that means out of the people. "There is all the difference in the world, both in immediate and in ultimate results, between the dangerous diagnostic process of 'telling people things' and the therapeutic process of helping people to 'recognize things for themselves,' that is, between doing things *to* others, or even *for* others, and in doing things *with* others."[3]

## REVERENCE FOR LIFE—IN THE INDUSTRIAL SCENE

To be able to do things *with* others, one must in some way speak a common language, one must use the same daily jargon. But much more important still: one must share a fundamental conception of life. Far removed as it may sound, Albert Schweitzer's *Philosophy of Civilization* supplied this common ground. Since the basic ideas underlying our group discussions were derived from Schweitzer, I quote those passages which we read in an early meeting. Fundamental is Schweitzer's conception of "Reverence for Life":

Wherever there is lost the consciousness that every man is an object of concern for us just because he is man, civilization and morals are shaken, and the advance to fully developed inhumanity is only a question of time.[4]

The development of such a consciousness is not a matter of abstract thought, but can only be the result of "a thinking experience of life":

It is in reason that intellect and will, which in our nature are mysteriously bound up together, seek to come to a mutual understanding. The ultimate knowledge that we strive to acquire is knowledge of life, which intellect looks at from without, will from within. Since life is the ultimate object of knowledge, our ultimate knowledge is necessarily our thinking experience of life.[5]

Granted that a full understanding of this passage requires a deeper knowledge of analytical psychology than the workers had, the explanation of this passage to the effect that thought and life had to be closely related made sense to them. They could feel the difference between intellectualism unrelated to life and a reasoned understanding of life. And whatever puzzlement may have been left in their mind was dispelled when they listened to this idea:

The unlearned man who, at the sight of a tree in flower, is overpowered by the mystery of the will-to-live which is stirring all round him, knows more than the scientist who studies under the microscope or in physical and chemical activity a thousand forms of the will-to-live, but, with all this knowledge of the life course of these manifestations of the will-to-live, is unmoved by the mystery that everything which exists is will-to-live while he is puffed up with vanity at being able to describe exactly a fragment of the course of life.[6]

Workers could feel the depth—and the immediacy—of thought expressed in this passage, they were pleased to find science subordinated to ethics, and they were grateful for the acknowledgement that they—"unlearned men"—can experience something more profound than the achievements of the academic world with which they identified me at the beginning of our acquaintance. They literally acclaimed this statement which touched off something very real in them—as shown by a remark made many months later in one of the group discussions, in an entirely different context. Out of a discussion of the role of work in our life, came the following pronouncement:

. . . there is such a thing as being too interested in your work. Scientists, for example, are just connected with their own little world, they don't stop to compare it to creation as a whole . . .

The practical implication of the experience of "the will-to-live which is stirring [around us]" is the primacy of an ethical conception of man, or—to be more specific—of an ethical conception of human relationships. A great deal of the present-day literature on "human relations" in industry is unsatisfactory because it does not come to grips with the problem of the ethical nature of man. As a result, man is cut off from the life-spring of his being and scientific thought becomes shallow. It becomes often an instrument to implement existing power positions and to manipulate people to make them satisfied with a basically undemocratic industrial organization. This is the ultimate result of a spurious "objectivity"—the worst idol worship of the *status quo* a scientist could be guilty of.

The ethics of "reverence for life" does not need such idol worship. Nor is it based on metaphysical speculations of any kind. It can rest in itself, since it grows out of an immediate experience of and thought about life. And it can be expressed very simply:

> . . . everything which in the ordinary ethical valuation of the relations of man to each other ranks as good can be brought under the description of material and spiritual maintenance or promotion of human life, and of effort to bring it to its highest value. Conversely, everything which ranks as bad in human relations is in the last analysis material or spiritual destruction or obstruction of human life, and negligence in the endeavour to bring it to its highest value. Separate individual categories of good and evil which lie far apart and have apparently no connection at all with one another fit together like the pieces of a jig-saw puzzle, as soon as they are comprehended and deepened in this the most universal definition of good and evil.[7]

Such a conception of good and evil is general but it is not vague. Indeed, the ethics of "reverence for life" is the most universal and the most concrete yardstick for life. Since it expresses itself in our relatedness to life and to people, it fulfills the dual criterion of generality of thought and concreteness of approach which is essential for the group discussions. General enough to be used without an attempt to indoctrinate, it can be applied realistically to the organization of the work process.

GROUP DISCUSSIONS AND DEMOCRATIC CONSCIOUSNESS

Our exploration of the nature of a democratic work process will follow closely the path we traveled in our group discussions. These discussions led to ideas not representative of those generally prevailing among the Hormel workers. Whereas in the preceding sections I have always given the opinions of various groups of workers who were typical representatives of the Austin situation, we shall now listen to those who best express the potentialities rather than the reality of the democratic consciousness of their fellow workers. My own thought will be presented in connection with the ideas of the workers who attended the groups since it has been developed in intimate contact with them.

No attempt can be made here to show the actual course of the group discussions. Only here and there will I refer to the proceedings proper. It is, for example, important to note that an attempt to come at the very beginning of our work to a clearer understanding of what democracy in industry means, was a failure. We got bogged down on such elementary confusions as between "democratic" and the "Democratic party." And the exploration of certain basic propositions about democracy in industry aroused fears of radicalism, if not communism. These fears were only slowly dispelled as our discussions went on and they were aroused consistently whenever a new worker was brought in contact with our ideas. "When I talk to fellows in my gang about what we are doing here, they say it sounds like communism"—a situation which highlights how remote most workers are from the experience of a democratic work process. It is not accidental that a rumor arose, when I left town for a prolonged weekend, that I was picked up by the F.B.I.—at exactly the spot where I actually took a Greyhound bus to Minneapolis. The rumor was so persistent and widespread that a call was made to the Minneapolis F.B.I. to verify—or deny it. No wonder one of the workers came one evening with great relief to our meeting, waving the printed evidence that ours was not a subversive undertaking: he had a short article in his hand, entitled "Can Factories Be Christian?" The article, written by John C. Cort, was originally published in *Commonweal* and reprinted in the *Catholic Digest*. It came indeed as close to our own trend of thought as anything we were familiar with.

These incidents show that it took time to realize the objectives of the group discussions which we formulated as follows:

1. To develop thinking out of the experience of our own life in the factory, the community, the church, and society at large.
2. To give to our thinking an ethical foundation by relating it to the principle of "devotion to life resulting from reverence for life."
3. To apply this kind of ethical thinking more specifically to the problem of a democratic way of life, a democratic way of organizing work.

As I look back on the group discussions, the ideas which emerged from them show, if not success, at least progress in that direction. I want to quote only one illustration. About nine months after the beginning of our sessions, one of the workers told me while we relaxed after our discussion: "Now I know how life could be if we could do something else than living up to the Joneses." This statement is also indicative of the potentialities of an intensive group work approach and the scope of the problems with which it must deal.

What has been achieved so far in regard to a clarification of a democratic work process will be presented within the frame of reference which underlay our whole discussion of workers' attitude towards work. These attitudes, workers' feelings, and the underlying relationships may be classified as follows:

1. Feeling of creative self-expression. This feeling may be derived from the following types of relatedness:
   a. Relatedness to the people, the product, the machinery, the place of work, the work process itself. Such a relatedness to the concrete aspects of work—the "technical" process of production—leads to corresponding work process identifications.
   b. Relatedness to and participation in some aspect of the organized work process leading to identifications with the goals and values underlying the organization of work.
   c. Relatedness to some community of people and ideas or to some goal and value outside the organized work process proper.
   The less workers are related to any of these three spheres, the more they approach a situation in which:
2. Work has lost any meaning and the feeling of creative self-expression does not arise.

This scheme allows us to apply the basic postulates of the ethics of "Reverence for Life" to the industrial scene: Any of these types of relatedness, which are ultimately "relations of man to each other," are good if they are in agreement with the "material and spiritual maintenance or promotion of human life and of efforts to bring it to its highest value." If there is no such positive relationship, or no relatedness at all, the situation is incompatible with democratic values because it does not allow a free, creative self-expression and self-realization of the individual within a group fostering the greatest possible development of man's emotional, intellectual, and aesthetic capacities.

### HUMAN VALUES IN THE CONCRETE-TECHNICAL WORK PROCESS

Starting with the concrete-technical types of relatedness, the present organization of work has been discussed by Bud in these terms:

I don't see how anything could be changed too much without cutting down efficiency. Then we would have less free time, now we have leisure more than working time. If we work 35 hours and get out at 2 o'clock we really have some free time. As long as working conditions are good, decent pay to earn one's livelihood . . . a decent livelihood, we have every opportunity to engage in a hobby afterwards. I don't see many changes, of course the windows. If we had any, it would make it more a place where humans are kept than where machines are kept . . . and the stink in the locker rooms and toilets, stuff like that could be changed. Most of them are far less modern than the plant itself is . . . they don't make it a pleasant place to hang around. The new cafeteria was a big step to make it a more dignified place to work in . . . much better than the old one. . . . It would be a better place if they would pay more attention to how hard a job is, one thing I had in mind, trucks, some terrible trucks. A man should not be pushing at all. They have rubber tires to save the floor, it seems that there should be different way of saving floor than make the job too hard. . . .

The specific issues are only mentioned here to preserve the original freshness of the statement. They do not matter and their merits will not be discussed. The orientation of this worker's thought is most significant. He does not want to tamper with the technical efficiency of the present organization and he sees work in connection with the life off the job. Hence his emphasis on short hours. After having read a summary of certain findings of my research showing that work in itself had "no meaning" and that "the most important values giving meaning to work consist in its ability to make family life possible and to give freedom for creative activities," all workers agreed that "this is why short hours are necessary—otherwise it (work) is drudgery."

In view of the widespread tendency to blame the machine for the ills of modern industrialism, the acceptance of efficiency in order to make the working time short and the pay high, should be underlined. Workers know too well the old "drudgery" of long hours and their former difficulties to make ends meet, to have much understanding for the armchair anti-machine reformists. For them "the idea of mass production is too important, we don't want to sacrifice income." If there is any possibility to express craftsmanship—all the better. But you can also derive satisfaction from other sources. Our whole discussion has, therefore, been based on the acceptance of efficient machine production.

Such an acceptance, however, does not exclude many possibilities of giving more meaning even to the technical-concrete work process. The work environment is of great significance. Bud mentioned windows. The animal psychology of work incentives is still so prevalent that it is often assumed workers would look out of the windows and forget about their work if they had the opportunity to do so. Actually anything that increases human relatedness is good since it will add joy to the work. The coloring of the room is very important and the potentialities of art are completely unexplored. Sculpture and painting belong right in the factory and the machine itself is an art form with many possibilities. Only music was mentioned by the workers, yet with certain reservations which are important:

> *Max:* [discussing various hobbies] We should have music as a hobby.
>
> *Joe:* And we should have it down there [meaning the plant] too, every day, when the fatigue comes on, it creates a mood.
>
> *Bud:* Music is good for milk cows, why not good for human beings?
>
> *George:* I am not sure, I have to listen to that at home, I want to get away from it. . . .

Whatever problems may have to be solved before certain art forms can be used, there is no question about the desirability of the greatest possible contact among the work group. Talking to their fellow workers has often been mentioned as a factor giving meaning to work. There is no doubt that once our thinking is oriented towards people, many possibilities of increasing contact among workers by changing the layout of working equipment could be discovered without the slightest injury to productive efficiency. Indeed it may raise it.

Even more fundamental is the spirit of work groups. Many times workers would complain about the "dog-eat-dog" attitude and the widespread absence of an informal democratic group process. If "a few king pins run the whole gang" there is indeed not too much democracy in the work group. Even if the situation is not as extreme, there will be no democratic work process until something else than conceit relates workers to each other. The following conversation illustrates this point:

> *Otto:* Each one thinks that he is smarter than the other, that's a way of putting them below.
>
> *Fred:* Maybe.
>
> *Joe:* I think I am smarter, but I can see from the expression of their faces that they think they are. . . .

The absence of anything to share besides a common interest in money does not improve the situation. Again discussing hobbies, a worker said, "If the whole department had a hobby like that, they would share; that would make work a hell of a lot better."

Interestingly enough, the idea of a genuine human relatedness to the foreman occurs only exceptionally. Under present conditions the line between having a good free relationship to the supervisory staff and "playing up to the boss" is so fine that it can scarcely be drawn. And this is the reason why the foremen appear, as we have previously seen, in an unfavorable light—much less favorable than they deserve. Without real authority and yet symbolizing the authority of management, the foremen are in a difficult position, lost somewhere between management and the workers. They earn not much more than the workers, sometimes less than the best-paid workers whom they supervise. This is bound to create envy. And the bonuses which the foremen get to make up for this situation do not endear them to the workers. Cut off from the organized work process, the workers project all their fears and misgivings on the foremen with whom they are in daily contact. Hence the abuse of the supervisory hierarchy as a depository of workers' unresolved conflicts—a situation which explains partly their acceptance and approval of the "I.M.

Rumbling" column, a column in the union paper which attacked the foremen violently. All these factors combine to make it impossible for the foremen, even with the best of intentions, to do much better than "handle" workers well—a far shot from a democratic relationship.

It is, indeed, amazing to what extent "handling people" and "running gangs" are the accepted frames of thought—and action —for workers, management, and the union. Only as we learn to think in terms of a democratic group process can these attitudes be overcome and the foreman-worker problem be solved—by the abolition of their traditional positions and roles. As Claire Bishop put it so sharply in *All Things Common*: "A 'good' boss is a menace to the development of the desire for freedom, because of the tragedy that people can be happy in slavery."[8] To be free and democratic, leadership must grow out of the gang and must be task- and not personality-oriented. That means whoever is best qualified to discharge certain functions of the group is delegated to do so. While he does it, he remains responsible to the group. If there are several equally qualified workers in a gang, they may rotate in taking charge of certain problems the gang has to solve. All problems are shared, discussed, and thought through together.

How remote workers are from such an ideal is indicated by the inability of the company to improve foreman-worker relationships by making grievance men foremen. Assuming that men in whom workers had enough confidence to elect to the Grievance Committee would also be able to get along well with the gang, management made them foremen. Yet it found that they were more inclined "to run the gang" than foremen brought in from outside. Many workers are, even today, sceptical about having "insiders" become their foremen "because they know all the tricks." This is a sad comment on workers' acquaintance with a democratic work process—and a great challenge to the union.

DEMOCRATIZATION OF THE ORGANIZED WORK PROCESS

While starting to discuss the concrete human relationship between workers and foremen, we slipped imperceptibly into problems connected with the organized work process. This is unavoidable because the nature of the man-to-man relationship between workers and foremen is determined by their positions within the industrial organization. The problem of making the work experience more democratic by giving more meaning to workers' human relatedness can, therefore, not be solved apart from a reorganization of the work process proper: human relations in industry get their peculiar quality from the nature of industrial organization. And the absence of relatedness to the *organized* work process and the very limited possibilities of participation were sharply criticized by the workers.

George put the problem clearly when he said: "For one thing, the grievance setup is wrong. All you do is to gripe about something after it happened; we should know before." To overcome these shortcomings he suggested "to incorporate the Business Improvement Committee right in the grievance setup. . . ." The problems posed by this suggestion will be examined in the following chapter. Suffice it to state here that the grievance machinery as it is now constituted does not allow a creative self-expression of the workers since its orientation is not sufficiently positive. It has a tremendous positive value because the elimination of dissatisfaction is essential, but it does not give an opportunity for the kind of participation which relates workers meaningfully to the organized work process.

How the problem of participation affects the whole work experience is strikingly illustrated in a discussion which grew out of some remarks about the passing of time:

*Joe:* For the farmer the time flies because this is where his interests are.

*Fred:* How can a man be interested in cutting the ears off the hog?

*George:* Especially if he does *not know what they do* with the ears after he has cut them off.

*Joe:* I agree with that 100 per cent.

*George:* If we knew, for example, how much they sell for, in comparison with other products, or their problems . . . these bigwigs wouldn't think to tell some of the workers what they are looking for, they sometimes monkey around for three days to find out what workers could tell them in three minutes. Management thinks they would lose face. . . .

*Joe:* [interjecting] If they wouldn't have something to *tell* us . . . job important if we know how much job netted, what it is worth, saving livers . . . it is better now; before my attitude was just making them wages. . . .

*George:* It all gets down to this . . . if they are going to have workers, there can't be the difference where management thinks that they can make all decisions without consulting us at all. . . . Things like whether save livers . . . how much beef to kill. . . .

The difficulties of identification with the organized work process because of the lack of relatedness to any of the goals in view of which work is organized comes out strikingly in this discussion. If you do not know what *they* do with the ears after *you* have cut them off and you are not consulted, you have no objective which could bestow meaning on your work and you have no mechanism through which you can make your ideas known.

The dual remedy for this situation—to find new values and to create broader channels of participation—recurs again and again in workers' ideas about a democratic work process. I quote another discussion:

*Joe:* You should participate in management.
*Fred:* How do you feel about this?
*Max:* You can't do it, too many different ideas.
*Joe:* I disagree with you . . . the foremen get cut out. . . .
*Bud:* If people were consulted, if the Business Improvement Committee was in every department, people could bring their ideas to some use . . . the only thing they are concerned with now is to save the company some money, if it costs more money, they are not interested.
*Fred:* What about participation in management?
*Max:* Capitalist idea involves the idea that somebody manages it . . . Rockefeller had money and equipment . . . you do the job.
*Bud:* What about workers elect some people on the Board of Directors, the capitalists can dictate, they can shut down the plant . . . that's why communist idea because capitalists have the whip . . . where did he get his money from?

The confusion of "somebody manages it" and having "the whip" is understandable in view of workers' lack of experience of a democratic group process—and/or a democratic organization of the work process. It is the outgrowth of an authoritarian conception of authority which is best expressed in the following statement of management: "The fellow who said 'cooperation means to do what I tell you' wasn't kidding, because you can't have more than one quarterback calling signals if you want to win ball games."[9] No doubt that "management can't grab business opportunities unless it can make quick decisions and move fast."[10] But the necessity of "authority on the top" does in no way preclude the development of a democratic authority which is based on superiority of ability, knowledge and experience, and which makes those who exercise authority somehow responsible to those who have to submit to it. Basically, "management is a delegated and assigned power and function."[11]

The best form of selecting management and relating it closer to workers is a difficult problem not to be discussed here. But nobody who believes in democratic ideas can take issue with the workers' suggestion that those who give a significant part of their life are—in principle—entitled to some kind of say-so in management, as well as those who give their money.* Unless authority and control are exercised democratically, democratic attitudes cannot arise. And control is only democratic if it is delegated by the people. Democratic control emanates from below, not from above. But it brings—through a democratic group process—the best and most qualified people to positions of authority. Without selection and renewal of an "aristocratic" leadership, control from below does not lead to a democracy centering around individual self-realization but to a "mass" society in Ortega Y Gasset's sense.[12] Yet no "democratic aristocracy" allows authority and control to be based on status; nor does it admit a leadership position involving more control than responsibility to those who delegate the control.

Workers differ as to how far that responsibility should go:

*George:* A worker has to have some feeling of ownership in tools, machines, and in the product he produces.

*Joe:* Something to say in management.

*George:* At least some way to express his ideas. . . .

* This is a somewhat modified version of a statement to which Mr. Hormel objected. I agree that the relationship of the worker to the firm may be considered as a purely contractual wage-service relationship but such a position would be clearly in disagreement with the basic value position taken in this book—and with many pronouncements and actions of Mr. Hormel himself.

But they do agree that the most important changes in the work process must be made in "the over-all organization" as Max put it, rather than in the technical sphere. Or, as Bud said: "To make it a place in which you could be more interested, give them something to say in management. . . ." Without such an opportunity to be interested, most workers quite naturally feel "that they are just working there" and they do not feel responsible towards those who are not responsible to them:

I used to get drunk, thought what's the difference. I am not getting anywhere anyhow. That's why I believe that it's a mistake not to let workers be capitalists in a small way. . . .

There are other instances to show that workers feel more participation would make them more responsible. A discussion which started by Joe saying:

. . . workers are lots of times wrong, they say it [a new idea] won't work, but it does eventually, but since they said no, they buck it. . . .

ended with George pointing out:

. . . they [management] don't act like you were responsible when it comes to decision. . . .

Nobody would deny the manifold difficulties in the way of building up a democratic work process. And more than once did workers point out, as Otto did: ". . . company has to look out for its own interest; not each of us can tell them what to do . . . we are not always right . . . they can see further than we." Under present circumstances this is certainly true in many instances. But as workers' capacities are being developed and mutual responsibilities established, the situation will or at least can change. Democracy does indeed imply a faith that the creative potentialities of people can and should be developed and that—if an attempt is being made to develop these potentialities—recourse to reason is the best method for making decisions and winning consent. A democratic work process must, therefore, be based on much more than a purely mechanical participation, like voting. It implies an emotional involvement into a group—a community—and an intellectual insight into the problems which concern the group. It is only democratic if it allows the highest development of workers' emotional, intellectual, and aesthetic potentialities and fosters the greatest possible participation in all decisions affecting their life—according to their potentialities of insight. Only if these conditions are fulfilled can consent be won democratically since democratic consent is based on full use of our rational faculties, the greatest degree of consciousness, and participation in the formulation of values to which allegiance is demanded.

As significant as the provision of adequate channels of participation is and as imperative a reorganization of the work process in order to make possible a democratic give-and-take, the values underlying the organization and the general ideas and ideals which give meaning to the participation are even more important. They are more important because they will determine the nature of the participation, its meaning—and the genuineness of its democratic character. To grasp this problem, we shall again listen to what George has to say:

> Now we produce meat to make a profit. You get your share, that's why you are more interested than the guy at Wilson's. But if you felt you contributed your share to raise the standard of living, you would have a different feeling . . .

The desire that "the company does well" certainly means progress as compared to a situation in which workers thought, as Bud formerly did, "If they go in a hole, I might as well get out as much as I can before they go into the hole." But is it enough to develop workers' potentialities?

Here is a conversation emphasizing the question mark:

> *Bud:* Our system of education is wrong . . . it makes kids expect to make their living easily, the money angle is drilled in them . . . no reason given for work.
> *Joe:* Except for becoming a foreman, a supervisor.
> *Bud:* One reason why people stress the money angle . . . the depression, many are from farms, they lost their farms . . . they want security . . . enough money to fall back upon. . . .

A COMMUNITY OF PEOPLE AND IDEAS

In raising the question as to the values which will give meaning and orientation to workers' participation in the organized work process, we have crossed a new invisible border which links the organized work process to the community of people and ideas in which industry is embedded. Just as the machine is subordinated to the goals in view of which industry is organized, so are these goals, in turn, subordinated to the values of the cultural and ultimately the human collective.

When Bud said that our system of education is at fault because "no reason given for work," he directly refers to a culture which does not have too much use for manual labor while glorifying the "white collar." How far-reaching the influence of these values is can be clearly seen from the following conversation:

*George:* Maybe the whole darn thing comes from our school system. The further they go, they give them to understand that if they work with their hands, they are a failure. . . .

*Joe:* That is certainly true.

*George:* Our whole school system gives the wrong idea. Maybe a guy doesn't want to be a big executive. He doesn't have ambitions of that kind. Maybe he just wants to raise a few tulips in his back yard. I happened to see my tulips today. It gives a different valuation of life. I think of the guys whom you see sitting in the front doors of the little cabins in the Smoky Mountains. They contribute as much to civilization as the big executives who are destroying our civilization. If they were given a free hand, they would destroy our democracy. . . .

Consciousness of a contribution to civilization—this is, indeed the outstanding factor determining the meaning of work: the values which give meaning to the life of the workers are also the values which give meaning and orientation to work. And what is wrong with work is not the repetitiveness *per se*. Rather, it is the fact that repetitive work is allowed to set the pattern for our whole life instead of being subordinated to a meaningful life. At present work takes place within a social, cultural, and ultimately human context which is meaningless: this is the ultimate "evil" of modern industrial work.

Repetitive work *in itself* is and will always be meaningless. But a certain amount of routine and repetitiveness is part of the most creative life. Even a genius cannot be creative twenty-four hours a day. What determines the creativity of our life is the degree to which creative or noncreative activities are dominant, as manifested both in the amount of time we devote to meaningful activity and the spirit in which we carry through these activities. The machine as such has not destroyed creative self-expression and self-realization for the large number of people. Quite to to contrary, it has made them possible by enabling us to do away with the drudgery of manual labor and the low standard of living of pre-industrialism. It is the *use* of the machine, the subordination of human values to the machine in the *organization* of the work process which has destroyed creative self-expression in industry because it has allowed the machine to set the pattern for our whole life.

It is quite true that work hours must be shortened in order to reduce a repetitive and in itself meaningless activity to such an extent as to make it possible for other activities and values to set the pace for workers' life. This is a necessary but not a sufficient condition for a democratization of the work process. Without a community ideal very different from the existing cultural collective, human values cannot become the center of the organized work process and work can neither be creative nor can it fulfill its role in a creative life. Instead of experiencing themselves as what Riesman so aptly called "The Lonely Crowd," workers must have some feeling of involvement in a group. As Ordway Tead said:

Modern democratic faith does not say that man is made for *the* community but that he is made for community—for attaining personal stature through communal relations and creative contributions.[13]

A system which, as Bud said, "is based on selfishness" or which, as George put it, "has nothing Christian about it, you should be your brother's keeper," is obviously remote from democratic values. "During the war we considered each other as brothers," Bud said in a different meeting. "Now we are too far to the materialistic side. We don't consider the Negroes equal. Religion and the brotherhood of man can help, we should get together and help everybody to live decently *because he is a man*." Though this sounds familiarly like one of the opening statements read when our discussions began, it was actually said six months afterwards, and its concreteness gives it a spontaneous character.

Only if these values which Bud mentioned and which find their deepest expression in what Albert Schweitzer called "Reverence for Life," imbue the community ideal—only then can workers find a creative self-expression. To be democratic, the community of people and ideas must be the outgrowth of an individual relatedness to a larger community, not the result of a blind acceptance of collective ideas and ideals. Workers must be involved emotionally, but their involvement must have an ethical content and be based on a reasoned understanding of the individual's relatedness to a larger group. And to be genuine the community of people and ideas must be the most concrete and the most universal expression of the our relationship to life. Without a human relatedness to one's fellow worker and fellow man any community ideal becomes abstract and false, and without an awareness of an involvement in mankind it becomes shallow. Ultimately, it must spring from our peculiar individual relatedness to life in all its infinite manifestations.

## *EPILOGUE*

# *Toward a Democratic Work Process*

After having listened to a summary of my manuscript dealing with workers' experience of their work and its impact on their life, George said: "What you just read to us is quite true: this sort of thing can't possibly go on for generations." Indeed, it cannot if we are to develop the potentialities of our democratic way of life rather than to submerge a creative self-expression in the compulsive emptiness of an industrial mass society.

In exploring these potentialities, I go beyond the role usually assumed by a scientist engaged in reporting on his research experiment. I am speculating on philosophical and ethical implications. A great deal more research and experience are necessary to test the concrete suggestions which I will presently set forth. This epilogue I am sure will be found controversial and I hope that it will be sufficiently provocative to lead to further inquiry into the socio-economic and human implications of the proposals made.

### THE SCARCITY AND ETERNITY OF TIME

A brief discussion of the role of time in the life of the workers will give an idea of the human problem of our industrial society and contribute to an understanding of the proposals made in this chapter. As all those familiar with the historical develop-

192

ment of the work process know, attitudes toward work, toward time—and toward life—are closely related. To understand their inter-relationship, we must point to the dual aspect of—and hence relatedness to—time. This duality may be expressed in the paradox: Time is eternal and time is scarce.

Time is as eternal as space because life is embedded in a continuum whose beginning or end is beyond our finite rational faculties. The experience of this eternal-infinite element has always been contingent upon a certain amount of contemplation, upon relatedness to something in us and something around us which allows us to partake of the "aesthetic-feeling continuum" rather than channeling our energy towards an activity yielding immediate result.[1]

The experience of this eternal element is well expressed in Chinese painting in which the unity of the picture is not attained by anything rational like perspective, but by the light and the atmosphere of a universe which permeates all being. A similar experience is expressed in the sand drawings of certain American Indian tribes. The Indians know that the wind will destroy their drawings but they do them nevertheless because it strengthens their creative attitude towards life. Time to such people does not matter, because they experience its eternity. The cathedrals of the Middle Ages bear witness to the same attitude toward time: they were built for the "glory of God," though those who started to build them never saw the completed product of their work.

Time becomes scare as soon as we cease to contemplate and begin to be active. It is for this reason that no age has experienced the scarcity of time as much as our own. When Benjamin Franklin said: "time is money," he proclaimed the advent of an era in which men became oblivious of time as eternity, and emphasized more and more the scarcity of time. This change in the attitude toward time was accompanied by a fundamental change in the attitude toward work. Success, the immediate result of work, became the criterion for evaluation, and man became engaged in a feverish activity. At the beginning, this activity had still a religious, or at least a transcendental, foundation: it was a justification in the eyes of God; it was proof of ultimate salvation. When the transcendental element disappeared slowly under the blows of the rising industrial system, only the striving for success remained. The emphasis on the immediate result minimized contemplation and channeled human energy toward activity, toward work.

There are few workers, indeed, who enjoy "lying on the grass and looking at the clouds in the sky." The simple enjoyment of life, without doing something, without "having fun," is beyond the reach of most workers. It is significant that the question which I was most often asked in regard to my European experience was: "How is it possible that these people [particularly in France] are happy? They are poor and yet they sing—nobody sings around here." Many a G.I. was bewildered about the "contemplative" satisfaction with the simple things in life which the workers observed while being overseas.

They were bewildered because they have lost the experience of time as a—positive—eternal element. When the development of "modern" industrial organization deprived work of its meaning, time again became eternity. But this eternity is not experienced as a deep relatedness to life and the universe. It is merely experienced as monotony. Time drags—one of the deepest fears of the workers. Hence, "the need to be occupied" as a carry-over of a typical work, and general cultural, attitude. Indeed, the word "occupy" comes in its intransitive, passive form closest to the Webster definition of something "that takes up space or time." In so far as the eternity of time can only be experienced as boredom, workers run away from it. As soon as they are on the run, time begins again to fly by—since the experience of time and space is relative. It seems, therefore, that workers are satisfied only if they are "occupied," or "busy." This would be true if their efforts "to make time go by"—the prime motive underlying the game of work—were only to alleviate the monotony of work and the fear of dragging time. Actually, they also create new fears, deep anxieties emerging from the emptiness, the meaninglessness, of the very activity that makes time fly by: it creates the fear of life flying by without having really lived it. To live life means to face it, to experience its eternal element, whereas the tendencies created by the organization of the work force workers to run away from it. The mood which such an experience of life creates is well expressed in a song to which I listened many a time when I tuned in the radio after work: "Enjoy yourself, enjoy yourself, it's later than you think."

The tendencies created by the organization of the work process have reached their climax: life is reduced to an automatic compulsive performance—a race with time and from time. Even "time off" the job becomes filled with "pastime" activities, rather than with any activity which has an inner meaning. "The eternity of time" no longer elevates. It oppresses. I once told a worker in an uptown bar who was playing a slot-machine: "Come along. What's the use of losing your money?" He answered: "It passes the time."

The vicious circle is complete. The compelling desire to be "away from it all" and the necessity to engage in new activities in order to get away from it, leads to a race whose whole object is never to meet time, never to meet life!

## WORK IN AN INDUSTRIAL CULTURE

The forces engendered by the organization of the work process could not have as great an impact if they were not reinforced by the values of a whole culture. Only a culture oriented toward activity could allow work and busy-ness, rather than inward development and contemplation, to play a central role in the life of most people. And only in a culture which gives a premium to rational economic activities could work attitudes permeate all spheres of life. Ours is, indeed, an industrial society in which cultural attitudes merge imperceptibly with work attitudes, each reinforcing the other. This is particularly true of the attitudes toward time and life. The race from and with time has as its counterpart a lack of consciousness of values which give meaning to life. And the absence of any ideal transcending the desire to get ahead contributes greatly, in turn, to the absence of any ethical conception of work.

The full impact of these forces will become manifest in the forthcoming study on "Apathy and the Democratic Process." It leads to a general lack of relatedness and a feeling of being lost. Like "a little duck in a big pond," workers feel exposed to forces which seem beyond their control. "Being nothing in the mass," as another worker put it, is not only a feeling which brings little personal happiness. It also constitutes a danger for democracy. If these statements came from workers who were untypical representatives of the values of their culture and society, we could disregard them. But, quite to the contrary, they come from people who are the most pronounced exponents of industrialism: they have made competition, ambition, and the desire to get ahead their central values.

Granted that any sweeping generalizations about the impact on an individual worker of these forces originating in the presently existing organization of the work process and reinforced by cultural trends, are bound to be misleading. Nevertheless, it remains true that we have given an accurate description of the *tendencies created by the relatedness to work.* These tendencies are diametrically opposed to those forces which make for a productive orientation toward work and toward life. Asked what it means to be a producer, one worker expressed the potential meaning of work in a simple and beautiful language: "You further life, you make it possible for people to live." Is it accidental or is it of symbolic significance that this was said by a worker to whom a personal fate has denied development of her creative potentialities? It is undoubtedly symbolic of the small degree to which the existing system of organizing work encourages the development of workers' creative potentialities.

Individual destiny does allow some workers to escape the social-collective forces emanating from the present organization of the work process. The "Christian Gentleman" is a good example of a man who is deeply rooted in the "human collective" and who derives his strength from the creative experience of something greater than himself: a religious experience of life allows him to withstand the social-cultural collective.

But the forces emanating from the organization of work—and reinforced by cultural trends—make it extremely difficult for the majority of the workers to experience life creatively. To expect the average individual to transcend his society and culture is to ask the impossible: the average will always be more strongly shaped by the social and cultural collective than he will be by the creative possibilities of the human collective.

The worker who succumbed to a "Foe Unseen" has indeed sacrificed his creativity at the altars of industrialism. And the "Would-Be-Salesman" is torn by conflicts created by his culture, his society, and a personality which is not strong enough to derive nourishment from the deeper sources of his real self.

The need for a reorganization of the work process becomes, therefore, vital. Whether the ideal of a creative self-expression growing out of a meaningful relatedness to life—which is implicit in our preceding discussion—can ever be fully realized is a moot question. What matters is whether we move towards the ideal or whether we move away from it. And to be able to orient our actions towards the eventual achievement of what now seems a remote ideal, we must have a concrete starting point and a method of dealing with the problems which are bound to come up as our efforts get under way.

A MEANINGFUL LIFE

These efforts should, from the beginning, be oriented towards two objectives: (1) to integrate work into an over-all life pattern which is meaningful, and (2) to give to human values a central place in the *organization* of the work process while fully exploiting the potentialities of modern technique. "Industry and society," to use W. F. Whyte's expression, must be conceived as a unit. A similar idea is expressed by O. Tead when he says: "Industry, integral as it is to well-being in life, can no longer remain divorced from the aims of life itself."[2]

The first objective—which amounts to the creation of a new community of people and ideas relating workers meaningfully to time and life—is so complex and so wide in scope that we must limit ourselves to record some suggestions of workers. Their repeated emphasis on hobbies points the way to a concrete starting point: "If a fellow can experience something about a hobby, he is interested, keyed up." Bud wants the company "to promote hobbies, diversion." George asked for an educational program organized by the union but not "the kind of stuff where they just try to put something over."

The real significance of such programs and activities becomes clearer as we follow the thought of a worker who feels more is necessary than a hobby. He said, "Everybody should have an avocation." Since "a job is a job" rather than a vocation or a "calling" in the Puritan sense, it makes sense to search for the vocational element in activities outside the factory gates. A hobby is more likely to be of peripheral significance, whereas a vocation implies a more central orientation. And as its meaning is related to a wider community of people and ideas, it can become an important focal point for an integration of the avocation and work into a greater unity of being which bestows meaning on both. Unless such an orientation occurs, the avocation may at best counterbalance the evil effects of a meaningless work process.

These few remarks must suffice to point to the staggering task ahead. It is a task which can only be solved by a coordinated effort of various community groups and organizations.

## HUMANIZATION OF WORK

The second objective, the reorganization of the work process proper, can and must be examined more adequately. It is again the suggestion of a worker—of George—which tells us what the first step should be: to incorporate the Business Improvement Committee into the grievance machinery. In this concrete form, George's suggestion is only applicable to the Austin situation since few committees comparable to the Business Improvement Committee exist in American industry. However, stripped of its technical aspects, George's suggestion is of the most general significance: it is a proposal which would transform the grievance machinery into a genuine instrument for self-administration of the work process and the supervisory function would become an outgrowth of a democratic group process in which workers delegate the function of supervision.

At present, the social-psychological function of the grievance machinery is to make workers sufficiently satisfied to accept a basically undemocratic organization of the work process. George's suggestion would make it the most important instrument through which workers would eventually find a positive self-expression.

As we examine the proposal in terms of the power structure

of industrial organization, its crucial significance and the generality of the problems it raises will become obvious.

The diagram on p. 200 illustrates in broad outlines the first stage of a democratization of the work process. The basic change consists in the merging of the supervisory hierarchy with the grievance machinery and the resulting emergence of a new kind of work-committee structure.

Each gang forms a group with a leader or group steward: the rank-and-file work committee. The group stewards represent the group in the departmental committees which have a departmental steward at their head. The departmental stewards, in turn, function as a group with a divisional chairman as a group leader. These divisional committees are directly related to the "Central Work Committee" which consists of the Seniority Board —regulating specific work assignments—and the "Clearing Committee." The latter's primary function is to assimilate, digest, and pass to management and to the union officers whatever ideas and suggestions emerge from the rank and file of the workers as well as to communicate to the workers management's and union officials' problems and ideas.

How democratic such a work process is depends upon the quality of the group process on each committee level. A mere change in structure is not sufficient: administration of the work process through workers' committees is a necessary but not a sufficient condition for a democratization of work. In addition there is a need for basic changes in attitudes among the workers, a new conception of a democratic group process—particularly of the leadership function—and a new ethics of interpersonal relationships.

The Central Work Committee may be a joint union-management body, or management may be connected with the new machinery at a higher level, such as the Personnel Director-Bargaining Committee. There is, however, no reason to exclude management representatives from participating in the same way in which they now participate—to give a concrete illustration—in the procedures of the Seniority Board at the Hormel company. There management never interferes as long as somebody who is competent is assigned to do the work; *who* is being assigned is

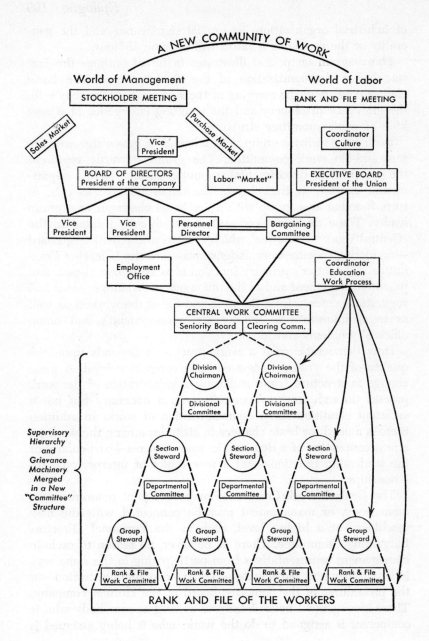

A NEW COMMUNITY OF WORK

World of Management

World of Labor

STOCKHOLDER MEETING

RANK AND FILE MEETING

Sales Market

Purchase Market

Vice President

Coordinator Culture

BOARD OF DIRECTORS
President of the Company

Labor "Market"

EXECUTIVE BOARD
President of the Union

Vice President

Vice President

Personnel Director

Bargaining Committee

Employment Office

Coordinator Education Work Process

CENTRAL WORK COMMITTEE

Seniority Board | Clearing Comm.

Division Chairman

Division Chairman

Divisional Committee

Divisional Committee

*Supervisory Hierarchy and Grievance Machinery Merged in a New "Committee" Structure*

Section Steward

Section Steward

Section Steward

Departmental Committee

Departmental Committee

Departmental Committee

Group Steward

Group Steward

Group Steward

Group Steward

Rank & File Work Committee

Rank & File Work Committee

Rank & File Work Committee

Rank & File Work Committee

RANK AND FILE OF THE WORKERS

considered to be a union problem. The extension of this principle to all the human aspects of the organized work process indicates the role of management on the Central Work Committees: it acts as a watchdog—with veto power as long as this is considered necessary—making sure that the terms of the agreement are being kept and that the agreed-upon flow of products is forthcoming. The basic features of such an agreement between the union and management are: management pays so much for a unit of work, can expect so many units of a certain quality during a designated period of time, and has the right to introduce any technological improvement provided earning opportunities are maintained.

The problems thus raised cannot be explored here. Suffice it to emphasize the central shift in the management-union relationship. The new machinery administering the work process confronts the managerial hierarchy without the cushion of the supervisory hierarchy which previously linked management and the workers. Instead of acting as a counterweight to the supervisory structure of the company, the internal organization of the union—though fundamentally changed in its nature—is now face to face with management. As the diagram on p. 200 indicated, and as should be emphasized, the managerial hierarchy itself and management's functions in regard to the conduct of the business, particularly the sales and other markets, are not affected by the proposed first step in the democratization of the work process. The union, however, takes on immediately the important new function of administering the work process through the new committee structure. Hence the need for new offices arise. One, called here "Coordinator of Education—work process," has as its main task to help in the formation of a genuine democratic group process within the various committees and to evoke the greatest possible development of initiative and participation in all the committees. Another function performed by the "Coordinator— cultural activities" relates work activities to off-work interests and helps to create a new community of work by developing the whole personality of the worker and integrating "work" and "life" in a way fostering the greatest self-expression and self-realization.

PROBLEMS TO BE MET

The closeness of top management and union brought about by these modifications would raise serious problems. Management may be afraid of an eventual encroachment on managerial "prerogatives" as regards the conduct of the business. The union, on the other hand, is likely to be afraid of too close a connection with the company, and eventual loss of its identity. These are legitimate fears which have to be reckoned with. They are, furthermore, deep-seated fears because they are a heritage of the dualism inherent in the traditional organization of the work process.

The traditional differences in regard to control and authority are absolute: those who organized the corporation had the power to express their own values, while workers were mere means in the organized work process. Yet the differences in regard to freedom and security were of a more complex nature. A simple division into two groups, one having both security and freedom and the other having neither ignores a basic psychological fact, namely that freedom and security for one group which implies lack of freedom and security for another, creates anxiety and fears in the "top" group. The existence of such—usually unconscious—anxiety is clearly shown by the insistence on managerial prerogatives which, psychologically speaking, is a rationalization of insecurity. Men who feel secure in a free society do not need such exclusive group prerogatives. Nor do men who feel secure have to keep such a "distance" from groups to whom they are, functionally speaking, very close.

Since the balance of power is with management, managerial fears and insecurity are particularly important. They find their strongest expression in the spectre of "workers—or union 'bosses' —taking over and running the show," a spectre which creates attitudes similar to those expressed in the famous query: "Would you like your daughter to marry a Negro?" It is a spectre quite irrelevant for the merits of the first step of the reorganization under discussion. But it is significant precisely because of its seeming irrelevancy: it shows that little progress towards a democratic reorganization of industry is possible as long as the widening of the sphere of workers' self-expression raises immediately fears as to the ultimate control of the work process.

## WAYS OF SOLVING THESE PROBLEMS

There is no way of alleviating these fears within the confines of the traditional power struggle. If the union has enough force to shift the balance of power to its side, modifications of the work process such as George's proposal which give workers greater self-expression could be instituted. But their success is more than doubtful as long as management remains hostile to the idea. And unless the change in power position does more than change power positions—unless it transcends the power struggle while fully recognizing its existence—it is not a really democratic change: if the union "runs the show" there is not the slightest guarantee of a greater self-expression of the workers than if the company "runs the show." Only a truly democratic conception of an organized work process and truly democratic methods of change will assure progress towards the ideal outlined in the preceding chapter.

The exploration of truly democratic methods of change would lead us beyond the subject-matter of this book. Suffice it to state their essence: To fight *for* something *without* hatred; more than that, *with* respect for those who obstruct the realization of one's goal. That means: To fight for an organization of society which gives to *everybody* the greatest chance for self-expression and self-realization.

There is an important managerial function to be performed in industry and those best qualified should administer it—while being responsible to those who delegate authority to them. Only such a conception of the goal allows democratic methods to come into operation at all—a striking illustration of the intimate interdependency of means and ends.

The absence of any truly democratic conception of the work process among labor is, therefore, as serious—if not a more serious—obstacle to the reorganization of the work process as is the fear of management to give up traditional power positions. As long as the concept of a democratic group, of joy and self-expression in work, are as conspicuous by their absence as they now are, there is little chance of a democratic reorganization of industry even if management would hand over its power position to the union on a silver platter.

This, however, is a hypothetical assumption. More realistic is a situation in which unions will ask for more and more participation and management will be as certainly forced to give in as it has been forced to accede to major wage demands, pension plans, etc. Yet there is one important difference in the situation: wage demands may be won on the picket line; real self-expression and self-realization of the workers in the work process require more than that: it presupposes a give and take and a new conception of industrial organization which will require a peculiar kind of cooperation, a cooperation to transform the corporate form of industrial organization into cooperative enterprises. Only a cooperatively organized work process can be a democratic one and only a new kind of labor-management cooperation can avoid the pitfalls of the traditional pattern which stifles individual growth and real participation and leaves workers subject to an organization of work which creates compulsive tendencies and destroys a meaningful relatedness to life.

BLUEPRINT OR EXPERIMENTATION?

The implications of this new type of "cooperation" are being examined in a forthcoming study on social action and the democratic process. A concrete illustration of the general possibilities of change rather than of the methods to bring it about must suffice here. When the union forced the company to accept seniority, the company felt, as a top-management official told me, "that it would be impossible to 'run the plant' in this manner." Less than twenty years afterwards, Mr. Hormel referred to the seniority setup as an example showing how workers can participate in the work process to such an extent that "an actual voice in management can come later, by natural development, without even being considered as a right which has been conceded."[3] Management did undoubtedly give up a managerial "prerogative" when the union demanded seniority. But today it does not feel that this is a "right which has been conceded" since management is happy to be able to devote its energy to its market functions rather than to the administration of the work process. Once George's proposal has been realized and the supervisory hierarchy has been replaced by a democratic group process, management will have the same feelings about the new setup as it now has about the seniority board.

To bring about these changes democratically they must be part of a gradual process, new ideas may even be introduced in certain departments only, and the area as well as the nature of participation may expand slowly. Limitations to suggestions is a legitimate safeguard until a genuinely democratic group process is developed. What is needed is *experimentation* with a reorganization of the work process rather than an elaborate blueprint of a "brave new world." The diagram on p. 200 should, therefore, be considered as a basis for thought—and action, rather than as a specific plan.

There are several reasons why such a blueprint is neither possible nor desirable. First of all, it has not been the tradition of the American social scene to follow schemes which, by the very nature of their comprehensiveness, must be rather abstract. American pragmatism has, as all approaches, certain disadvantages but it does have the advantage of leaving the door open for an experimental approach which keeps in close contact with the problems arising from day to day. And the technical details of a democratic organization of industry must be explored by experience rather than be determined by preconception. It is, for example, an open question to what extent procedures common in the political arena of parliamentarianism would be most suited to achieve workers' participation in the work process and self-expression in it. The proper methods and corresponding institutions must be developed out of a new conception of a *democratic group process*. We do know in general terms that this process is superior to what we now have in industry—in regard to technical efficiency as well as in regard to the realization of human values. But we do not know enough about the problems which will arise to make any detailed statement as to the machinery which must be built up to give it the best chance. George's proposal—and the diagram on p. 200—are concrete and clear-cut as a first step but leave many questions unanswered. And once we have accomplished the integration of the grievance machinery and the foremen setup—through absorption of the Business Improvement Committee or, more general, through making the grievance machinery an instrument for self-expression of the workers—and a real self-administration of the work process is a reality, problems even more difficult to answer now will arise. To elect management, for example, may be the worst method to get efficient management—and any kind of industrial organization needs the very best in managerial ability it can develop.

A COOPERATIVE COMMONWEALTH OF PEOPLE

To forgo a blueprint does not mean to work in the dark, without a goal. There is a world's difference between the experimentation suggested here and the approach of the new species of human relations experts who want to give workers a "sense of participation" and "a sense of belonging." Under the guise of making industry "more democratic" they manipulate workers in order to make them more "corporation"-oriented. They do not come to grips with the problem of having workers really participate, and really belong because they do not deal with the problems of values, power, and their expression in the organization of industry. Let it, therefore, be said that no group skill, no ingenuity and imagination can create genuinely democratic attitudes within a social framework which gives to those who invest their money in industry a say-so about it and denies even a nominal voice to those who "invest" a significant part of their life.* And let it also be said that alienation from work, time, and life and hence ultimately self-alienation can not possibly be cured within the corporate structure of industry.

Yet the new cooperative system which must eventually replace the present organization of industry must be developed democratically, which means *with* and *out of* the workers. It can neither be imposed nor can it be done *for* the workers—by either management or the union. Since, however, industrial organization is essentially a group or collective organization, the union—the formal instrument of the work group—will play a strategic role in any genuinely democratic industrial organization. Unions

* See Footnote on p. 186.

must, therefore, establish a minimum of democracy within their own organization before they can legitimately ask management to begin the reorganization of the work process by expanding the functions of the grievance machinery. But—and this is an important but—to ask unions to develop a genuinely democratic consciousness among the workers as long as the union is cut off from the organized work process as much as it now is, is an unfair request because it is an impossible one. Workers cannot develop a consciousness of democracy without an experience of it. The experimental group work discussed in the preceding chapter has shown the possibilities of developing a democratic consciousness out of and with the workers. But it has also shown the limitations: to be effective and lasting, this must be done in connection with actual participation of workers in the daily decisions to be made in their working life. The proposed transformation of the grievance machinery into a positive instrument for workers' self-expression is, therefore, essential.

But it should not obscure a wider problem as to the general objectives and values of the unions. Labor has entered a new historical era. Having gained a great deal of power, it has not yet decided what to do with its power. Consume it in a sheer struggle for power? Waste it by adopting traditional business ideology? Or use it constructively for a democratic reorganization of industry?

There is no room in the American social scene for a labor ideology which separates workers from other social groups. But there is a desperate need for a "labor" ideology which develops the slumbering democratic consciousness of the workers and relates them to a larger community of people and ideas. The core of the American tradition—the idea of freedom, of the dignity of the individual, of democracy—must be the nucleus out of which a cooperative commonwealth of people is developed. Granted that it is "radical" to advocate a transformation of the corporate structure of industry into a cooperative organization. It is radical because it goes to the *roots* of the American tradition and is dedicated to its fullest realization.

# Earning Opportunities and Other Benefits of the Hormel Worker

## WAGES

The Working Agreement contains the basic wage stipulations. It states: "Each employee will be employed on an annual basis and shall receive the regular weekly rate of pay provided for him in a work schedule established for his department. . . . in no case shall any such employee be employed for more than 2000 hours within the applicable 52-week period . . ." (Article III, Section 2). The regular weekly rate is equal to the scale rate—an area rate established by collective bargaining—multiplied by the number of hours guaranteed. In order to give the company some leeway in the administration of the guarantee, the number of hours guaranteed amounts to 38 or 36, depending upon the department, rather than 40 hours per week. If the scale rate for Joe Doe is $1.50 per hour and his department has a 38-hour guarantee, he has a minimum weekly pay of $1.50×38=$57.00.

In addition to his minimum weekly guarantee, Joe Doe will get his incentive earnings. He is a member of a group which has a contract with the company—called the work schedule—stipulating the amount of work to be done during each hour in order to earn the $1.50 per hour. If the group produces less, it will get into trouble for "bad workmanship." If it produces more, it is paid in direct proportion to the increase in group production. Let us assume that Joe is a hamboner and that the group standard requires boning of an average of 50 hams per hour per man. Joe Doe may do a little bit more than his share during that week or he may have not felt too well and have done somewhat less. In either case, his pay is determined by the total output of the group divided by the number of workers in the group, e.g., by the group average. If Joe Doe is a perfectly average worker and he bones 75 hams per *clock*-hour, he has to his credit 1 and ½ *production* hours and his weekly earnings—provided he works at the same rate all week—will increase correspondingly. This is why Joe, when asked, "How much production did you make this week?" will answer: "I made 19 hours." He means to say that he got credit for "an additional" 19 production hours besides his regularly scheduled 38 hours of work. His weekly check would be equivalent to 57 instead of the 38 hours which he actually worked. It is computed as follows:

1. guarantee of 38 hours: scale rate $1.50
   (minimum guarantee)                              $57.00
2. incentive earnings: 19 hours @ $1.50             28.50
                                                    ———————
                                                    $85.50

Since the hours actually worked every week differ, the weekly earnings over and above the minimum will vary. Some weeks Joe will work only 25 hours and his opportunity "to make production" will be much smaller than during the long winter days when he may work 50 hours per week. If the end of the company year approaches and Joe Doe "put in" his 2000 hours, he will be sent home in order to avoid overtime penalty payments. If, at the end of the year, he did not quite put in his 2000 hours he is that much "better off"—at least in terms of leisure time.

Yet all kinds of things affecting his pay may happen to Joe during the year. He may be transferred to another job or he may take the initiative and transfer himself. In both cases seniority rules will determine whether he must leave a gang in case of gang reductions or whether he has "enough rights" to bid for a job in case of an opening in a gang. The mechanism through which he puts in his bid is called the "posting in" system: Job openings are posted at a bulletin board. If a worker feels he has enough seniority to have a chance to get the job, he writes his name on the bulletin announcing a particular job opening. He thus tries to "post in." Among all the workers who list their names, the one with the highest seniority will get the job. According to a new system adopted in 1952, jobs are posted on a plant-wide basis.

There are still other things which may happen to him. A new machine may be introduced or changes in the work schedule—his contract with the company—may become desirable or necessary. The Working Agreement stipulates that "(1) no revised schedule lessening the possibility of rate of gain within a department shall be put into effect on less than 52 weeks' notice," and (2) that "whatever changes are made, the gain opportunity of an individual worker cannot be lessened as long as this worker remains on his job." This rule assures Joe the same production gains as long as he and his gang work equally hard—and he stays in his department.

If there is anything Joe Doe does not like about whatever changes may occur, he can go to his shop steward and have him write a grievance. Just about everything that may happen in connection with his job may become the object of a grievance and be processed through the regular grievance machinery, following the clearly laid-out procedure. But if Joe does not like the speed of his work—which is determined by the whole gang—he must bring up the matter at his departmental union meeting. The company has nothing to do with such matters.

JOINT EARNINGS

At the end of the company year, just before Thanksgiving, Joe will receive a certain fraction of his earnings in the form of a "joint earnings" check. Though the Working Agreement acknowledges the existence of the Joint Earnings Plan—which has been in operation since 1938—and "contemplates [its] continuance and recognizes the necessity of renegotiating many of the provisions of the Agreement in case the joint earnings plan is abandoned or materially modified in form," it states explicitly that the disposal of the joint earnings is not part of the collective agreement but under the exclusive control of the board of directors of the company (Article II).

The plan treats "for accounting purposes, the business . . . as a joint enterprise of the stockholders as one group and the employees as the other" (The Hormel Annual Wage, Wage Incentive and Joint Earnings Plan). The "Joint Earnings Amount" is computed as follows:

. . . from the gross income of the company all expenses are paid, including wages and salaries of non-participating employees, but not including wages and salaries of Joint Earning Employees. Thus, all sales and miscellaneous income are credits to, and expenses are deduction from what we call the Joint Earnings Account.

Let us assume the company had a sales and miscellaneous income of $350 million and all expenses other than wages and salaries of participating employees amounted to $322.50 million. The Joint Earnings Amount would then be equivalent to $27.5 million. The division of this sum between the stockholders and employees is computed on the basis of a sliding scale which gives the workers a *relatively* greater share during bad years and the stockholders a relatively better deal during good years:

> . . . the stockholder, having the mechanism of the corporation, is organized to build reserves in a way which the employee cannot do. Thus, partly because such reserves are a protection for the employee, and partly because the stockholder is entitled to a greater share of the earnings as he provides the facilities and the management which afford the employee an increased earnings opportunity, the stockholder's *rate* of participation increases as the joint earnings amount increases with relation to the basic joint earnings pay roll.

The Joint Earnings Pay Roll—or the total pay roll of the participating workers—may have amounted to $25.00 million. Joe Doe's share in the total earnings would then amount to $50.00 computed on the basis of the following scale:

| (1) Joint Earnings Amount up to 100% | (2) Employee's | (3) | (4) Stockholder's | (5) |
|---|---|---|---|---|
| | Share | Amount | Share | Amount |
| 101 | 99.10 | 100.09 | 0.90 | .91 |
| 102 | 98.25 | 100.22 | 1.75 | 1.78 |
| 103 | 97.37 | 100.29 | 2.63 | 2.71 |
| 104 | 96.50 | 100.36 | 3.50 | 3.64 |
| 105 | 95.70 | 100.49 | 4.30 | 4.51 |
| 110 | 91.80 | 100.98 | 8.20 | 9.02 |
| 115 | 88.25 | 101.49 | 11.75 | 13.51 |
| 120 | 86.50 | 103.80 | 13.50 | 16.20 |
| 125 | 85.00 | 106.25 | 15.00 | 18.75 |
| 130 | 83.50 | 108.55 | 16.50 | 21.45 |

The Joint Earnings Amount in this schedule is expressed in percentages of the Joint Earnings Pay Rolls. A rate of 100 per cent means that all earnings of the company have been paid out during the year to the workers in the form of wages and that nothing is left either for the workers or for the stockholders. If the amount earned is greater than the pay roll, the percentages in Column 1 increase according to the relative surplus of earnings over the pay roll. As the surplus increases, the employees get a *relatively* smaller share, as indicated in Column 2, which shows the percentage of the Joint Earnings Amount allocated to employees; yet the absolute amount increases: its increase "as percentage of the Joint Earnings Pay Roll" is indicated in Column 3. Columns 4 and 5 give the respective figures for the stockholders.

To illustrate: The Joint Earnings Amount was $27.5 million and the company books show a Joint Earnings Pay Roll amounting to $25 million. Of the Joint Earnings Amount $2.5 million are thus left at the end of the year after deduction of earnings paid out in wages. As $2.5 million amount to 10 per cent of the pay roll, the Joint Earning Amount in percentage of the Joint Earnings Pay Roll is, therefore, equal to 110 per cent. In this case the workers' share is almost 1 per cent (to be exact, .98) of the pay roll, or $250,000.00. Of this amount Joe Doe gets a fraction determined by his weekly *guaranteed* pay check. If Joe Doe is an average worker all through, his share would be equal to the total employee's share divided by the number of workers. A total share of $250,000.00 divided by 5000 workers would give him a share of $50.00, an amount just about equal to one weekly base pay check.

If Joe Doe has been with the company since 1939, he would have actually received since that time the number of weekly pay checks indicated in Column 2 as his Joint Earnings checks, while all Joe Does together received the amounts shown in Column 3:

| (1) | (2) | (3) |
|---|---|---|
| Year | Joint Earnings in terms of the number of weekly pay checks | Amount of Joint Earnings paid to employees |
| 1939 | 1.529 | $ 147,186.05 |
| 1940 | 1.719 | 166,846.56 |
| 1941 | 1.133 | 120,850.03 |
| 1942 | 4.315 | 611,210.72 |
| 1943 | 7.013 | 1,041,791.52 |
| 1944 | 8.017 | 1,195,140.29 |
| 1945 | 2.4 | 346,670.66 |
| 1946 | 5.153 | 1,063,093.17 |
| 1947 | 7.131 | 1,831,419.15 |
| 1948 | 7.452 | 2,401,586.00 |
| 1949 | 1.028 | 367,364.00 |
| 1950 | 2.019 | 839,364.00 |
| 1951 | 2.241 | 1,017,699.00 |

PROFIT-SHARING TRUST

This addition to his yearly income does not, however, exhaust the benefits Joe derives from working for the Hormel company. He also takes part in the Hormel Employees' Profit-Sharing Trust. This trust was approved by the Board of Directors of Geo. A. Hormel & Co. in 1944. It has never been mentioned in any of the amendments to the Working Agreement.

. . . the purpose of the trust is to provide some money which may be added to the individual's own savings, insurance and Social Security benefits, upon retirement or disability. Participation in the plan is based on length of service. An employee must have completed four full years of continuous service before he begins to share in the trust . . .

As one's years of service increase, his rate of participation in the trust increases. The rate of increase grows very slowly during the first five years of participation and very rapidly as he approaches 26 years of service, which entitles him to the maximum annual participation under the plan.

The trust establishes a fund to which only the company, but not the workers, contribute. Company contributions may come (1) from stockholder's share of the Joint Earnings, or (2) from savings of income and excess profit payments.

The technicalities of computing the company's yearly contributions are rather complicated. Suffice it, therefore, to state that in a "normal" year the company contributes about $4.50 for a worker with four years of service and $200.00 for a worker with twenty-six years of service. In a very good year, its contributions are much higher. In 1944, for example, the company contributed $84.15 for a worker with four years' seniority and $3,600.00 for a worker with twenty-six years' seniority. The limits to which any one worker can accumulate credits in the trust "amounts to $20,000.00, or to the equivalent of six years' base pay, whichever is smaller." If this limit is reached, the worker "gets no further apportionment until 30% of the participating employees have accumulated apportionments equal to three years' base pay." The worker or his family may get the money accumulated for them in the trust (1) upon death, (2) upon leaving the employ of the company, or (3) upon retirement at 65 years of age.

If, in December, 1950, Joe Doe had been with the company for four years, he would have had $275.00 in his trust account. But if he had been there for over twenty-five years, he would have been one of the one hundred-odd workers who had—after six years of operation of the trust fund—more than $10,000.00 to their credit!

# Research Methods

This book is a first report on an action-research project which was started in Austin, Minn., in the summer of 1948. So far there have been three distinct periods of field work: summer of 1948, summer of 1949, and all of 1950. An extensive memorandum on the field experience is available to those interested. Part of the memorandum has been published in the *Journal of Social Issues*, Spring, 1953, under the title "Getting individuals to give information to the outsider." Other aspects have been examined in *Action Research and Industrial Relations*, Proceedings of the Second Annual Meeting, Industrial Relations Research Association. The methodological implications of action research have been examined in a paper entitled *Action Research—a scientific approach?* (prepared for the spring 1953 meeting of the Pacific Sociological Society, Stockton, California). The following remarks are, therefore, limited to a few basic points which are essential for an understanding of the material presented in this study. An adequate evaluation of the data, however, would necessitate an examination of material not included here.

THE NATURE OF THE OBJECT OF INVESTIGATION

Factory life was examined as an integral part of a larger unit—as a microcosm which is part of a macrocosmic social structure and the psychic forces which it expresses. The basic concepts corresponding to such an approach are the personality and the social structure.

Society is understood as a field which is structured according to purposeful goal-oriented human activities. The field consists of a network of relationships whose configuration depends upon the distribution of power, the manner in which control is delegated, and the kind of values implemented by the system of control. Personality can best be understood as a clearly structured pattern of "inner and outer" relationships resulting from activation of certain libidinal forces within us. Personality and social structure are "continuously interacting. Each influences the other selectively towards change."[1]

The interrelationship between personality and social structure is well illustrated by the fact that people's status, the roles they play, the control they exercise, and the authority to which they have to submit are determined by their relatedness to the social structure. Moreover, "the integrity and continuity of the system"[2] can only be maintained if those who are part of the organization are in general agreement with its purpose—a consent which is being won by (1) selection of certain attitudes in people (channeling of libidinal forces into certain directions), and (2) by selection of people with certain attitudes. This dual selective process is one of the most important manifestations of the social organization.

THE RELATIONSHIP OF THE SCIENTIST TO HIS OBJECT OF INVESTIGATION

The scientist is a participant observer who is part of the personality-social-structure field which he investigates. Whether he tries to change the relationships existing in this field or not, he cannot help but influence them by being involved in it and therefore needs the greatest possible degree of consciousness of himself and the role he plays in the field.

A project whose purpose is to contribute to a fuller realization of democratic values must be conducted in agreement with the ethics of a democratic way of life. Accordingly, a concerted effort has been made to meet people as human beings, not as guinea pigs, and to involve them in the research by sharing as much as possible with them. During the year and a half which I spent in Austin I was practically every day in the plant, often working there. I met regularly with groups of workers and had close contact with a considerable number. The research was, furthermore, designed in such a way as to allow people the greatest degree of participation.

RESEARCH DESIGN

The project has a diagnostic and a therapeutic phase. The former analyzes the existing situation, the latter explores possibilities of change and tests hypotheses through a change experiment. The data presented in this book are predominantly from the diagnostic phase; they only touch the therapeutic phase in the group discussions.

Planned as a comparative study, the research has so far been limited to one factory. An "ex-post experimental design" in Chapin's sense[3] has been approximated in this research.

The nature of this project required a combination of "deep insights" into the personality structure and an "extensive insight" into social-cultural forces. It also necessitated a give-and-take experience in the development of a democratic consciousness. Depth-interviews, group work, and research tests have therefore been used.

The data presented in this book are primarily based on interviews with workers—though foremen, supervisors, management representatives, and union officials have also been interviewed.

SAMPLING

In selecting workers for the original interviews, a dual purpose was pursued: (1) to gain an insight into attitudes most frequently occurring in the microcosm under investigation, and (2) to have a wide cross-section of attitudes significant for a democratization of the work process—even if numerically of little importance.

The *size of the sample* was determined by trial and error. First a 1 per cent sample was chosen for intensive four- to eight-hour interviews. The adequacy of this sample was tested (1) by a near-random sample of workers met in the cafeteria, and (2) by an experimental 3 per cent sample which was discontinued after some time because (a) it did not show any new attitudes changing the over-all picture, and (b) because of a shortage of research funds.

*Stratification* of the sample was based on those factors primarily responsible for systematic differences in attitudes: (1) the kind of work done, (2) sex, (3) age, (4) certain socio-economic characteristics (e.g., farmers who work in the plant).

*Selection procedures* were as follows: the first worker who—according to the predetermined stratification—fitted the sample was chosen through personal contact while working in the plant. A more detailed description of this approach can be found in the paper on "Getting individuals to give information to the outsider," referred to above.

The choice of particular workers within the systematically predetermined groups approximates a random choice since the circumstances under which I worked in different departments were so varied that the meeting of the first worker was pretty much a random phenomenon. But a *bias* was introduced by about 20 per cent of the workers declining the invitation to cooperate on the project. This bias was accounted for in the analysis.

RESEARCH TECHNIQUES

*Participant observation* was primarily an expression of the researcher's willingness to share his life with others. The problem which the researcher meets is to maintain an "inner distance" which allows him to see "the field" clearly while establishing a genuine mutual human involvement.

The *interview schedule* is a standardized schedule built up in such a manner as to yield checks on the consistency of certain responses. All the questions are open-end questions. Some are very concrete, often referring to specific events (Example: How do you feel about the recent strike?). Others are vague (Example: What does it mean to be a producer?). The schedule was pre-tested and several changes were made.

The *interview conversation* is an adaptation of the more traditional methods of administering interviews: the interviewer shares some of his own experience with the interviewee and thus establishes a closer relationship to him. Pitfalls in regard to the scientific validity of the data thus obtained are avoided by systematic spacing of conversations initiated by the interviewer, etc. The reader is again referred to the article in the *Journal of Social Issues* referred to above.

Any satisfactory discussion of the *group work* would have to deal with (1) the group leader and his relationship to the group, (2) the structure of the group, (3) the material with which the group is dealing, (4) the basic values underlying the group interaction, and (5) the procedures used. Since the general aspects of the group work have been discussed in the text, only one remark should be added: The group sessions were not only of great importance as experiments in the development of a democratic consciousness; they were also of invaluable help in obtaining data, developing hypotheses, and verifying results.

ANALYSIS OF THE INTERVIEW CONVERSATION

The data obtained were classified as follows: (1) in a "personal" file, each containing all information about one person (40 workers from the 1 per cent sample plus 30 additional interviews and about 100 conversations); (2) an "area" file containing all data pertinent to a specific problem area, e.g., the union (15 areas); and (3) a "question" file consisting of ten thousand 5" by 8" cards, each containing the answer of one person to one question.

The analysis begins with a reading and rereading of "personal files." This first step leads to a broad general understanding, the formulation of "hunches" and hypotheses. It is influenced by the general frame of thought and the basic attitudes of the researcher.

The second step—the analysis of the area files—gives a more concrete impression of worker's attitudes. Hypotheses may be added or formulated more precisely.

The third step—the technical analysis proper—consists in the analysis of the question file with the help of tables based on categories taken from the code. The code consists of a list of criteria and categories which facilitate the ordering and classification of the interview material. These criteria and categories were specifically developed for each of the 200-odd questions contained in the interview schedule. They were derived from (1) theoretical insights into the interrelationship between the personality and social structure, and (2) categories suggested by the interview material itself.

At least one table has been drawn up for practically every question analyzed in this study. Orders of magnitude have usually been indicated but no attempts at precise quantifications were made. In many instances the number of cases in specific code categories would have been too small to give statistically valid results. Moreover, the general purpose of this study was to get intensive insights and to develop significant hypotheses pointing a way to change—rather than to get extensive quantifiable data of a more "shallow" universe.

The conclusions drawn from the empirical material can be checked relatively easily by anyone who would like to do so. The code, the table, and file cards are at the disposal of any interested and qualified person.

# Notes

INTRODUCTION

1. Erich Fromm, *Escape From Freedom*. New York: Farrar & Rinehart, 1941, p. 96.
2. J. M. Clark, *Studies in the Economics of Overhead Costs*. Chicago: University of Chicago Press, 1923, p. 7.
3. Max Weber, *Gesammelte Aufsätze zur Wissenschaftslehre*. Tübingen: J. C. B. Mohr, 1922, p. 479.
4. H. Freyer, *Soziologie als Wirklichkeitswissenschaft*. Leipzig: B. G. Teubner, 1930, p. 123.
5. Jacob Burckhardt, *The Civilization of the Renaissance in Italy*. London: Swan Sonnenstein & Co., 1892, p. 129.


CHAPTER 1

1. *Squeal*, Hormel news magazine, Souvenir Number, November, 1941.
2. *Ibid.*, p. 9.
3. *Report of the Joint Committee on Labor-Management Relations*, Congress of the United States, 80th Congress, 2nd session. Senate report No. 986, Washington, 1948, p. 94. This Report will be quoted from now on as *"Senate Report."*
4. *Austin Daily Herald*, June 26, 1950.
5. Polk's *Austin City Directory*, p. 17.
6. *Ibid.*, p. 18.
7. *Ibid.*, p. 18.
8. *Senate Report, op. cit.*, p. 94.
9. *Sales Management*. The Magazine of Marketing, May 10, 1950.
10. Information given by the company. The turnover figure refers to 1951.
11. The stock is listed at the Chicago Stock Exchange.
12. The wording of the original text has been slightly modified in order to meet some objections from the company.
13. *The Unionist*, Austin, Minn., Friday, July 3, 1949, p. 8.
14. See letter of the President of Local 9, dated August 24, 1951.
15. The lowest wage any worker was getting during the week when the meeting in the Sutton Park took place was $15.80 since workers had a minimum guarantee at that time. Earnings of $9.00 or less were due to irregular employment.
16. *Mower County News*, Austin, Minn., Thursday, July 20, 1933.
17. *The Unionist*, July 15, 1949.

18. *Austin Daily Herald,* Saturday, September 23, 1933, p. 1.
19. *Ibid.*
20. See letter of Mr. O. J. Fosso, President of the I.U.A.W., written on September 22, 1933.
21. *Austin Daily Herald,* Saturday, November 11, 1933.
22. *Ibid.,* p. 1.
23. *Ibid.,* p. 1.
24. *The Unionist,* July 22, 1949, p. 3.
25. *Austin Daily Herald,* Monday, November 13, 1933, p. 2.
26. *Ibid.*
27. *Ibid.*
28. *The Unionist,* July 22, 1949.
29. *Ibid.*
30. *Ibid.*
31. Report on the Industrial Commission, see *Austin Daily Herald,* Saturday, November 18, 1949, p. 3.
32. *The Unionist,* July 22, 1949, p. 3.
33. In July, 1937, a sit-down strike took place in the hog-kill. Most sit-down strikes, however, preceded the union shop agreement.
34. *The Unionist,* September, 1942.

CHAPTER 2

1. *The Hormel Annual Wage, Wage Incentive and Joint Earnings Plans,* Geo. A. Hormel & Co., Austin, Minn., pp. 1, 2.
2. See *Guaranteed Wages,* Report to the President by the Advisory Board, Office of War Mobilization and Reconversion, Washington, 1949, p. 323.
3. The whole plant was on straight time for a few weeks during 1933. After the formation of the union, the guaranteed wage was discontinued. It was then reintroduced, department by department. It took several years until most of the workers were again on "straight time."
4. These difficulties were closely related to the fact that workloads were determined on an *annual* basis at that time.
5. Conversation with Ralph Helstein in Chicago, May, 1950.
6. *The Unionist,* September 2, 1949. The meeting at which the Working Agreement was approved took place December 5, 1940.
7. *Working Agreement,* Article I, Section 1.
8. *Ibid.,* Section 2.
9. *Senate Report, op. cit.,* p. 98.
10. *Working Agreement,* p. 7.
11. The president chairs all meetings, prepares the executive board meetings, and carries out the policies of the executive board. For further details see *Constitution of Local 9.*
12. *Working Agreement,* Article III, Section 2.
13. *Ibid.,* Article XIII, Section 1.
14. *Ibid.,* Section 2.
15. *Ibid.,* Section 3.
16. *Ibid.,* Article VIII, Section 1.
17. Information given by the union, verified by union records, and checked by management which suggested various changes in the wording of the list given above.

18. Quoted in *Guaranteed Wages, op. cit.*, p. 325.
19. *The Hormel Annual Wage, Wage Incentive and Joint Earnings Plans, op. cit.*
20. *Ibid.*, pp. 23, 24.
21. *The Hormel Annual Wage, op. cit.*, November 24, 1943.
22. *Squeal*, January 1, 1947, pp. 8, 9. See also *Squeal* of May 1, 1945.
23. In regard to remuneration policy see *Squeal*, January 1, 1947.
24. *Ibid.*, January 1, 1947.
25. *Ibid.*
26. *Ibid.*, May 1, 1947.
27. *Ibid.*, May and December, 1947.
28. *Squeal*, January 1, 1947.

CHAPTER 3

1. *The Unionist*, July 29, 1949.
2. *Ibid.*, p. 3.
3. George Sorel, *Reflexions sur la violence*. Paris: F. Alcan, 1936, esp. Ch. IV.
4. *Ibid.*, August 26, 1949.
5. *Ibid.*, September 23, 1949. The meeting was on May 14, 1945.
6. According to a letter of the President, Frank W. Schultz, dated September, 1949.
7. *Senate Report, op. cit.*, p. 356.

CHAPTER 4

1. Originally, the publication was a salesman publication and was called the *Dairy Advocate*. After a few months (1917) the name was changed to *Squeal*. Any further reference to the *Squeal* is limited to the period from 1934 on.
2. See Alvin Zander's unpublished paper on interpersonal relationships, Research Center for Group Dynamics, University of Michigan, Ann Arbor, Mich.
3. Letter from the files of the Geo. A. Hormel & Co.

CHAPTER 5

1. Henrik de Man, *Joy in Work*. London: G. Allen & Unwin, Ltd., 1929, pp. 110 ff.
2. Information obtained by the head nurse in the first aid station.
3. Henrik de Man, *op cit.* p. 66.

CHAPTER 6

1. See Frances G. Wickes, *The Inner World of Man*. New York: Henry Holt & Co., 1948, esp. pp. 132 ff.; also R. S. Lynd, *Knowledge for What?* Princeton: Princeton University Press, 1946, p. 46. Lynd pointed out that the modern emphasis on money is partly due to an attempt to integrate the various spheres of activities by dragging them down to a common level: money.

2. I am referring here to Baynes' observation that the incidence of nervous breakdowns during the landings and fighting at Gallipoli during the first World War was much greater among British than among French soldiers. The French soldiers showed their fear and excitement openly, while the British went into battle composed and "brave."
3. This interpretation was suggested to me whils reading Frances G. Wickes' unpublished manuscript on *The Creative Process*.

CHAPTER 10

1. *The New Yorker*, July 1, 1950, p. 22.

CHAPTER 11

1. "Guaranteed wages, high C.I.O. objective is a 17-year-old fact at meat packing firm," *The Wall Street Journal*, December 20, 1951.
2. Data based on company records. For further data given in this chapter see also "Security Plans Hinge on Profits and Production," *The Austin Daily Herald*, December 14, 1949. For average earnings of a worker in the packing industry see *Facts and Figures*, Vol. II, No. 12, March 25, 1949; also *Monthly Labor Review*, August, 1950, and July, 1951.
3. The firm is the Rath Company at Waterloo, Iowa.
4. Ordway Tead and Henry C. Metcalf, *Personnel Administration*. Third Edition, New York: McGraw-Hill Book Co., 1933, p. 247.
5. Ordway Tead, *New Adventures in Democracy*, New York: McGraw-Hill Book Co., 1939, p. 177.
6. James C. Worthy, "Democratic principles of business management," *Advanced Management*, Quarterly Journal of the Society for the Advancement of Management, March, 1949.
7. Cited by Sumner H. Slichter, *Union Policies and Industrial Management*, The Brookings Institution, Washington, D. C., 1941, p. 165.
8. Max Weber, *Die Protestantische Ethik und der Geist des Kapitalismus*. Tübingen: J. C. B. Mohr, 1934, p. 204.

CHAPTER 12

1. For a further discussion of the problem of objectivity in social science see, by the same author: "Max Weber's postulate of 'freedom' from value judgments," *The American Journal of Sociology*, July, 1944.
2. See Erich Fromm, *Man for Himself*, New York: Rinehart & Co., 1947, partic. Ch. II.
3. A.T.M. Wilson, "Some implications of medical practice and social case work for action research," *The Journal of Social Issues*, Vol. III, No. 2, spring, 1947, p. 13.
4. Albert Schweitzer, *The Philosophy of Civilization*. New York: The Macmillan Company, 1949, p. 14.
5. *Ibid.*, p. 55.
6. *Ibid.*, p. 308.
7. *Ibid.*, p. 310.
8. Claire Bishop, *All Things Common*. New York: Harper & Brothers, 1950, p. 55.

9. *The Hormel Annual Wage, Wage Incentive and Joint Earnings Plans,* *op. cit.,* p. 23.
10. *Ibid.*
11. Ordway Tead, *New Adventures in Democracy.* New York: McGraw-Hill Book Co., 1939, p. 182.
12. Ortega Y Gasset, *The Revolt of the Masses.* New York: Mentor Books, 1950.
13. Ordway Tead, *op. cit.,* p. 222.

EPILOGUE

1. For an elucidation of the concept of an aesthetic-feeling continuum, see F.S.C. Northrop, *The Meeting of East and West.* New York: The Macmillan Company, 1946.
2. Ordway Tead, *New Adventures in Democracy.* New York: McGraw-Hill Book Co., 1939, p. 148.
3. "Write your own ticket while you can," address given by Jay C. Hormel at the General Session Meeting, American Meat Institute's 45th Annual Meeting, Palmer House, Chicago, October 3, 1950. Mimeographed Release of the American Meat Institute, 59 West Van Buren Street, Chicago 5, Ill., p. 6.

APPENDIX II

1. *The Social Responsibility of Psychiatry.* A statement of orientation formulated by the Committee of Social Issues of the Group for the Advancement of Psychiatry, Report No. 13, pp. 1 and 2.
2. P. Selznick, "Foundations of the theory of organization," *American Sociological Review,* February, 1948, pp. 25 ff.
3. F. Stuart Chapin, *Experimental Design in Sociological Research.* New York: Harper & Brothers, 1947, esp. Chapter V.

# Index of Subjects

Accomplishment, feeling of, 119, 130
Action Research, 214-216
Alienation, 122, 205 ff.
American Meat Institute, 19
Annual Wages, see Guaranteed Annual Wages
Apathy, 47, 195
Arbitration, 24, 33
Art, in industry, 181
Aspiratons, see Level of aspirations
Austin, 1-3
Authority, 30, 68, 186
  see also Foreman; Democratic group process; Democratic work process; Democratic leadership; Participation

Boredom, 81, 84, 124, 136, 147, 164

Chamber of Commerce, 19
Check-off, 18
CIO, 12, 17, 21, 45
Committee for Constitutional Government, 34
Communism, 178
Community of people and ideas, and the company, 121
  and democracy, 189, 190
  its ethics, 191
  the need for, 197-198, 201, 206-207
  and the union, 121, 170
  and work, 40, 47, 51-52, 65, 122
Competition, 52, 110, 196
Control, and the company, 19-29
  democratic, 186, 202, 203
  power struggle, 34-35, 133, 170, 186

Control—(Continued)
  and the union, 19-20
  workers', 18, 29, 31-32
  see also Authority; Democratic group process; Democratic work process; Democratic leadership; Democratic methods of change; Working Agreement
Cooperation, in general, 52
  labor-management, 32-35, 160
  and organization of industry, 204-206
Creativity, and democracy, xix, 169-180, 187
  and grievance machinery, 184
  and industrial organization, 168, 196-197
  and machine production, 75, 189-190
  need for creative self-expression, 96, 104-108, 110, 112, 116, 119, 130-131
  and reorganization of industry, 204
  and self-expression in work, 92, 170-171, 180, 191, 193, 201

Democratic consciousness, 175 ff.
Democratic group process, and the company, 31, 162, 169
  experience of, 68-69, 73, 153, 182-183, 185
  and guaranteed wages, 165-166
  new conception of, 198, 202-205
  and security, 161
  and the union, 151, 170
Democratic leadership, 183, 186, 199, 202-203

225

Democratic methods of change, 203, 205-206
Democratic values, in general, xviii, xix, 174, 176-177, 180, 187-188, 190, 196, 201 ff.
and research methods, 215
*see also* Community of people and ideas
Democratic work process, xvii-xxi, 157-208
*see also* Grievance machinery; Guaranteed wages; Hormel Business Improvement Committee; Hormel company; Participation; Security; Union
Depression, of the thirties, 188
Division of labor, technical and social, 112-113, 120

Earnings, 158
Education, 188-189, 197

Family life, 95
Fatigue, 79-81, 92, 100-101, 103, 137, 146, 168
Fear, of losing one's job, 159, 161, 163-165
of a speed-up, 159, 161
Fishing, 101, 108-111, 124, 143, 144, 145
Foremen, attitude toward, 126-127, 139-140, 150
and the company, 59, 71
their role, 5, 7, 16, 19-24, 29, 56, 114, 182-183
and the union, 41
and work, 86, 159-160
*see also* Democratic group process; Democratic work process; Grievance machinery; Hormel Business Improvement Committee; Hormel company; Participation; Union
Free Enterprise, 4, 73

GI Bill of Rights, 148
Grievance machinery, and Business Improvement Committee, 31, 170, 184, 198, 206
and a democratic work process, 169, 207-210
structure of, 19, 21, 23, 24, 32

Grievance machinery—(*Continued*)
functioning of, 24, 27, 33, 114, 151, 160
social-psychological function of, 198
*see also* Community of people and ideas; Hormel Business Improvement Committee
Group incentive system, attitudes, 124-125, 149
development, 16
and productivity, 159
the system, 208-210
and work incentives, 160-161, 164-165
*see also* Guaranteed wages
Guaranteed wages, and the company, 57-58, 61-63, 129, 149
and feeling of security, 42, 61
first experiments with, 8
and group incentive system, 17
and human values, 166
meaning of, xix
operation of the plan for, 22, 26-27, 208, 212
original plan for, 15-16
and overtime, 16
and OWMR study, xi
and productivity, 159
and social responsibility, 47
underlying ideas of, 14
and the union, 16, 46, 135
and work discipline, 126
and work experience, 114, 124-125
and work incentives, 160-161, 164-165
*see also* Democratic group process; Hormel company; Union; Work incentives

Hobby, 105, 180-182, 197-198
Hormel Business Improvement Committee, and cooperation, 34
and democratic work process, 31, 68, 161, 169, 198
and grievance machinery, 31, 170, 184-185, 198, 199, 206
and participation, 69-71, 114
and the *Squeal*, 66
and workers' attitudes, 65, 134

Hormel Business Improvement Project, 28, 169
Hormel company, conception of, 56-57
development of, 1-4
and democratic work process, 162, 169, 171
general feelings about the company, 57-61, 157, 159
identifications and partnership feelings, 62-65, 113-114, 115, 120-121, 124, 139, 145, 149
information about the company, 65-66, 68, 141, 152
organization, 14-35
participation in company, 65-68, 69-72, 153
*see also* Community of people and ideas; Control; Creativity; Democratic group process; Foremen; Group incentive system; Guaranteed wages; Management; Participation; Security; Work incentives; Working Agreement
Hours of work, 83, 85, 158

Incentive system, *see* Group incentive system
Integration of personality, 98-99
Interviewing, 217
International Workers of the World, 40

Labor Day, 51
Labor-Management Relations, *see* Cooperation; Control; Working Agreement
Level of aspirations, 85, 93
Local 9, *see* Union; United Packinghouse Workers of America

Management, function of, 68, 186, 199-201, 205
prerogatives of, 202, 204
*see also* Hormel company; Democratic group process; Democratic work process
Mechanization, 75, 80, 83, 190
Money, 87, 91-93, 115, 120
Monotony, 76-78, 80-82, 84, 86, 93, 147

National Association of Manufacturers, 19
New Deal, 8

Objectivity, 173-176

Participation, in the company, 28-32, 49-50, 64-65, 69-71, 73, 161, 171
and a democratic work process, 31, 161, 185, 187-188, 204-205
and the social division of labor, 113
and the union, 36, 47-50, 151
and work, 169
Pension Plan, *see* Profit Sharing Trust
Personality structure, 214-216
Play, and work, 105, 132
Political attitudes, 50
Process of rationalization, 52-53, 72
Productive efficiency, 114, 115, 157, 163-168, 171, 182
Productiveness, 113, 153-154, 196
Profit sharing, attitudes toward, 61-64, 125, 140, 149
operation of, 26-27, 210-212
Profit Sharing Trust, attitudes toward, 61, 125, 149
operation of, 27, 212-213

Repetitiveness, 76-78, 92, 106, 189

Sample, 216
Satisfaction with work, 87, 89, 91, 116-117, 124, 130
Security, and the company, 61
and a democratic work process, 161
in general, 91, 148, 157-158
and productivity, 165
and the union, 41-42, 50
and work incentives, 70, 114, 159, 164, 202
Seniority, 41-42, 50, 53, 61, 160, 204, 209, 213
Sick-leave, 61-62, 140, 149
Skill, 75, 88, 89, 113, 120
Social Structure, 214-216
Speed of work, 83, 86
Squeal, 65, 66, 134, 153

Strikes
  1933, 10, 13
  1936, 12
  1946, 33
  1948, 33, 44-47, 135, 142
  1951, 33
Supervisory Hierarchy, *see* Foremen; Democratic group process; Democratic work process

Taft-Hartley Act, 128, 141, 152
Time, passing of, 82-84, 86, 101-102, 109, 124, 136, 147, 184, 192-195
  perspective, 78
Time study, 33, 114

Union, and Business Improvement Committee, 32, 134, 170
  and check-off, 18
  development of, 5-12
  and democratic work process, 161, 169, 170, 202, 203, 206
  and education, 197
  general feelings about, 38-39
  and guaranteed wages, 16, 46, 135
  identifications and partnership feelings in, 39-43, 50, 53, 121, 127-129, 134, 135
  ideology, 37-38, 51, 113, 207
  meetings, 47-50
  political action, 13
  protection, 41-43, 139, 145
  strikes, 33
  Structure and functions, 19, 21, 36, 39-40, 54, 151, 157
  and work process, 36, 41-43, 52, 54, 113, 121, 157, 197, 201, 206, 207
  *see also* Community of people and ideas; Control; Democratic group process; Democratic

Union—(*Continued*)
  work process; Foremen; Grievance machinery; Guaranteed wages; Hormel Business Improvement Committee; Participation; Strikes; Seniority; Security; Working Agreement
Union-shop, 12, 18, 29, 43, 125-126
Unionist, 13, 34, 36-37
United Packinghouse Workers of America, 12, 17, 38, 41, 127, 139, 151

Vacation, 61-62, 100-102, 106, 108, 125, 131, 140-141, 144-145, 149, 154, 167
Values, 18, 31, 34-35, 52-72, 114-115, 132-135, 165-166, 171, 190 ff.

Wage Stabilization Board, 33
Weekends, 99-100, 107-108, 130, 143-144, 154
White Collar, 132, 133
Wilson & Co., 40
Work, flow of, 83-84, 87
  meaning of, 77, 83-85, 87, 91-93, 95, 97-98, 115, 117-119, 121
  *see also* Community of people and ideas; Creativity; Democratic group process; Democratic work process; Foremen; Grievance machinery; Group incentive system; Guaranteed wages; Hormel Business Improvement Committee; Hormel company; Participation; Security; Union
Work incentives, 163-166, 181
Work Progress Administration, 136
Working Agreement, 17, 22-23, 208-213

# Index of Names

Ball, Ruth, xv
Bakke, E. Wight, xiv
Bishop, Claire, 183
Brownlee, Fred L., xii

Chapin, F. Stuart, 216
Cort, John C., 178

Dunham, Carol, xii

Eastman, Eva Hills, xii
Ellis, Frank, 10

Franklin, Benjamin, 193
French, E. R. P., xiv
French, M., xii
Fromm, Erich, xii

Gasset, Ortega Y, 186
Gray, R. F., 70

Heinz, Gretl, xiv
Helstein, Ralph, xii, 17
Hogle, Lois and George, xiii
Hormel, George A., 1, 4
Hormel, Jay C., attitudes toward
  company, 59
  democratic work process, 161,
  186, 204
  general, xii, 4
  guaranteed wages, 14, 125
  and the Master Plan, 25-26
  strike of 1933, 10-11
  and the union, 9, 12, 17, 41, 127,
  129
  and the workers, 8, 26

Kennedy, Van Dusen, xiv
Kerr, Clark, xiv

Landauer, Carl, xiv
Lewin, Kurt, xiv
Lewis, John L., 12
Lippitt, Ronald, xiv

Man, Hendrik de, 75, 92
Mankiewicz, Joseph, xix
Mead, Margaret, xiv
Mills, C. Wright, xiv

Nisbet, Robert, xiv

Olson, Floyd B., 11

Peterson, George, 1
Phifer, Miriam, 15

Riesman, David, 190

Schultz, Frank W., xiii, 37, 46, 49
Schweitzer, Albert, xiii, 175, 191
Sherman, Fayette, xiii
Sorel, George, 46
Sullivan, Harry Stack, xii

Taylor, Paul, xiv
Tead, Ordway, 190, 197

Weber, Max, xviii, 52, 174
Whyte, W. F., 197
Wickes, Frances G., xii
Windisch, Richard P., xii

Zander, Alvin, xiv

*Set in Linotype Caledonia*
*Format by Edwin H. Kaplin*
*Manufactured by The Haddon Craftsmen, Inc.*
*Published by* HARPER & BROTHERS, *New York*